D1507518

Independent Living

Being On Your Own

Independent Living

Being On Your Own

Craig M. Pearson
Contributing Editor

Helen Magnuson Galgowski
Instructor, Home Economics
Keigwin School, Middletown, Connecticut

Joseph R. Marfuggi
Coordinator, Program Development
City Institute
University of Hartford, Connecticut

Deirdre C. Pearson
Instructor, Home Economics
Department of Children and Youth Services
Connecticut Valley Hospital

Virginia Safford Strain
Home Economics Specialist
Orange Unified School District, California

Carleen Hoyt Crowley
Instructor, Home Economics
Carle Place High School, New York

Lorraine Hensel Bailey
Instructor, Home Economics
Cuesta College
San Luis Obispo, California

Gregg Division
McGraw-Hill Book Company

New York Atlanta Dallas St. Louis San Francisco Auckland Bogotá
Düsseldorf Johannesburg London Madrid Mexico Montreal New Delhi
Panama Paris São Paulo Singapore Sydney Tokyo Toronto

Also available as individual softcover modules

THE GREGG/McGRAW-HILL SERIES FOR INDEPENDENT LIVING

On Your Own/Pearson—Galgowski—Marfuggi—Pearson
Caring for Kids/Norris
All About Clothes/Crowley
A Place of Your Own/Strain
Time to Spare/Bailey
Food and You/Pearson—Galgowski—Pearson

Library of Congress Cataloging in Publication Data

Main entry under title:
Independent living.

(The Gregg—McGraw-Hill series for independent living)
A collection of 5 works originally published separately.
Includes index.
(CONTENTS: Pearson, C. M., et al. On your own.—
—Crowley, C. H. All about clothes.—Strain, V. S.
A place of your own. [etc.])
1. Home economics—Collected works.   2. Single
people—Collected works.   I. Pearson, Craig.
II. Galgowski, Helen Magnuson.   III. Series: Gregg—
McGraw-Hill series for independent living.
TX7.I53   640   79-16892
ISBN: 0-07-049061-9

1 2 3 4 5 6 7 8 9 0   DODO   8 7 6 5 4 3 2 1 0 9

Contents

Preface

"Independent living" is a goal not easily reached. Part of the difficulty is that many people are confused about what independent living really is. For example, independent living *doesn't* mean mere freedom from the influence and orders of other people. Independent living means something more: having freedom and knowing what to do with it. People have a lot of admiring ways to describe this ability.

"You know your own mind."
"You know where you're going."
"You're a self-starter."
"You've really got yourself together."

Of course, the attitudes and skills of independent living are as important to the young adult as they are to the senior citizen, to people living alone as well as with others.

The number of people who do, in fact, live by themselves has greatly increased in the 1970s; one-person households have grown faster than any other type. The increase between 1970 and 1975 alone was almost 30 percent. At the end of that period, almost fourteen million people lived alone. They made up one out of every five households in the nation. (One-person and two-person households together added up to *more than half* of all U.S. households for the first time ever.)

Not many years ago, living alone was neither a popular nor an approved way of life. Young people, especially, were expected to stay close to home and family. Ways of living have changed a great deal since then. For one thing, distances aren't what they used to be. We all move faster and farther. Sons and daughters who move to another city or another state (or, for that matter, another continent) are only a few hours away. Jobs are more varied, better paid, and often demand long moves. For a whole set of reasons, the pressure to marry young (or to marry at all) has been eased. "Everyone's Lib" has sold the idea that young women and men are right to make their own way.

Independent Living looks at the new responsibilities raised by this new freedom. As the saying goes, freedom is often "easier said than done." People who live alone discover that they must be their own cooks, repairers, launderers, housekeepers, teachers, planners, counselors, friends, and more. When you're on your own, you are responsible for what you do with your freedom—and for what freedom does to you.

Responsibility means learning to think about yourself in two parts. You're a giver and taker, servant and served, judge and defendant, counselor and patient. Living on your own can be dreadful if both parts of you are constantly at odds with each other. When you've got yourself together, on the other hand, independent living can be free and good. Even such small matters as sewing on a button, serving a decent meal, or dusting a room can be important signals of self-respect. You find out who you are by adding up such personal favors into a lifestyle and a life plan. Each part in this book is designed to help you do this.

Part I, *On Your Own,* is about setting goals and reaching them. Each of us has the chance to make daily decisions about food, dress, money management, work and play, home care. The evidence suggests that such decisions are best made by people who know their own needs, motives, and values. *On Your Own* opens up these questions.

Part II, *A Place of Your Own,* is designed to serve as a guide for those of you who will be moving into your own apartments for the first time. It's assumed, however, that any ideas pertaining to apartment living also apply to brownstone, flat, condominium, duplex, townhome, or any other similar rental. Housing needs and facilities vary from place to place, and values differ from person to person. Therefore, the general rules presented here may not always apply.

Planning and setting up a place of your own will be a source of much pleasure and satisfaction. But there may also be some feelings of uncertainty and insecurity. *A Place of Your Own* seeks to help you cope with these problems in a confident and effective way.

Part III, *Food and You,* is about one of humankind's main interests. Food means survival, strength, health, and healthy good looks. At another level, food can set the scene for graceful and gracious behavior. The preparation of food can be an essential task, a hobby, an art. "You are what you eat," the old saying suggests, and it rings true in many aspects of independent living.

Part IV, *All About Clothes,* will enable you to answer "yes" to the following question. Are you spending your clothing dollars wisely? Have you taken a clothing inventory recently? Are you aware of the *building on basics* principle? Do you understand the three F's of selection: function, flattery, and fashion? Do you know what your measurements and proper sizes are in both customary and metric units? (Metric units are rounded off slightly for practical application.) Do you know the best wash and dry techniques for each of your washables? Do you know how to repair and alter your clothes? The way you look is a crucial part of the overall impression you make on others. *All About Clothes* will help you determine the look that is right for you.

Part V, *Time to Spare,* explores the major possibilities open to each individual in using leisure to make dreams come true. In addition, practical vacation and travel information is presented so the student can make the most of opportunities. We do have time for leisure, and all that it implies, but we really have no time to spare in living our life to the fullest.

Independent Living is firmly based on the real experiences of many young people who have told us about their own problems, hopes, and ways of truly living independently. We thank them for sharing this kind of information which often can't be found in books.

PART ONE

On Your Own

Solitude and Self-Awareness

If a cure for loneliness had to be stated in just four words, they might be these: *Learn to like yourself.*

Talks with a hundred people who live alone will reveal hundreds of ideas about avoiding loneliness. But the people who consider themselves happiest seem to agree on this one point:

George "For me, there are three big *L*'s in life: *L*iking yourself, *L*iking other people, and *L*uck. If you don't like yourself, you're never going to get across to other people. You can have plenty of faults. You have to see them and accept them. But you have to be able to let yourself and other people see what's good about you, too."

Lucy "I've lived by myself for a long time, and I wouldn't have it any other way. I think of myself as a private person. I want to do my thing whenever I want to do it. You have to know your limits, of course. I know I'm never going to be a Billie Jean King or a Carol Burnett or a Congresswoman Barbara Jordan. I still have a lot to offer myself and others. I like people. I like to 'read' people, and oh what a good listener I am. This has to start with yourself. If you don't start accepting yourself and your own faults, you can't accept other people and the faults that you see in them. I have one friend who thinks everyone who comes into her life is terrible. She's looking for perfection in other people. She has no openness for human weakness, no understanding that that's the way the person is. And she's miserable. In a way, she's not really very healthy. That's important. Both physical and mental health. If you have poor health—or if you *think* you have poor health—everything looks wrong to you. That includes other people."

2

What is "Self"?

"Self" is an old word, used easily and often. Yet people who study the human mind do not agree about what "self" means. Differences of opinion about that have indeed grown far wider in the past century.

These differences might be illustrated by an imaginary fellow named Adam. Adam is troubled by his behavior. He might think about his problems in any one of three ways:

1. "I don't know why I act the way I do sometimes. I just seem to get these childish feelings that make me do foolish things. I've been trained to behave better. But sometimes I can't seem to stop myself."
2. "I can't help being who I am and acting the way I act. All sorts of people and events have made me what I am today. It would take an awful lot more to change me."
3. "I do many things, good or bad, because other people expect me to act that way. They don't know the real *me*. I'd be a lot better off being myself."

Adam's thoughts very simply represent three important psychological viewpoints:

1. This first statement fits the ideas developed by Sigmund Freud in the late 1800s. Freud was the first world-famous psychoanalyst. He said that the human personality was shaped, in the person's infancy, by family love or conflict. He saw the inner mind as something he called the *id*. The id had no sense of good or evil. The id wanted pleasure, and it wanted its own way. The id was unconscious—not really known to the person who owned it. Another part of the mind, the *superego,* stored up the rules of correct behavior given by parents and the world. The wild, selfish id and the stern, proper superego fought for the upper hand. The person's *ego*—the personality seen by others—reported the results of the battle to the outside world.
2. Adam's second statement fits the views of the *behaviorist* psychologists, who came after Freud. They denied that there was any inner self of any kind. The personality, they said, was

formed completely by outside influences on the person. The person was conditioned by other people and events to behave in certain ways. These ways of behaving told all there was to know about a person.

3. This third statement fits the ideas of the *humanistic* psychologists, who have become more widely known in the past 30 years. They believe that *personality* and *self* may be quite different. They see the self as a rich inner world of feelings and powers the person can explore. People may be very unhappy when they ignore or cover up this self and shape their personalities only to suit what the outer world seems to want. Many psychologists now believe that people are healthiest when they can put self and personality in tune with each other—when they can show their true feelings and try to be what they really want to be.

Whether we've studied psychology or not, most of us are likely to be affected by one of these views. Without a sense of self, we become what others make of us—for better or for worse. A strong view of self, on the other hand, prods people to take charge of their own lives.

Alone with Self

People who believe in themselves value aloneness. For writer Hugh Prather, "Solitude . . . means putting the parts of me back together." Long before him, the poet William Wordsworth wrote about "that inward eye/which is the bliss of solitude."

However valuable it may be, time to be alone is scarce in the early learning years of most people. When children have it, they seem to use it well:

"Watch a child playing on the seashore by himself: dumping sand into water, and water into sand; studying a shell, a crab, tasting seaweed, laughing at the foam that tickles his toes; lifting his gaze briefly to the far rim of the world and saying aloud to nobody, 'That was a big one,' when the surf booms. Is he lonely? In one exact

sense, yes; but invade it and he will yell. Never to be lonely is never to be free."[1]

The Uses of Solitude   Aloneness can be used in many ways to multiply a person's chances for self-awareness and independent living.

Some of these uses are simple. The plain tasks of daily living—like cleaning, mending, paying bills—are often best done alone. Other people may insist that *they* are more important than such dull duties. But the little things, left undone, begin to mess up your place, take up your time, and generally interfere with your sense of running your life well.

Solitary hobbies such as photography, painting, cooking, stamp collecting, sewing, and reading give you a chance to enjoy your own company. Liking and accepting yourself is an important part of independent living. (Sepp Seitz, Magnum Photos)

[1]Michael Drury, "The Gifts of Solitude," *Woman's Day*, October 1969, p. 41.

Time alone is very important for knowing where you are and for making decisions about where you're going. In the language of the 1960s the word "together" meant a person who knew. And you can only "get it together" alone. Otherwise, your life may be run by a committee including one to a hundred other people.

Finding yourself is solitary work. If you're not pleased with the you that others seem to see, you have to look alone for the real you.

People who live alone say that a rewarding search may start in very simple ways:

Joe   "I want a little time to myself to do nothing. I mean nothing. No television. No reading. No working. No sleeping, either. But it's not a negative thing. I'm not trying to escape the world or blot out problems. Maybe you'd call it meditation, or peace and quiet. I really don't see why you have to call it *doing* anything. It's just a good feeling of owning your time—time for nothing."

The pace of work and play leaves little time for solving problems—or even for deciding what things are problems and what are not. Solitude is useful for sorting out the issues in a person's life:

Dee   "Once, in college, I remember wanting to be alone so badly that I went into my big old closet and sat there for half an hour. I had to be away from the swirl of girls in the dorm. It was great. I really had a chance to put some of my thoughts in order. Today I like my time alone for the same reason. Of course, I don't have to hide any more."

John   "I need time to come to my own rescue and save myself. I have to be alone to decide if what I'm doing is what I should be doing. Sometimes it's just simple stuff, like trying to figure out better and cheaper ways of feeding my face. Or thinking about whether I should be watching more good TV and fewer lousy movies. Sometimes it's serious, like thinking about how I deal with other people."

Solitude may offer better chances to think about long-term problems and hopes:

Linda "I was an only child, and I'm used to being alone. You spend a great deal of time by yourself. If you're surrounded by busy adults, you learn to make up games and occupy your own playtime. You do become—I did—more imaginative. I'm still pretty adventurous when it comes to finding out about my head and my body. I'm learning to like jogging now. It's not like trying to find partners for tennis or for talking and listening. I like the challenge, but there's no best or worst to worry about. I'm not really athletic, but energy is energy and it needs an outlet. Just sitting and talking isn't always the way.

"Did you ever get into a conversation with someone who's talking 90 miles an hour and you can only listen at 10 miles an hour? You get away from that problem with a book. That's why I like reading. I'm into photography too. I think a lot of the reason people are getting into photography is that they can have a place to be alone—in the darkroom. Your photographs are your views of things. They're the way you see the world. It's a very personal thing. Do you know what I mean?"

The Right to Be Alone Wanting solitude is one thing; being allowed to have it is another. Few people want to be alone all the time or most of the time. But most people who live by themselves comfortably have suffered from wrong-time visitors. The drop-in might be a lonely neighbor, who can't believe that anyone else could not want company. It might be a fun-loving friend from across town, who wants to start a party. Or it might be the apartment-house politician, who wants to talk about the great issues of the day. And tonight's the night you wanted to read, or balance your checkbook, or plan out the month ahead, or just think. How do you say "go away" without hurting or losing a friend? People who live alone suggest several do and don't rules:

1. You have to be willing to take the phone off the hook. You should also cover up any welcome signs—like a light shining outside your door or through it.
2. Don't be cute. A DO NOT DISTURB sign outside your door wouldn't work any better than a NO SMOKING sign inside your apartment.

3. Most important, learn to be more honest with other people about your needs. Tell them directly that you have things you must do. On the other hand, you don't have to explain in detail what you plan to do. You don't owe that to others.
4. You *can* be a little bit tricky without being dishonest. Lay out a set of props—like a stack of open books and papers—that pop-in visitors can see. You may do this even if you just want to do nothing.
5. Follow the golden rule. Respect the right of other people to be alone when they want to. Telephone to ask if you can visit. If you do drop in and find a person busy, leave gracefully. Help other people to be alone when you sense they need it, and they'll help you.

Meeting You   Being alone is no joy, of course, when you find you are a stranger to yourself. You're uneasy. You've never been properly introduced to yourself. Millions of Americans are spending millions of dollars for books and training courses that are supposed to arrange such a meeting. Yet it's really something only you can do. Isn't it odd, though, that you feel foolish about it? Forget that feeling for a while and try some of these no-cost stunts:

1. Look in a mirror and tell yourself how wonderful you are. You don't have to make believe the flaws aren't there. But think harder about your good points and the things about yourself you want to make even better.
2. Listen to your own voice. You can do this in a crowd, but it's better alone. If you must, use a tape recorder. Hear the tone and your way with words. Note the phrases you like and those that could be replaced.
3. If you're tense, take a big deep breath. Then make the muscles of your face relax. Loosen up around the eyes. Let your tongue and cheeks and jaw sag. If necessary, let the same feeling happen all the way from your shoulders to your toes. Try the same thing again sometime when you don't *think* you're uptight.
4. Pick out some words to praise yourself. Most of us have favorite words for self-scolding when we make a mistake: "You dummy." "Jerk." "Stupid." Isn't it only fair to have other words for self-congratulation when we do something well?
5. Make a "self" collage. Cut out and collect pictures and head-

lines from newspapers and magazines that are in tune with what you know about yourself. Paste them up, artistically overlapped, on a large sheet of cardboard or hardboard.

6. Write an advertisement about yourself that "sells" the best features of the real you. Use the most colorful words, pictures, and designs you can.

None of these exercises is medical or magical. You should be able to invent many more by yourself. But this isn't such an easy thing to do. Most people are uncomfortable with ideas that seem too self-centered. Yet self-knowledge requires paying a great deal of attention to yourself. This self-knowledge is needed, in turn, to make the kinds of decisions discussed in the next chapter: How much time should be yours alone? How much time should be shared with others?

THINKING IT THROUGH

1. "You have to like yourself before you can like other people." Do you or do you not agree with that statement? Why?

2. How important is it for a person to know what others think about her/him? Do you know who you are by what other people say? Do you know who you are *only* by what other people say? How accurately do people see what other people are like? Some people frequently say such things as, "My parents don't understand me," and "My wife doesn't understand me." Does this mean that these people have inner qualities that cannot be seen or explained to others?

3. Consider this mental health idea: The "healthy" person is the person who's got the inner self and the outer self operating in harmony and moving along on the same track, the person who doesn't feel any serious conflicts between these inner and outer selves. Do you agree with this idea? Or do you feel that a person has inner qualities that can't or shouldn't be expressed to other people and the outside world?

4. Is it good or bad for a person to spend some time doing nothing? Should people have more time for, and devote more time to, doing nothing at all? Why or why not?

5. Give examples of things you *must* do, things you *ought* to do, and things you *want* to do. Do most people have conflicts among these kinds of things? Why or why not?

Action against Loneliness

Few of us would want to spend *all* our free time alone—even if we had the chance. Aloneness is a scarce resource. But it can cause feelings of restlessness or boredom, and it sometimes does so for almost everyone. The most popular advice then is this: Do something. Or even: Do *anything*.

Writer Christopher Morley once put it another way. "No person is lonely," he said, "while eating spaghetti. It requires so much attention." Various kinds of "spaghetti" activities can fill our lives. They keep us—for better or for worse—from thinking about ourselves and our problems. Here is a handy list of silly ideas for filling lonely time:

1. Play a game of solitaire. If the ones you know bore you, learn a new one. There are several hundred kinds of solitaire.
2. Do a 300-piece jigsaw puzzle.
3. If you have any kind of collection, sort it out in a different way from the way it is sorted now. For example, you may have jars of buttons sorted out by color. Sort them out by size instead.
4. Straighten all the pictures on the walls.
5. Write down the words of two of your favorite songs. Count the words to see which one has more. Which song has the most letter *e*'s in it? Which has the most letter *w*'s?
6. Do a 500-piece jigsaw puzzle.
7. Write down the names of all the characters who have appeared in your favorite soap opera in the past year. Try to recall all that has happened to each one.
8. Rearrange your furniture.
9. Flip a penny a hundred times. Count the number of heads and tails.

10. Change the places of cans in the cabinet, books on the shelves, bottles in the medicine cabinet, etc.

Useless things to do? Maybe not. Compared to idle loneliness, almost any action looks great. "Spaghetti" things can help a person tune out bad feelings and get ready to tune in better feelings. But many of us do too many "spaghetti" things for too long. Some people use them as full-time time killers. Then they wonder why so much of their time gone by seems dead. Most of us finally wonder how that past could have been made more alive.

Choices of Action

A type of telephone conversation that starts in the teens, but often goes on for many years more, sounds like this:

"Hey, what say we do something tonight?"

"Yeah. What do you want to do?"

"I don't know. What do you want to do?"

"I don't know. . . . How about a card game or a movie?"

"Aaaah, I'm getting sick of cards. And there isn't a good movie for miles around. How about a little bowling?"

"That doesn't sound too deep-down thrilling. How about you calling Joel and Mike, and I'll call Kerry and April. See what they want to do."

[20 minutes later] "Hey, Joel doesn't answer, but Mike wants to hear that new group playing at the Lion's Den."

"I was down there Tuesday. Tell Mike the group reeks—a waste of time. Listen, April just washed her hair, but Kerry wants to go to Giovanni's for a pizza."

"OK, I could force down a slice or two. Let me call Mike and see if he'll go along with pizza. Hey, give Lisa a call. She might want some too."

And so it goes. The polling method results in plans that may please everyone a little and nobody a lot. Sometimes nobody agrees and nothing happens. The poll itself becomes the main activity of the evening. For some people, that's something—enough to fill a few lonely hours.

There are improved ways, of course, to telephone around for consensus—that idea on which everyone in the group can agree.

"...I don't know. What do you want to do?" The phone-around poll can become the main activity of the evening—for some people, it's enough to fill a few lonely hours. (Thomas Hopker, Woodfin Camp Associates)

One way is to start with a clear question: "Pizza? Yes or no?" That will almost always limit the size of the group. Another way is to list many possible things to do and agree that the most popular thing will be done. But people who lack ideas to start with find a list like that is hard to make.

Looking for a Leader   All the troubles of the phoning-around habit are erased when someone else plans free time for you. That is the selling point for the singles clubs or singles apartment buildings that abound in many cities. Many have full-time directors. They promise there will *always* be much to do. That, many live-alone people complain, is just what's wrong with the singles club outlook:

Joe   "Everyone deserves some fun as a payoff for hard work. But I wonder about people who seem to live only for the good times.

Most of them seem to think that having a good time is the most important thing in the world. They don't seem to do much thinking about who they are or what they'd really like to do with their lives. They're too busy running off to singles bars, ski trips, beach parties. I think most of them keep jumping from one party to the next because, deep down inside, they really aren't having a good time. But they keep trying. Lots of the 'swinging singles' are too insecure to believe that they could have a good time by themselves. They end up giving up their *identity* to the group. They wear the same kinds of clothes. They go to all the same places. They all talk about all the same things. It's an empty kind of life, as far as I'm concerned."

Club members defend their life-style on the grounds that it won't really last too long:

Jody "Look. Don't worry about it. As my mother used to say, it's just a phase. There are plenty of years ahead to be serious. And I *am* thinking about that."

Bill "Sure, it's a little phony. For one thing, we live half our time without ever seeing older people or kids. It's like the whole world is all one age every night and weekend. That's unreal. But I'm not trapped in the singles scene. I have the choice of spending time alone, and I use it a lot. But I'm having fun too."

Changing Pace People who live alone well seem to agree on one rule for low times: Do something different. Sometimes this means trying to change the person's view of self:

Henry "No matter how much you like your work and your way of life, you start to get bored sometimes. The trick for me is to get out and do something new. I change my points of reference, my frame of mind. I try not to be so aware of myself. If I've been reading and thinking a lot, I turn to sports. If I've been working with my hands a lot, I change to a book, watch TV, listen to music, go for a walk. Boredom gives me a signal to try new things or new thoughts."

Singles clubs, such as this one, offer people programmed activities and a group identity. (Harrison Conference Center)

Sometimes the something different means closer attention to self:

Lucy   "I had this real lack of confidence after my divorce. I moved to this city, where I didn't know anyone, and I felt very sorry for myself. Then I decided I had to forget about myself and start doing things. I joined the 'YW' and got into every course going. I made silver jewelry. Then I got into weaving. You name, it, I studied it. But the circle of people I knew, and enjoyed being with, kept widening. Strangely enough, the more people I knew, the more I enjoyed my time alone. Now I figure that loneliness is just self-pity. You want someone else to beef up your life for you. But I tell myself that I can do it myself. You've got to be creative, come up with some ideas for yourself. For example, on a mucky Sunday I might treat myself to a concert on my stereo. I put a lot of thought into the music I want to hear. I set up the program carefully. And I sit and give it my complete attention and enjoyment."

Helping Hands People who think well of themselves may have a little extra self to share with others:

Carl "To me, loneliness doesn't have that much to do with living alone. I know a lot of lonely people who are married and living together. To me, loneliness is a case of not being able to share with others. Take the people who live in this apartment building. They have some important things in common. For starters, they all chose the same place to live in. Some sharing is in everybody's best interests. If one of my neighbors is out of town, I'll volunteer to pick up the newspapers and mail. As you know, piled-up mail could tell thieves that no one's home. When people look out for each other, they probably cut down the threat of crime. Of course, there's a fine line between being neighborly and stepping on someone's privacy."

Being able to *ask* for help may be just as important as being able to give help. Lonely people often feel helpless. They may dwell on the thought that "nobody cares," making their loneliness deeper. Seeking help when it's needed can be a sign of self-confidence:

Marilyn "My first place of my own was a little bit of a house out near the end of the bus line. The only heating system was a big stove. The fuel was gas, which was in a big tank outside. Well, the men from the company brought the gas tank but didn't light what they call the 'pilot' on the stove. I didn't know anything about doing that. When the stove didn't work, I called the gas company. They said they'd send someone right out. Nobody came. I called them twice a day for a whole week, and nobody came. I just sat there at night freezing and feeling sorrier and sorrier for myself. None of the houses down the street seemed to have gas tanks. I was a little bit shy about knocking on their doors, anyway. But finally I sat down and asked myself who'd know something about something like pilot lights. The fire department! I called them. They sent two people out in about five minutes. I was an expert at lighting my stove in about five minutes more."

John "Having to take care of yourself all the time can be frightening. Being medium sick—and alone—is awful. What I mean by that is you're too sick to do anything but not sick enough to go to the hospital. You just have to remember that most sicknesses run their course. I had this cough once that felt like I was being stabbed in the chest. That one only lasted a few days. But it made me quit smoking, so it did some good. But the people around you can't do much for you. There are times, though, when you must have help. I have this mental file of friends I can call on when something or somebody is giving me trouble. It might be something about my job, or the landlord, or my car, or repair people. When I call for help, I'm not looking for a lot of sympathetic talk. Or for free work. I just try to remember people I can trust who have had that same kind of a problem. They can give good advice. What I mean by that is that a woman friend who's been ripped off on car repairs is a kind of expert. She may not be a mechanic. But she knows plenty about being a victim.''

Getting into Focus

The field of action (Figure 2-1) against loneliness is very broad, and it can be baffling.

Loneliness is the thin, dark edge of the field. People can hide there in self-pity and confusion, doing nothing that matters.

Solitude is a bigger, brighter area. It's the place where we can meet ourselves on equal terms. We can learn to know ourselves and like ourselves better. That *self-awareness* is a great start toward joining the big action world of friendship, work, learning, and service. It's a world of millions of possible decisions about what to do and who to be. It's full of promise. It's also full of traps and snags and roads to nowhere special:

Linda   "There's an old saying about busy hands being happy hands. I don't really buy that. Busy minds are better. A lot of people I know keep so busy they never have time to think about what they ought to be doing with their lives. There's always something they've *got* to do. Even when they're alone, they have a list of tasks a mile long. It seems strange to me to hear someone living alone say they've *got* to wash curtains or they've *got* to do cleaning tonight. As though they had someone else standing over them, making them do it. It seems stranger yet to hear someone say they've *got* to crochet or macrame or go to a hobby class or movie. I mean, it's great to be well organized. But there's a point when these people seem to be always running. And they're always going partway in 20 different directions but never really getting anywhere.

Self-centered Action   A person stepping into the field of action has some big choices to make all at once. One major choice is the balance between self-centered (or selfish) action and sharing. The person may choose to spend all free time doing "my own thing." Every free moment, that is, will be given to the person's own pleasure or growth.

This leads to a second choice. How much time should be spent alone with daily tasks, books, hobbies, and solitary thoughts? How much time should go toward self-amusement or self-growth in the world outside your place? There are courses to take, friendships to make, shows to see, games to play. Which of them satisfy your best interests? Which of them make you think of yourself as a better person? Which—if you're ambitious—help you get ahead in work? Which help the people you like to like you more?

These are all self-centered questions and choices. Each looks easy bv itself. Added together, they may be harder to answer.

Selfless Things to Do   Beyond self-centered action is the still bigger field of sharing. All of us live in some kind of community. We may see it as a group, a neighborhood, a city, a nation, or the world. We feel that we owe part of ourselves to our communities. Or at least we've been told so: "Be a good citizen." "Join up, help others, and feel good." How? The list of groups to join is almost endless. It is filled with possibilities in politics, church work, youth work, professional and fraternal activity, community betterment. Some groups help the needy or elderly. Others fight against diseases or for causes from civil rights to education to the environment. Volunteers pitch in to help the paid workers at hospitals, police and fire departments, museums, schools, and other institutions. Such volunteer work sometimes opens up (self-centered) career opportunities.

People who share often have to ask themselves what they can really afford to give and what satisfactions they want:

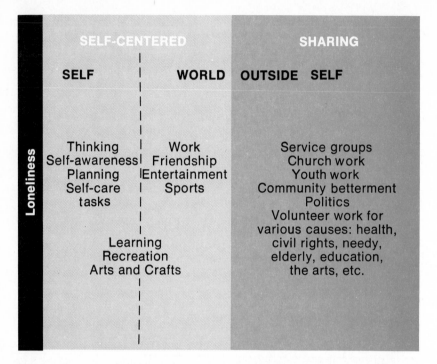

Fig. 2-1 The field of action against loneliness divides into self-centered action and sharing action. Self-centered action is what you do for your own comfort, convenience, knowledge, and fun. Sharing action is what you do for the comfort, safety, and pleasure of others.

Joe "I used to have a lot of dead time. Then I got into a group that was getting up a block party. That led to neighborhood people talking to each other for the first time about problems. Some were afraid. Some were lonely. Some wanted the street to look better. Some wanted better service from city workers. From that we started an association. Now I'm up to my armpits in work. I help put out a newsletter. I'm serving on about five study committees, going to hearings, getting into politics a little. *Now* I wish I had some dead time just to sit back and put up my feet. I don't want to get tired of working for the neighborhood. But sometimes I think I am."

For better or for worse, choices like these may start to add up to a life-style. Few people can do everything they'd like to do. Few can even do all the things at which they'd be very good. Choices have to be made. Some people, as a matter of fact, don't ever make these choices for themselves. Some choose very poorly and don't know how to undo their choices. How can they improve? The old Chinese proverb says that a journey of a thousand miles starts with a single step. The choice of a satisfying life-style, as the next chapter suggests, may start with a single day.

THINKING IT THROUGH

1. "Boredom is. . . ." Finish this statement in ten words or less. Now complete this statement: "When I'm bored, I. . . ."
2. What do you do for time-killing and busywork activities? The class may want to take a vote to decide the most imaginative time killer, the most absolutely useless, the most endless, and so on.
3. Would you ever join a singles club or something like it—an organized group designed to provide a variety of entertainment three or four nights a week, plus weekend days? Explain why you would or would not join.
4. Suppose that you were starting a club designed to occupy the time of a great many people who had no special interests, like hobbies or sports, in common. What sorts of things would you provide for them to do? Work up a program for a typical week.
5. Refer to the telephone conversation in Chapter 2. Have you ever been part of a conversation like that? How did you feel about it? Did it work out effectively? What ideas would you propose for improving the telephone polling method?

Planning a Day

"Where were you at 9:27 on the morning of August 5?"

"What were you doing at 1:13 on the afternoon of December 12?"

The courtroom lawyers of stage, screen, and television sometimes get answers to questions like these. In real life the probability of getting such answers is very small indeed. Most of us grow foggy after a few days about just what happened when.

We may remember the best and worst events of our lives by date and time. Holidays, birthdays, weddings, and graduations are easy to remember. Deaths and funerals are hard to forget.

We may also be able to pinpoint the dullest events in our lives: "What was I doing at noon on Wednesday? I was eating a cheese sandwich at the Ajax Lunch. How do I know that? Because that's what I'm doing *every* Wednesday at noon."

In-between events, neither extraordinary nor dull, make up much of our lives. They go by and melt together into one big time period called the past: "Was it Monday or Tuesday when I bought these apples?" "Was it March or April when you first applied for your job?" "Was it spring or summer when we first met?" "Was it last year or the year before when we started to fall in love?"

It's often hard to remember when things happened. And does it really matter?

"What will you be doing at 8 in the evening on July 16?"

If it's an invitation, that question can be exciting. When the asker is someone beautiful or important to us, we know that the answer is that we'll be there. If it's only a general question, we probably don't know the answer. Who looks ahead that far? Maybe people who have vacations or tickets to a big game or concert. Without hopes like that, we may give one of these answers. "Who knows?" "I don't know." "Nothing."

Perhaps these answers are only partly true. No one knows about the future for sure. But most of us, if we thought hard about it, might be able to make some good guesses about the doings of any plain old day ahead.

Time Presses On

Many people seem careless about the details of time in the past and future. Surprisingly, the same people may look worried about the present day. They are pushed and pulled and bothered by the idea of *now* and the few hours just gone by:

Sarah "I know that I'll feel better if my time is organized. I'll have a feeling at the end of the day that I've accomplished something. My problem is being organized enough to organize. You have to fight those 'I don't care' feelings first. Then you have to figure how much you have to do to feel you've done something worthwhile. That's mixed up, isn't it?"

Chris "I can sit in a chair for an hour thinking about all the things I've got to do. And then I decide I don't have time for them. And then I realize I *had* the time I spent sitting and thinking about the time I didn't have."

Sam "On some Saturday mornings I try to make out a list: 'Take shoes to repair shop. Cash check before bank closes at noon. Dry cleaner. Do laundry. Make up grocery list. . . .' Sometimes it runs up to 15 or 20 things. I feel pretty good as I cross them off. Then time starts to run out and I start to panic. I get really surly if anybody interrupts."

Linda "I really started thinking about taking charge of my time after my car was stolen. All of a sudden, everybody else's time had to be my time. When a friend with a car was ready to go the supermarket, I had to be ready. When another friend suggested going to a movie after I hadn't been anywhere for a week, I went, even if I didn't really feel like going. It made me believe that I'd have to find time for *me*."

These people on their own share some widely held views of time. Time is for doing; it measures work. Time is freedom. Time—as Benjamin Franklin said long ago—is money.

It may be clear at a glance that these views don't square neatly with each other in all cases. One person might agree that work leads to money, which leads to freedom. Another might protest that time is used for work and money *or* for freedom. Such interesting views deserve a test.

Accounting for Time Supposing that Benjamin Franklin was right, we ought to be able to handle time as we do money.

But we can't really *save* time by putting it aside for later use. That's out.

We can, on the other hand, *spend* time for many things. And time, like money, is in much shorter supply than all the things we could use it for. It's certain, then, that we have to make choices of what we "buy" with our time. Making a budget—a spending plan—seems a good way to get the best use out of time as well as money.

The model form in Figure 3-1 may help in taking the first step toward budget-making. It serves as a record of how time is actually spent during half of a single day. (One form might be used for "prime time" or two for a whole day.) Use it to note what you actually did in time spans as short as 15 minutes. Wait until later to fill in the three columns at the right.

What's the point? People start to budget money because they don't know where the money goes. The first step in deciding what *ought* to be done with money is finding out what *is* being done with money. So families and single people preparing to budget often keep records for several months of what they actually spend for what things. The same ideas seem useful in finding out what happens to your time.

A financial spending record shows a number of important things. It identifies how much money goes for *fixed spending*—those bills that must be paid in about the same amount every month or every few months. These might be things like rent or insurance or installment payments.

The record also identifies *variable spending*. This would include money spent for things like food and clothing. These things are

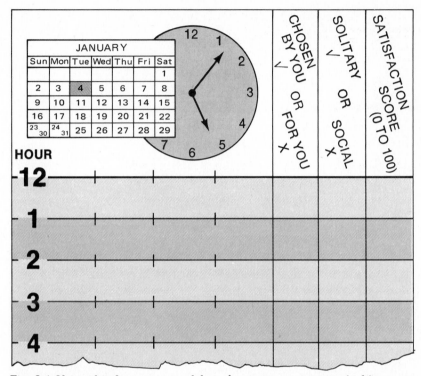

Fig. 3-1 Using this form as a model, make up your own record of how you spend your time. Carry it with you all day and note everything you do. Later, rate each activity as shown in the columns on the right. A time record can help you decide if your time was well spent, or how you think it could be better spent.

important, but spending for them may be increased or decreased from month to month.

The money that's left over has been saved or spent for extra things. It may have gone for movies, magazines, household repairs, or any one of a hundred other items. The spending record often shows that surprising amounts have gone for certain things. A *time* spending record may be equally surprising.

What Happened?   The spending record of time can tell a person a lot about life-style that may not have been clear before. The sample hours shown in Figure 3-2 describe three different kinds of people and happenings.

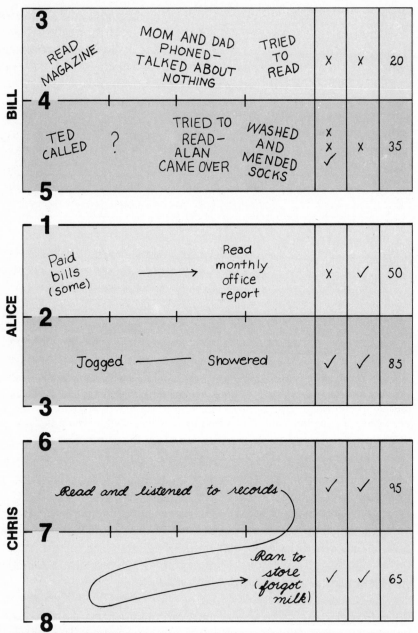

Fig. 3-2 These three people—Bill, Alice, and Chris—each spent two hours of their time very differently. The columns on the right reflect how they feel about their spending records.

Bill   has recorded a sad-looking stretch of afternoon. His time has been broken up, perhaps wasted, and a little of it has even been lost. Records of spent money and spent time may be alike in these ways. No matter how much attention the recorder pays to the task, some dollars or minutes may slip away unnoticed. When the useless spending is added up, the total amount may be alarming.

Alice   has recorded mixed results. She's spent a halfhearted hour writing checks and trying to do some "homework" from her office. Both tasks have not only been unpleasant but have remained unfinished as well. Perhaps these tasks would fit better in a different time slot than Saturday afternoon. The change of pace to jogging certainly seems to have improved the record.

Chris   had a good thing going until his own mistake caught up with him. A long spell of almost perfect solitude turned into a mad dash to reach the store before closing time. The spending record might remind him to make his morning shopping list more complete next time.

Such spending records provide a realistic basis for making a better time budget. Both the records and the budget are very personal, of course. The budget maker is the best judge of what uses of time may be changed and what uses must be kept. The spending record offers some good starting points:

1. How much time goes for *fixed spending*? Many large and small duties use up regular blocks of time. You're signed up for an adult education course, and you give it the same hour once a week. You do your grocery shopping at a certain time. It probably can't be done any faster. Your time for paying bills is about the same each time you do it. You also spend various little bits of time in small talk with neighbors. You happen to believe that you owe them that much time. So the amount of small-talk time, in your case, is fixed spending.

2. How much time goes for *variable spending*? The amount of time you spend for meals, newspaper reading, volunteer work, and other things may be very different on different days. In your case, grocery shopping may take 20 minutes one week and two hours the next for about the same list. Why? The spending

record may start you thinking about the right amount of time for it.

3. How much time seems to be spent uselessly? The record shows time spent for unwanted or unremembered reasons. This is the kind of spending that needs the most attention and gives you the chance to choose. What would you rather be doing instead of what you actually did?

Meanings of Time

"What would the ideal day be like?" "What is the best possible day I can make for myself?" The second question, not the first, is the better one for the person budgeting time. A spending record shows that some uses of time can probably be changed, while other uses cannot. Some of the must-do tasks are hardly ideal. The best a person can do is keep them in their place in the budget. Yet beginning budgeters often tend to forget the record and start dreaming. The Saturday morning samples in Figure 3-3 show how it happens. Dora has thrown away some time for tasks—time that will surely come back to haunt her. Eric, on the other hand, has put himself on a production-line budget. His timetable is so stiff that a few interruptions may throw it off completely. Budgets need some room to bend.

Eric's way of budgeting his time is similar to the mistake families most often make in budgeting their money. The family puts every cent of income into many accounts. Every account is cut down to the smallest possible amount that might be spent. Then a surprise guest arrives. Some fancy food is in order. So the food account is overdrawn. Then an appliance breaks down. That causes the household account to be overdrawn. This starts a string of changes. Money is taken from account A to cover a shortage in account B. Then account A goes dry, and money must be switched to it from account C. Finally, the family tires of it all and throws the budget away.

It is wise, with money or time, to allow some space in which things can go wrong. Eric tries to fill every minute of every hour. There's no minute to spare for a slip.

Eric's budget can be seen in another way. He has set it up as though he were a worker on a factory assembly line. His budget is

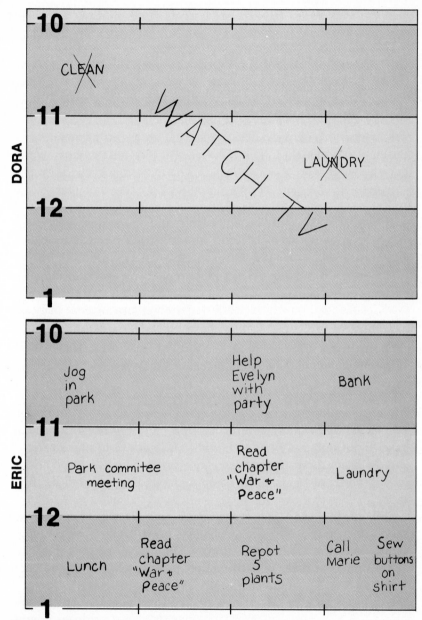

Fig. 3-3 These two time budgets, planned by Dora and Eric, show common mistakes made by beginning budgeters. Dora has decided to watch TV rather than do her household tasks and Eric has crammed his day with too many activities.

designed to increase the amount he gets done in every hour. This method is well known, but it may not fit a personal time budget.

Time and Efficiency   The idea of efficiency has a high place in American thought. However, it has really taken hold only since the early part of this century. The workday used to run from sunrise to sunset, which made it different from season to season. Each worker had a personal way of doing the job. The movement called *scientific management* changed all that. It sought the "one best way" to do any given task in the factory. Split-second studies were made of each worker's every movement. Time-motion people (also called efficiency experts) then drew up the one way the task should be done in the least time and with the least wasted motion.

Time-motion studies helped make American workers the most productive in the world. The same ideas were also applied, with good results, to household work. A person's use of time at home may improve after a little thought about better ways to do small tasks. Minutes can be saved by using better ways to sweep the floor, empty garbage, stock the shelves with canned goods, wash dishes, etc.

These ideas should be used with care, however, in budgeting time or in making a life-style. Efficiency can help to get some dull daily tasks over with in a hurry. On the other hand, efficiency can make things dull that needn't be dull. (Should we judge our use of time by how many books we read and how fast we read them? Does it matter *what* we read?) Some enjoyed things can't be measured.

Each person may also feel that all hours are not equal to all others. In recent years, some scientists have studied the *circadian rhythms* of living things, including people. These rhythms might be called, simply, a daily pattern of ups and downs in the way each person's body and mind works.

You may think of yourself as a "morning person" or a "night person." A morning person may jump out of bed at dawn, happy and full of pep. About the time a morning person is ready to go to bed again, a night person is just beginning to fill up with energy and ideas.

Until recently, this was thought to be a simple matter of habits. Many scientists now believe that the morning person and the night person are truly different in the way their bodies work and change from hour to hour. Thus, a morning hour is *bigger* for a morning person. The midnight hour is *bigger* for a night person.

THINKING IT THROUGH

1. What was your best-remembered day of the last year? Why do you remember it more than others? Was it a good day or a bad day? Do most people tend to remember good days or bad days more?

2. Where were you and what were you doing last Thursday? A month ago today? Six months ago today? Some people have much better recall of their uses of time than others. What do you think are the reasons for such differences in people?

3. Do you think more about the past than about the present or future? How many people in your class think most about the present? How many think most about the future? Are there broad differences of style apparent in these answers? If so, why are people so different? Or perhaps practically everyone has indicated a tendency to think largely about one of the three. If so, why is this group of people so much the same?

4. Time appears to affect all people equally. Yet it is valued in very different ways by different people. Complete the statement "Time is . . ." in ten words or less. Why do people like or dislike the idea of ongoing time?

Needs, Values, Goals

A record of spent time offers a look at several interesting questions:

- How much of your time spending goes for what *you* choose?
- How much time do you spend with others? How much alone?
- How much of your time is spent in satisfying ways? How much is spent for things that do not please you? Why?

Those questions answered, you try to budget time for a better (if not ideal) day. If you pay attention to your spending record, you find there are some things you must do, like them or not.

But you also find you have some time to spare to make new choices. You choose. Then a couple more questions arise:

- Did you budget time for things you think you *should* do?
- Or did you budget time for things you really *want* to do?

Those two kinds of things, the ones you should do and the ones you want to do, may be exactly the same in your view. Or they may be quite different. The questions about them make up a test of who you are.

Suppose you chose to do what others wanted you to do (or what you *thought* they wanted). You didn't think about yourself. The name for that is *respondent behavior.* You *respond* to other people's wants or wishes. You strive to please. You listen to advice and almost always take it.

Maybe, on the other hand, you thought first about what *you* wanted. You just made up your own mind. You were ready to take the blame if your choice was wrong. The name for that is *operant behavior.* You *operate* your own life and try to make it work well.

Operant behavior is likely to be more satisfying than respondent behavior. It doesn't mean that you ignore other people's advice and wishes. It surely doesn't mean you always do the opposite of what others want you to do. (That's just another way of being respondent.) It does mean you know where you're going and why. You have strong values and goals.

Working for Self-control

Operant behavior is a mixture of many ways of thinking and acting. Here is how it looks in the words of two people who live alone and seem to have a good hold on their own lives:

Henry   "I plan most of my time. But I try to plan it flexibly enough so that I can make up my mind without a lot of heat. I have three offers of things to do next weekend. I can put off deciding—without troubling the people who asked me. I want to think about things I have to pay some attention to and things I want to do. So I've just told people I'll get back to them on Friday.

"I set goals for myself in the short range, like a week. And I set some goals in the long range, maybe five years. The far-off goals are quite a bit more general than the close-by ones. I set a goal of finishing work on my college degree after I got out of the Army. I did that. Then I set the goal of getting my master's degree. But I won't chase that with the same drive I needed to get the first degree. I'll get there someday. I guess I just wanted that bachelor's degree more.

"I reach my goals if I really want to. If they really *are* goals. Sometimes you set goals that become less important as you get closer to them. Once, I decided I was going to get up to a certain salary. When I reached it, I asked myself: 'Now what? Do I set another money goal?' I decided I was satisfied with the money I had. Money became less of a driving force. I decided that other kinds of things were more important to me. I wanted more satisfaction in other things I was doing, like reading and community projects. It was a trade-off of the company's time for my own time.

"I started college with the goal of becoming an engineer. I flunked out because that wasn't a real goal. I felt bad about flunking out. But I felt equally good when I finished Officer Candidate School and got my army commission. I blamed my failure in college on being too young and lacking self-discipline. OCS demanded much stricter control of yourself. I proved to myself that I could handle that. That was the turning point for me. After that, I had a lot more confidence in myself."

Lucy   "I've lived alone for a long while. It would take a very special person—and a *big* house—for me to change my mind about living alone.

"I want fair warning from people who want me to join them. I just don't understand people who call at 5:15 and ask me what I'm doing for dinner. You know, that may be the night I don't want to do anything for dinner at all. It may be the night I want to go to the library or spend hours doing my hair.

"When I was on a Monday-through-Friday routine, my life was more structured, set up for me. I always had Saturday off. I enjoyed spending a lot of time cleaning—*if* I had plenty of time to do it alone. Now I've got an executive sort of job. I travel a little. My time is less certain. When my time is limited, cleaning is not the kind of thing I really want to do. At this point in my life I hate what I call 'scutwork'—laundering drapes, scrubbing the bathroom, and all that. When I have just a little more money, I'll have a cleaning service come in. I used to think heavy cleaning was really, really important. I was conditioned that way by a mother and a mother-in-law. Now I'm sick of myself worrying about waxy buildup and ring around the bathtub. I mean, how dirty is dirty? Oh, I keep it neat. But I don't let cleaning run my life.

"I belong to the American Youth Hostel. One of the things we do is take blind people out into the woods on hikes. Or sometimes we take them for rides on tandem bikes. Or we might do a picnic at the beach.

"I wouldn't want to do these things as a really steady diet. But when I do them, I feel good about giving myself and my time. It's a kind of communion with other people, helping them enjoy different things that they couldn't without you. Some of us in the neighbor-

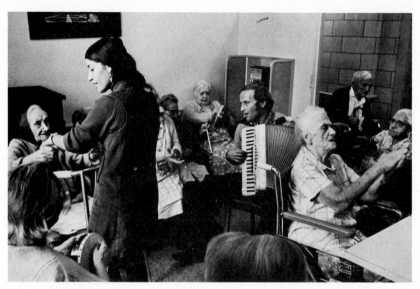

"I feel good about giving myself and my time. It's a kind of communion with other people, helping them enjoy things that they couldn't without you." (Metropolitan Jewish Geriatric Center)

hood get together every year and put on a Thanksgiving dinner for elderly people who are going to be alone on the holiday. Last year we served dinner to over 200, and it was a special night. We had candlelight and singing and a six-course meal cooked by volunteers. I like to do things like that, that make other people happy. Maybe it's an ego trip but it's a good kind of giving."

Elements of Self   People like Henry and Lucy seem to make the best of independent living. In quite different ways, they express good feelings about themselves. They seem able to talk clearly— and honestly—about who they are. They also speak directly about what they have, what they want, and why.

How do people like these put themselves together? Going back through what Henry and Lucy have to say, it's possible to see some of the "building blocks" that make them who they are:

Needs   People have some needs that must be met if they are to live at all. Food, air, and water head the list. Anything beyond these—even shelter, clothing, and tools—may at first be *wants* we can live without. Once material needs are met, economists say, the wants become needs, and new wants replace the old. In economic terms, this chain of events can grow almost endlessly. "I need bus fare; I wish I had a car." "I don't mind riding the bus, but I really need a car." "My car is OK. But I need a bigger, faster model." And so forth. People have psychological and emotional needs as well. "I love my Rolls Royce, but I need love and respect." These needs, of course, don't follow the laws of economics.

Goals   A need may be general. Hunger can be satisfied with all sorts of foods. A goal is a definite idea of what it takes to meet the need: "I'm hungry. I want a pizza." Or, more seriously: "I need to know more about computers. There's a great night course at Tech on computers." A person's goals may be quite dim: "I need money. I wonder if there are any jobs around." Or they may be very clearly seen: "I need better pay. I know I can make more as an auto mechanic." Goals may go well beyond money and things: "I need friendship. I know that people would like me better if I could stand up and .speak my mind."

Motives   The distance between need and goal often seems huge. Motivation is the force that helps a person see goals clearly and go for them. Psychologists suppose that every person has 20 or more different motives. Each one is a pattern of thoughts and feelings connected with a certain need. Survival is a strong motive in all of us. Curiosity is a motive almost all of us have, but many of us don't use it. Motives can be buried deep inside. The unmotivated person seems to be uncaring, unfeeling, turned off by just about everything. But motives can be turned on too.

Values   What is worth doing, worth having? What decides a person's self-worth and worth to the world? A person may have a set of beliefs, opinions, and feelings—all values—that help answer these questions. What does that have to do with the price of beans? Quite a lot. Beans are on the shelf today at 38 cents a can. That's a fact. Are beans *worth* 38 cents? That is the value given them today by millions of buyers. But you can take it or leave it. You happen to believe that beans are the greatest food in the world and a steal at that price. Many, many people will not agree. But that is your value, and only you can change it. Your values may come from you alone. It is more likely they have been shaped by hundreds of outside forces. Parents, teachers, friends, writers, political leaders, advertisers are just a few of them. Some of your values may be shared with millions of other people. Some are so widely held they seem like facts. But *all* values may need testing once in a while. Suppose you're thinking not about beans but about freedom. You believe in freedom. *Everybody* believes in freedom. Do you really? Do they really? One hundred percent? If not, how much? Having a value is more than saying it. You value freedom by the way you use it yourself and support its use by others.

It should be possible for you to draw a four-part picture of yourself, for yourself, by using these four "building blocks." No one is likely to draw a blank. You may find yourself stretching hard, however, for things you ought to know about you. A together person is likely to find needs, goals, motives, and values all in tune. Suppose you *need* a sense of your own worth. You set a *goal* of helping elderly people in town. You are *motivated* to call senior citizens centers to offer your services. One center invites you to come weekly as a crafts instructor. You *value* the dignity and spirit of your older pupils. Part of your life, at this point, seems to be working very well.

This story may be too neat, of course, but some thought about these ideas can bring real-life payoffs close to it.

I Need . . . Sigmund Freud's first studies of the human mind brought forth his view of the *id* (see page 3). It was the animal-like center of the mind. It wanted only raw satisfaction and pleasure.

More than half a century later, psychologist Abraham H. Maslow decided to look at the idea of self from a totally different point of view. Psychologists before him had largely attended to people who were troubled and sick. Maslow studied *healthy* people instead, trying to find out what being healthy really meant. He picked subjects who did much and seemed well connected to themselves and their world.

One result of Maslow's studies was the *Hierarchy of Needs* shown in Figure 4-1. Needs are pictured as a rising stairway. Most people try to climb it one step at a time. Only when they reach the first step do they think strongly about the second. Only when they

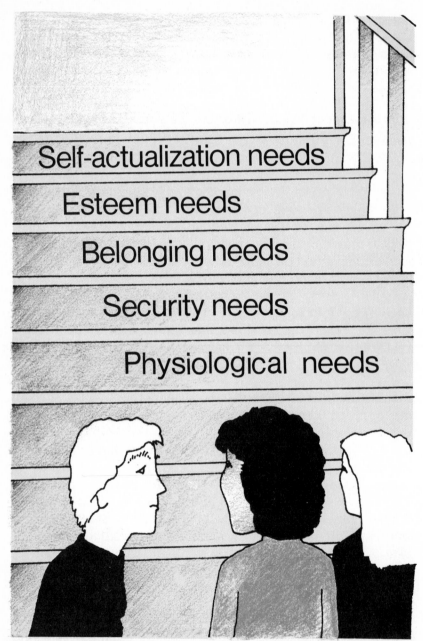

Fig. 4-1 The hierarchy of needs is a theory by A. H. Maslow about human needs. Here, these needs are pictured as a stairway because you must satisfy each level of need before you move up to the next.

reach the second do they think strongly about the third, and so on. Most of us have a view, however dim, of the stairway as a whole. A great many of us get stalled on one step or another along the way.

A clear view from the bottom to the top of the hierarchy might look like this:

1. *Physiological Needs*   These are the simple bodily needs that must be met to keep life going. Among them are thirst, hunger, rest, movement. When these needs can be satisfied, the person's attention is able to move on to

2. *Security Needs*   We want to be *sure* that our basic needs will be filled not only today but in the future. We want to be safe from attack and natural dangers. When the need for security is met, the person's attention moves on to

3. *Belonging Needs*   The person wants strongly to be part of a group. This means friendship and the giving and receiving of love. It means the pleasures of working with others. After these things begin to happen, the person's thoughts turn to

4. *Esteem Needs*   The person wants to be liked and respected as an individual by the group. The person needs feelings of self-worth that grow from what others in the group say. This need may increase to a need for *status*—high standing—in the group. Accepted in these ways, the person will turn to

5. *Self-Actualization Needs*   The person needs an *inner* sense of worth, of having done the best that could possibly be done. Self-actualized people are realistic. But they fully enjoy themselves and the world around them.

The first two steps—bodily needs and security needs—are fairly easy for most people in today's world. Either of the next two— needs for friendship, then recognition—may loom too large for most of us to see the highest step.

One point more must be made about the climb. People themselves are the judges of when their needs are filled. Many are stuck on the steps because they simply do not know how much friendship or praise or power they want. How much is enough? Since they have no clear goals, they do not know. Other rare people seem to be self-actualized with little in the way of goods or group esteem. Some artists are like that. They enjoy good things and other good people, but these needs are modest. Because of this, they have been able to move on to satisfaction and confidence in their own work.

Human Motivation

No serious study of human motives began before the 1930s. Most of the studies then and since have been built around people at work in factories and offices. The questions raised, however, often cover the full sweep of living.

The efficiency experts of this century (see page 28) believed—and may still—that workers were to do exactly as they were told. Each small work movement was mapped out. The worker was to obey the plan and even rest on its command.

The worker's satisfaction was to come from the higher pay that went with higher output. Pay often did go up in great leaps. Yet workers fought such changes or accepted them only grudgingly. Why couldn't they see that efficiency was meant for their own good?

Questions like that led to more. Why did some people work well and others poorly? What would motivate people to work more effectively? Pay was increased. Working areas were painted and lighted more brightly. Working hours were cut. Fringe benefits were invented. Vacation time grew. Bosses were even told to be more friendly to workers. Yet many workers remained unhappy and un-motivated. Why?

Behavioral scientists offered a surprising answer that remains the center of heated debate. The worker's satisfaction, they said, had to come *from the job itself*. Workers had to believe that what they were doing was worthwhile. If they could not take pride in their work, most other benefits did not matter.

Douglas McGregor made one of the best-known statements of this idea in a book called *The Human Side of Enterprise* (McGraw-Hill, 1960).

Most companies, he said, worked under "Theory X": *People really don't want to work. Workers have to be kept in line either by "hard" rules or a "soft" system of rewards.*

McGregor offered "Theory Y": *People want to work. They need the chance to take responsibility, to set their own work goals. Given the chance to give their best, they can help the company set and reach higher goals.*

Some people seem to have little need for material goods or group esteem. This artist may find self-actualization in his work. (Marc Weinstein, Pratt Institute of Art)

Theory Y is an idea whose time will not easily come. Few companies are ready yet to let workers take part in major decisions. Theory Y has led, however, to many programs for making work more interesting for workers. Companies have begun programs to enlarge and enrich certain jobs and to help workers advance. Great gains have been made by many of the people who take part. This does not prove, of course, that *all* workers would do the same.

The Achievement Motive   Achievement has been the most fully studied of human motives. Dr. David C. McClelland, the leader in these studies, did not try to study all sorts of people. Instead, he sought out people who seemed to have a high need to achieve. These were people trying to do things better, faster, extremely well. They often wanted to do things that no one had done before. McClelland wanted to learn how people like these thought, felt, and acted. He hoped that once he knew these things he could teach them to others who wanted to increase their own achievement motivation.

Thousands of people were tested for achievement motivation and two other important motives. The first of these was the need for *power*—the need to lead or control other people. The second was the need for *affiliation*—the need to have friends or help others. A person can act on several motives at once. In other words, motives don't have to crowd each other out. Fran may want to be club president because it takes skill and hard work (achievement motive). But she may feel she can make the club better for the members (affiliation motive). And she may enjoy being the leader (power motive). One of these motives, however, is likely to be *dominant*—stronger than the others.

McClelland's studies found people in every field who showed very high achievement motivation in their lives. From their real lives, he was able to draw the rich picture of achievement thinking shown in Figure 4-2. These 10 kinds of thought seemed to make up a pattern shown over and over again by people who prized excellence in what they were doing. As might be expected, some were very successful business leaders and athletes. But many others were teachers, musicians, clerks, housekeepers, artists—achievement has many expressions. Their 10-part way of thinking contained the following elements:

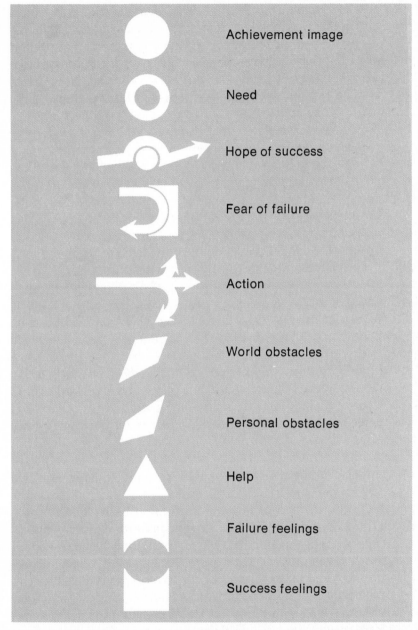

Achievement image

Need

Hope of success

Fear of failure

Action

World obstacles

Personal obstacles

Help

Failure feelings

Success feelings

Fig. 4-2 These symbols represent the ten parts of achievement thinking. (Adapted from Alfred Alschuler, Diane Tabor, and James McIntyre, *Teaching Achievement Motivation,* Education Ventures, Inc., Middletown, Conn., 1970)

1. *Achievement Image* The strong achievement motive makes the person's goal clear and sharp. It is not a goal of just getting something done. It is a goal of doing something important very, very well. It is always marked by *at least one* of four desires:
    a.   the desire to compete with self—to do something better than you have ever done it before;
    b.   the desire to compete with others in doing something or reaching a goal;
    c.   the desire to do something unique—something no one (in your family, school, town, or even the whole world) has ever done before;
    d.   the desire for long-term involvement—doing something well and improving results for a long time into the future.

2. *Need* The high achiever has a strong need to reach the goal. It is not a matter of thinking, "Wouldn't it be nice if. . . ." It is a real, powerful desire to get there. It is knowing what you want and how much you want it.

3. *Hope of Success* This is not simply a wish or a faint dream. It is a vivid picture of what it will be like, how good it will feel, to reach the goal.

4. *Fear of Failure* High achievers might have been expected to put thoughts of failure out of their minds. They proved instead to have greater fears of failure than other people. This is not just a matter of feeling uneasy or nervous. It is a vivid picture of how bad it would be to fall short of the goal.

5. *Action* The high achiever does something about getting to the goal. Action is planned, often a step at a time, to move toward the goal. The goal is clear. The high achiever works hard to make the path to the goal just as clear.

6. *World Obstacles* High achievers try to foresee those things outside themselves that may block the way to the goal. Lack of rain is a world obstacle for a gardener. Lack of jobs is a world obstacle for a person who wants to save for education. The high achiever tries to picture these kinds of trouble clearly—in order to overcome them.

7. *Personal Obstacles* High achievers try to face up to those things inside themselves that block the way to the goal. Smoking may block the way to the goal of good health. The lack of

certain skills may block the way to the needed job. The high achiever tries to picture these troubles clearly—again to overcome them.

8. *Help*   The person with a high need to achieve knows that some things can't be done without good advice and assistance. Help counts most in getting around world or personal obstacles.

9. *Failure Feelings*   When high achievers do fall short of their goals, they feel a very strong sense of loss. They can't just forget about it. But these feelings don't make them want to quit, but to keep trying for the goal in new ways. They learn facts from failure. They also learn they don't like the way it feels.

10. *Success Feelings*   When their goals are reached, high achievers have strong feelings of pride and happiness. They are satisfied. But they also are ready to keep improving. They've learned how good it feels to reach an important goal. They want to keep doing that.

All together, these 10 parts make up a full pattern of achievement thinking (see Figure 4-3). When people with a high need for achievement swing into action, they also use four important strategies.

1. *Researching the Environment*   The high achiever takes charge of the hunt for information. This means finding out everything possible about help or obstacles on the path from need to goal.

2. *Personal Responsibility*   The high achiever isn't ready to wait for luck or fate—or other people—to settle things. In case of failure, the high achiever takes the blame rather than pointing a finger at others or at "Lady Luck."

3. *Moderate Risks*   High achievers set goals that are hard, but not impossible, to reach. They do not like problems with surefire answers. Nor do they like dares so difficult that hardly anyone can do them. They would rather set goals where the chance of success is moderate—or medium—somewhere in the range of fifty-fifty. Such a goal is high enough to be exciting, but it is not so high that a person is defeated at the start.

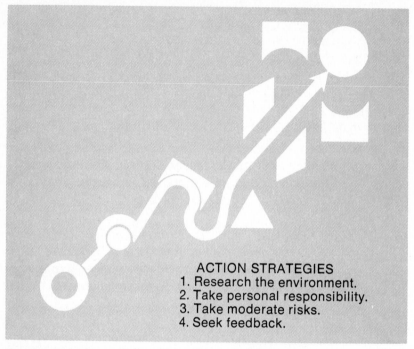

ACTION STRATEGIES
1. Research the environment.
2. Take personal responsibility.
3. Take moderate risks.
4. Seek feedback.

Fig. 4-3 When put together, the 10 parts of achievement thinking make up a model of achievement thinking and action.

4. *Feedback*   High achievers want to know how they are doing every step of the way. They seek feedback—facts and feelings about how well they are doing. They want to know about each right and wrong move as it happens. Listening to these signals helps them improve what they are doing and avoid making mistakes over again.

That big picture of a motive at work may seem too neat and right. Yet real-life people with high achievement motivation are daring in ways others of us won't try. Almost everyone dreams of doing *something* very well. We dream about standing out in sports, studies, art, work, crafts, or other fields. But then we smother the dreams, doing nothing or saying nothing about them. Others, meanwhile, turn dreams into plans. That's a difference between motives buried and motives at work.

Wide World of Values

Some people move along with their eyes fixed on clear goals. They tend to have their values sorted out to fit what they are doing. They truly believe in work for work's sake, in service to fellow humans, in art for art's sake, or in the duty to learn.

The rest of us, less ready to defend ourselves, are peppered with value statements from a hundred directions:

"Try Snookies. They're good—and good for you."

"Inflation is public enemy number one. We need a dollar worth 100 cents."

"It's getting so it's not safe to walk the streets anymore."

"Bright-o Toothpaste is good for you. Use Bright-o—and find love."

"This has always been, and ever will be, the land of opportunity."

"Looking for a job? Remember, it's not what you know, but who you know."

"We have to trust each other more."

"Try Snoozy sleeping pills. You owe a well-rested you to your family, your boss, and yourself."

"What I do with my body is my own business."

"Clothes make the man and woman. Good appearance is what it takes to get ahead."

"It's not the length of the hair that counts, it's what's in the head the hair is on."

"Anyone who really wants to find work can find it."

"You can't trust anybody anymore."

"I just don't like people, whatever their nationality, race, religion, age, sex, and so on."

"People are better than they're cracked up to be."

Look and listen hard enough and you'll find value statements covering every shade of almost every question. However, when they pile up around your eyes and ears, as in Figure 4-4, it may be hard to think clearly. How do you pick what's yours out of that big heap? Many people can't. With few values to call their own, they

Fig. 4-4 Headlines in newspapers and magazines and advertising on billboards, television, and radio all constantly bombard us with value statements. These statements often contradict each other. Sometimes, in the confusion, it's hard to think clearly and decide which are your own values.

stand unmoving. Or maybe they flutter back and forth in the winds of other people's opinions. People caught in that storm find it hard to use their own motives and to set their own goals. They don't know what they value. They don't know what they really want.

Trouble With Values   Some people seem to have few values. They act cool. They seem to care about nothing. Maybe not caring is what they value most.

More of us have trouble trying to choose among too many value possibilities. Some of us fall into *value conflicts*. We value—or say we value—ideas that actually fight each other. This is something like standing on both sides of the same fence at the same time. Value conflict can sound pretty silly:

"I believe in the rights of *all* people, but those (name of any ethnic group) don't deserve any."

"Honesty is the best policy, but you have to take what you can get in this life."

"These kids today need to be taught to think for themselves. And we've got to have tougher rules in the schools to do that job."

Value conflict is more often a matter of trouble in making choices between one good thing and another:

"That meeting tonight is really important. Matt's party sounds good too. But I need some sleep. Ought to be fresh for work tomorrow."

"The job offer is great. But it means giving up my art classes and the golf league. I need money. But you know that old saying about all work and no play."

"Being asked to run for office at my age is a great honor. I think I owe it to myself and to the party. But I have a private life too. And I'm not going to give that up."

Clearing Up   "What do you value most? You don't know? Well, sit down, think hard, and make a list." That advice is often given. It's so much easier said than done. People who don't know their values might as well be trying to write about some country they've never seen. It's their good fortune that there are other ways of trying to *clarify* values—make them clearer. One good starting point is a list of values that many people seem to hold, like this one:

A. Love; B. Health; C. Achievement; D. Adventure; E. Good Looks; F. Sports; G. Happiness; H. Money; I. Family Ties; J. Friendship; K. Freedom; L. Neatness; M. Safety; N. Honesty; O. Service to Others; P. Love of God; Q. Love of Country; R. Leadership; S. Skill; T. Power; U. Strength; V. Wisdom; W. Self-Awareness; X. Success; Y. Peace; and Z. Learning.

That alphabet of good things is a mere selection of values. (It is said that there are more than 7,000 good-value words in the English language!) Your job is to rank them in the order of their importance to you, from first to twenty-sixth. Or maybe it would be better to start with five or six values.

Another interesting way to do much the same thing is a forced-choice test of values. This is a sort of head-to-head contest. Each value on a list is matched once against each other. You *must* choose one in each pair:

1. To do things well   *or*   2. To have friends

1. To do things well   *or*   3. To do what is right

2. To have friends   *or*   3. To do what is right

The value most important to you is likely to "win" most often in these pairings. Another interesting way to look at values is one at a time. A value *continuum* (or scale) offers a fair self-test. Suppose that the value in question is hard work. If you had to rate yourself on the scale of 0 to 100, where would you be? What would be your score for friendliness on such a scale? For care in what you say? For taking care of your health? The number of possibilities is limitless.

There can be a broad line between listing values and doing something about them. Sometimes it may be very important for the person to declare the value to others and to put it into action. For example, Bill may put high value on friendship, yet he has been too shy to meet many people. Jill puts high value on privacy, yet she spends most of her time with other people. Both may have to take another look at what their values really are. It is better, psychologists note, to put high value on what you are and can be than on what you cannot be. Realistic values help to make people good in many different ways at what they do and who they are.

Values, needs, and goals put a new light on many questions about the uses of time. The next chapter moves on to a longer-range view of life-style.

THINKING IT THROUGH

1. Do you know any real-life people who are always doing what they think other people want (*respondent* behavior)? Or people who seem always to be doing what they want to do (*operant* behavior)? Which of these people do you personally like better? Why?

2. Do you think that most of your behavior can be called operant or respondent? Why? Do you expect that you will change that? When and why?

3. Look at the picture and description of the hierarchy of needs in Chapter 4. Which step beyond the first is the one you think is most important to you? Why? Try to explain your own needs more clearly by giving a score, anywhere from 50 to 100, to indicate what you want at each step. In other words, how much safety and security do you want? How many good friends do you want? How much skill do you want in doing things you want to do? What need is regarded as most important among members of the class?

4. Do you agree or disagree with McGregor's ideas as described in Chapter 4? He says, in brief, that people are treated as though they don't want to work (Theory X), but that most people really want to work and to take part in planning their work (Theory Y). What real-life examples can you offer to support Theory X and Theory Y?

5. In Chapter 4, ten elements of achievement thinking are described. Are you surprised by some of the thoughts that high achievers have, such as the fear of failure and the need for help? In what ways do you fit the ten-part model? In what ways are you different from the high-achievement model?

Planning a Week

One idea that is widely admired—or valued—is living "one day at a time." It is connected with people bravely rebuilding their lives. It is a motto for members of Alcoholics Anonymous. It has been used as the title of a TV show about a divorced mother. It has been borrowed by many others working to get their lives back in order. In that sense, each one day is part of the way to a big goal.

Many of us see our days differently. Each day is a just matter of getting things done or "getting it over with." A lot of the tasks we have to do stir up feelings like that. Even days that seemed happy and lively may leave no sense of lasting pleasure. Why? It is likely to be a matter of needs, values, and goals—or the lack of them.

Two people who live alone talk about trying to get organized:

Pete "Every once in a while I have this big urge to tie up all the loose ends. Usually what I do is make a general list of about 50 things I need to do. Things like clean up the refrigerator, write the letters I've owed for months, fix the toaster, and so forth. Then I divide them up into the days of the next week. I try to even them up as much as I can. I put down five or six things for Saturday, five or six for Sunday, and so on. Just making the list makes me feel like I'm getting a lot done. I feel better yet when I start to cross things off. Then I hit a day when I don't get anything crossed off. So I start feeling guilty and mad at myself. I'm really pretty disorganized. I'm not like my father, who used to plan things like that and make it work. Funny, the only time I really get it together is before Christmas. I'm into crafts, and I make a lot of gifts for the family and friends. Then I set my plan up *by the hour.* It goes something like this: 5 to 7, cut wood blocks; 7 to 7:30, eat supper; 7:30 to 8, make test prints; 8 to 9, set up copper enameling; 9 to 9:15, start kiln; and so on into the night. Now *that* works. I wish I could do it all year long."

Ellen   "I used to be Ms. Putoffski—put off everything until Saturday. You can't do that. You have to make a stern plan so you can be flexible. That sounds odd, but it's true. You plan it out by the minute all week. But you find yourself saving minutes. That means I get some free time for me whenever I want it. I used to think I was giving myself time by putting things off. Then I never had any time. Another way I save myself time and worry is by staying out of debt. Seriously. I don't get in debt. I keep my wants and needs where they belong. For one thing, clothes aren't all that important to me anymore. When I was living at home, they were the most important thing. But when you're young, alone, and low-paid, you have to make choices. So I decided being presentable was important, being fashionable wasn't. It depends on your income and your interests. Things like buying clothes carefully helped me get along OK when I was unemployed for quite a while. I didn't have any loans or installment plans to pay. Of course, changing some of your tastes isn't easy. I ate a lot of canned spaghetti before I learned to find other things that were cheap and good. But you can find things to do that are different and interesting and cheap—even free. And I do."

Time for Goals

In their different ways, Pete and Ellen say a lot about using time and working toward goals—seen or not. Pete seems to plan around values without knowing it. Ellen is aware of every valued minute. Some hours, depending on how we look at them, can be counted as part of an ordinary day or part of a lifetime.

That statement sounds clearer turned around: If _____ is your goal, what can you do *right now,* in this hour, to help you reach it?

For the Record   Studies of achievement motivation show that it is a good idea to ask, "Where are you going?" and, "How are you doing?" every day. People trying to increase their motivation got best returns when they kept accurate records of their own steps toward a goal. They set the goals. They set the time period for reaching them. But they gained when they were able to measure results daily in clear terms. If the goal was a distant one, the person could divide it into smaller time periods. For example, a person who wanted to be a banker could set a partway goal of reading books about economics. This could then be broken down again into a number of pages or chapters a day.

A week is a good amount of time for getting to a goal or partway goal. A week is quick enough for anyone eager to reach a goal. But it is also long enough for using feedback to change a goal that proves too easy or too hard. A week can be enough to quit smoking or cut down, lose a pound or two, read a book, write a song, improve a skill. A week is time enough to carry out some plans or to make new plans. There is time to make a budget, plan some interesting meals, develop a cleaning system that works, paint a room.

Some people will need the week to find out what they *think* their goals should be. They may decide they have no clear view of their own values. They will want to search for what their values are. Or they may want to find out if they have faults they want to correct. That may sound odd. Yet many people aren't sure whether their habits are bad or not. They feel a need to find out.

Searching for Values   One interesting way to bring values to light is by answering self-questions like those shown in Figure 5-1. An even simpler way to try to uncover values is to write down a few hundred "Things I Like." This can be done in spare minutes over several days. Different people make lists that are surprisingly unlike each other. Any one list may have likes as far apart as "thinking about life on other planets" and "hamburgers." But each list is likely to show a major number of things connected with one or two strong values. The value may be a job well done, helping other people, or being a leader. There's a fair chance the likes add up to a motive. That, in turn, is a sign of what the person's goals can be.

Faultfinding   The self-search for faults is at least as old as Benjamin Franklin, who tells about it in his *Autobiography*. As a young printer's helper of twenty-two, Franklin worried about his own attention to good habits. He listed what he thought to be the 13 great habits of the good person. Alongside each habit, he drew a square for each day of the week (as shown in Figure 5-2). He carried this

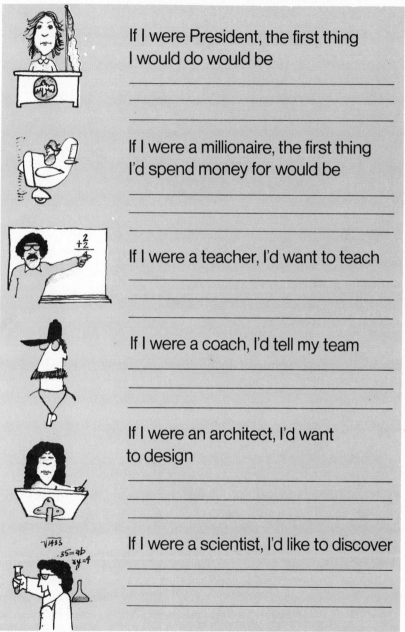

If I were President, the first thing
I would do would be

_____

_____

_____

If I were a millionaire, the first thing
I'd spend money for would be

_____

_____

_____

If I were a teacher, I'd want to teach

_____

_____

_____

If I were a coach, I'd tell my team

_____

_____

_____

If I were an architect, I'd want
to design

_____

_____

_____

If I were a scientist, I'd like to discover

_____

_____

_____

Fig. 5-1 Answering questions such as these can help you discover what are
your values. You can add other roles to the list, for example, a police officer
or a store owner.

VIRTUES	Mon	Tues	Wed	Thurs	Fri	Sat	Sun
TEMPERANCE	●						
SILENCE		● ●					
ORDER		●	●				
RESOLUTION	●		●				
FRUGALITY		●		●			
INDUSTRY				●			
SINCERITY			●				
JUSTICE		●					
MODERATION							
CLEANLINESS							
TRANQUILITY				●			
CHASTITY							
HUMILITY	●	●	●				

Fig. 5-2 Ben Franklin carried a chart such as this one with him. He kept track of his faults by marking down a black dot every time he failed to follow a good habit.

chart with him in a small notebook. At any time he thought he had failed to follow one of the good habits, he marked a small black spot in the correct square.

Keeping track of 13 things is hard. After a time, Franklin decided to give his main attention each week to just one of the virtues on his list. He would mark the others the best he could. "I hoped," he wrote, "to be happy in seeing a clean book at the end of thirteen weeks' examination."

But it wasn't that easy. There were no erasers in his day. Marks had to be removed with a knife edge or razor. Franklin soon found his chart full of holes "from scraping out the marks of old faults to make room for new ones." After he thought about that for a while, he decided that a good man should have "a few faults." A perfect man, he said, wouldn't have many friends—and might not even like himself too well.

Ben Franklin's system might be used today by a person who wants to do a self-check on faults. (Maybe not 13, but at least a couple.) Smoke too much? Talk too much? Snack too much? Some people suspect they do, but they do not know for sure. A black mark for each cigarette, each long speech, and each nibble will tell the story. And it may lead to a goal of correcting the fault.

One fault at a time can be checked out on the graph form in Figure 5-3. You may notice you say "y'know" a lot. Too much? Each time you catch yourself doing it, make a mark on a slip of paper. At the end of the day, put the total number of marks on the graph. As the week goes on, the graph line will show how you're doing. You may find you say "y'know" a lot more than you thought

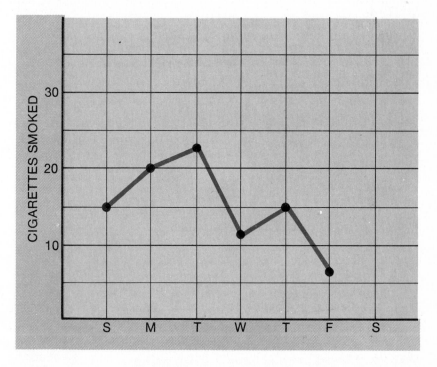

Fig. 5-3 Hank used Ben Franklin's system to keep track of one of his own habits—smoking. First, he made a chart and inked in a black dot for each cigarette he smoked during the day. Then, he made up a graph showing the total number of cigarettes smoked for a week. Although Hank thought he smoked about half a pack a day (there are 20 cigarettes to a pack), he was surprised to find that he had smoked an average of 15 cigarettes a day.

you did. Cutting down on saying "y'know" is a fair goal if you want it.

This type of self-testing may have a *Hawthorne Effect.* That is a scientist's term for an interesting human habit. People being studied by scientists often improve what they're doing *because they know they are being studied.* Something like that may happen to a person counting personal faults. They may somehow be cut down even as the person counts them from day to day. If not, cutting down on them becomes a potential goal.

Keeping Score   Competition with yourself may be the best game going. You can't lose badly, but you can win big. That's the idea of a kind of game designed to make sport of daily tasks. It starts with a list of the things you have to do or want to do in the coming day. (See Figure 5-4.) Using a value system of 1 to 10, you decide how much each thing on the list is worth. You'll want to think about how important the thing is and how much daily value or lifetime value it has. By this measure, going to the gas station to fill up might be worth 1 point. Going to the bank for a new-car loan might be worth 5. Reading a car manual to learn a new skill might be worth 8. Really doing a repair job for the first time might be worth 10. Those values, of course, are up to you.

Any day can be expected to bring unexpected tasks. Your values for the day include 10 points that can be spread out to cover tasks like that.

At the end of the next day, you score the results. If the task has been done well, it gets a score equal to its full value. If the task has not been done well, you have to decide how many points to subtract from its full value. For example, you may have repaired an open seam in your clothing. You valued this task at 3 points. But you think you did the job carelessly. You take a point away from yourself, scoring it only as 2. If the task doesn't get done at all, you take its *whole* value away from the day's score.

What's the sense of keeping score on yourself? Not much if it's only done for a day. It's something else when you keep a day-to-day scoring record for a week. (See Figure 5-4.) For one thing, it gives you an idea of what happened on the days you tried to do too much. Doing that is almost sure to make you feel bad and score

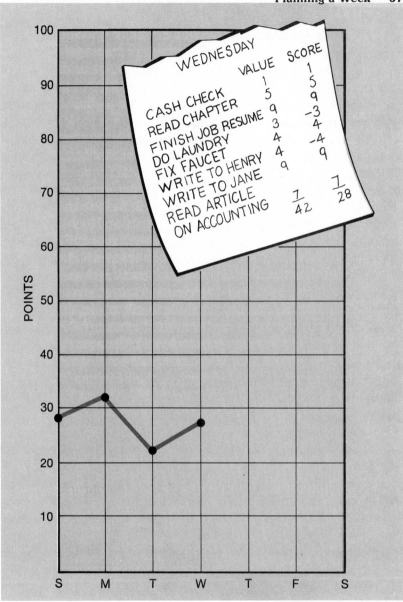

WEDNESDAY	VALUE	SCORE
	1	1
CASH CHECK	5	5
READ CHAPTER	9	9
FINISH JOB RESUME	3	-3
DO LAUNDRY	4	4
FIX FAUCET	4	-4
WRITE TO HENRY	9	9
WRITE TO JANE		
READ ARTICLE	7	7
ON ACCOUNTING	42	28

Fig. 5-4 Elizabeth has decided to keep a day-to-day scoring record. Every day she makes a list of tasks she wants to do and assigns a point value to each. At the end of the day she adds up the points for each task accomplished. Then, she plots her score on a weekly graph. Elizabeth's scoring record gives her an idea of how much she has done of what she planned to do each day of the past week.

badly. On the other hand, the record gives you a way of comparing very different kinds of days. A day when you had to do a lot of small tasks may have been worth almost as much to you as a day of big events.

You'll keep trying to raise your scores. You may also find that you don't really have bad days as often as you think.

There is good reason to warn against wanting to win this game every day. Most people punish themselves too much, psychologists say, for one slip from a good plan. A dieter who gains two pounds in a week, for example, may fall into sadness and self-blame. The whole diet may be given up. Yet that may be the very time the person should look back happily on five earlier weeks of weight loss. The *trend* is what counts in reaching a goal. People who want perfection fail to see that. But, as Ben Franklin reminded us, they're not very popular with other people or themselves.

A Week's Achievement Setting goals and reaching them is often a matter of personal style. Studies of achievement motivation (see pages 40 through 44) have brought forth an excellent all-purpose model. It can be used in trying to reach a one-week goal. It can be adopted and adapted for lifetime goals. The planning goes like this:

1. *Goal Image* Write your goal in as much detail as you can. How will you measure your success or failure in getting to it? Is it too easy or too hard to reach in a week? Does getting to the goal mean you'll be in competition with other people? In competition with your own best effort of the past? Are you trying to reach a goal that no one (in your family, your school, your town, or the world) has ever reached before? Is this goal part of a much larger goal? You should be able to answer yes to at least one of these last four questions.
2. *Need* Tell how important it is to you to reach this goal. How much does it really mean to you?
3. *Hope of Success* From here, you seem to have about a fifty-fifty chance of reaching your goal. How strong are your hopes of making it? Are you eager to get started? Excited about it?

4. *Fear of Failure*   If it is a fifty-fifty chance, you must also worry about *not* reaching the goal. How does that feel? Are you nervous or jumpy about the idea that you can fall short?

5. *Failure Feelings*   Do you have a clear picture of how bad you will feel if you actually do fail to reach your goal? Can you see yourself failing? How will you act? How will other people act toward you?

6. *Success Feelings*   Do you have an equally clear picture of how good you will feel if you actually reach your goal? Can you see how you'll act and how other people will act toward you when you get to the goal?

7. *Personal Obstacles*   What faults do you have that might keep you from reaching your goal? Do you have any doubts about your abilities or skills? List all the personal obstacles you know about.

8. *World Obstacles*   What things outside of you and beyond your control can block the way to your goal? List all you can think of.

9. *Help*   What have you learned from past successes and failures that can help you reach this goal? What kind of expert help will you need—from people, books, organizations—to overcome personal shortcomings and outside obstacles?

10. *Action*   Are you really ready to take charge of yourself in getting toward the goal? Are you ready to take all the blame if you fail, as well as taking credit if you succeed? List in the fullest possible detail what you will do to reach your goal. Tell about your actions step by step if you can. Do you know about any checkpoints along the way that will tell you how you're doing?

The kinds of thoughts, feelings, and actions suggested by the model may seem almost too strong for any goal that involves a mere week. Think about some kinds of things that might be done in a week:

• Learn 50 new words (in any language).
• Begin to learn how to speak better to people in groups.
• Learn how to cook three good casseroles.
• Learn the basic operation of a good camera and take 10 clear photographs.

- Buy some pigments, a canvas, and an easy instruction book. Do an original oil painting.
- Give an evening to each of two different youth groups. Make yourself really useful. Decide which group better deserves your time.
- Pick out one room where you live and make it better to live in.
- Begin a study of evening-school offerings. Decide which one(s) you would like to know more about.
- Learn about *all* the services of the library that serves you. Decide which of these services means most to you. Try it out.
- Cut down on the number of sounds without meaning—like "uh" or "y'know" or "Know what I mean?"—that you use in talking to others.

These are just 10 out of many thousands of possible one-week goal-reaching ideas. None of the 10 may fit your motives and values. If not, devise another you can really care about. The goal may seem modest to anyone but you, but it ought to deserve your intense feeling and effort. The reasons for caring, as the next chapter suggests, may go a long, long way into the future.

THINKING IT THROUGH

1. Have you ever kept a record of self-performance (measurements such as weight lost, points scored, amount of work done, amount of money earned, time to run a certain distance) from day to day or week to week? Did it help in improving what you were doing?
2. Do you think that keeping such records is needless or too self-centered? Why?
3. Some people may think that scoring doesn't make much sense unless another person is doing it. How many of you think that self-scoring serves a purpose? How many think it doesn't? Why?
4. Chapter 5 includes a list of ten goals that might be set and reached in a week. Try to make that list at least twice as long. Add things that you really want to achieve, and they should be things that aren't too easy or impossible to achieve.

Planning a Year

One more time: What is a goal? How can something that can happen in a week be called getting to a goal?

Think about what these different people say:

Rick "I'm flat. Out of cash. I've got to eat at the apartment Thursday and Friday. I guess I can scrape a few meals out of the cupboard. I've got a few cans of beans, a half-dozen eggs, and some canned tuna fish. I'll survive."

Rena "Come on over Saturday. I'll dazzle you with my chicken and rice. Believe me, nobody's ever turned down second helpings. You've got to try it."

Carla "I've got to get myself off this steady diet of frozen dinners. It will take time I don't have. And Mother never taught me to do much in the kitchen. But I'm going to do myself some meals from scratch. Fresh meat and fresh fish and fresh vegetables only. Do you have any recipes I can use? Something not too hard. But they should be good. I want to like my own cooking."

Chuck "Yeah, I know it's kind of a wild idea. But I'm going to have these three couples from the shop in for dinner. I'm doing everything myself. Yeah, I've never done anything like this before. But it seems better than taking them out to the kind of restaurant I could afford. I really want it to be good, though. These people have been real good to me. I want them to have a good time. I may have some cooking talent from my father. He used to cook a lot at home. Hey, steak is a good bet, isn't it? How do you pick out some good steak?"

A goal isn't likely to be a goal at all unless it involves true *caring* and true *risk* of failure. Rick's case doesn't seem to include either one. He's not excited, not sad, and his only risk is some dull eating for a few days. Getting through the week like that is a task, not a goal.

Lively Rena cares a lot, but she seems to have no worries about her prize dish. She's done it before. She knows what the praise of it sounds like. That's no risk. Having company may be her simple pleasure, but it's not a goal.

Carla and Chuck, on the other hand, have goals that mean a lot to each of them. Carla is ready to risk time and money on a plan for treating herself better. Chuck is risking money and his own feelings on a new thing that means a lot to him. Both, in fact, may flop in trying to do what they want to do. If they want to try again, they may have to choose better ways of taking the same chances. But they seem to be motivated people who would try again.

Futures and Risks

A week's goal may be no great loss from a lifetime. Yet many of us won't risk even that much. We're playing it safe. We do what we have to, or we follow our fates, letting things happen to us.

When a week of striving seems too dangerous, a one-year goal is going to seem unthinkable. That future may be something we'd rather forget. "I never think about the future; it comes soon enough," said Albert Einstein. The famous scientist could have been joking. His work caused hopeful change. It also helped shape a future—the nuclear age—that has raised the world's level of future fear.

But the future has to mean more than fear, said psychologist A. H. Maslow (see page 35). He believed that the future was an important part of the whole person. His idea can be put this way: Earlier psychologists pointed out that the *past* exists *now* in the person. It is there in the form of childhood memories. We must also learn that the *future* exists *now* in the person. It is there in the form of ideals, hopes, goals, and unused possibilities and talents. A person who cannot think about this future is helpless and empty. For that person, time must always be filled by others. That person cannot strive for goals and cannot organize a sense of self.

This advertisement was produced to warn the public about the world's dwindling reserves of natural energy. Problems such as these have raised people's level of uncertainty and future fear. (Courtesy Institute of Outdoor Advertising)

Mixed Feelings   How do people today feel about the future? How willing are they to look a year ahead? Five years ahead? Fifty years ahead?

A whole new field of study called *futurism* has grown up around questions like that. Most of the people in it come from other fields—science, business, science-fiction writing, and dozens of other occupations. They are all called *futurists* (or sometimes *futurologists,* which they don't like much). Some draw a gloomy picture of the world being emptied of its resources and filled with growing threats of war. Some see people unable to keep up with change, losing their sense and sanity. Alvin Toffler called this *future shock* and wrote a book about it. Some believe, with Buckminster Fuller, that the world can yet see its best days—if people learn to use well what they have.

Futurists have these very different views, but all of them have another view in common. They believe that people can make the future. They believe that people can change their world for the better and that people should not wait quietly while the future just happens. People should do something about it.

These are world-scale thoughts. What do they have to do with a single man or woman trying to go it alone in a new life? Quite a lot. For the world view seems to have a lot to do with the way that people, one by one, think about themselves. The man in the street is most likely to feel fearful and helpless:

"I'll tell you this. I'm glad I'm getting old, because I won't be around to see what's finally going to happen."

"I don't know if there's going to be any future for my children. We're in the process of destroying ourselves."

"There is no future. The cities, the schools, the economy are all falling apart."

People are troubled, of course, by warlike news and reports of the poisoning of air, water, and earth. They are bothered by news of unemployment, crime, and poverty. But they are also beaten down, Toffler says, by the ever faster pace of life and rate of change. This is caused even by the good news of science. We hear about more spare parts for the human body. We may soon have "smart pills" that help people learn faster. There is news of "electronic money": A person's pay goes right to the bank by wire. A supermarket purchase is subtracted from the account by wire. The landlord gets the rent by wire. Even a parking fine is taken from the account by telephone and computer. These are just a few of the thousands of wonders said to be in our near future. The present may be too crowded with wonders already. Consumers are faced with decisions about many thousands of goods. Dozens more new things reach the shelves each day. Students are told they will have to choose among more than 30,000 different kinds of jobs. Yet about half the kinds of jobs that will be available 10 years from now don't even exist today. Young people are urged to choose a direction early but also (as one guide put it) to "be prepared for any career direction."

The greater the number of choices, Toffler and others point out, the harder it is for people to make decisions. The push to make more decisions faster may be causing more people to make as few as possible.

Ways of Deciding   Futurism takes the world in view. Yet there is no small connection between futurists and the person doing a shopping list or making a job choice.

Futurists are troubled, for one thing, about the small attention given to helping young people think about tomorrow. One futurist-teacher found her junior high school students at first unwilling to talk about it: "They seemed to be weighed down with the awful feeling that their futures had been decided for them. And they could do nothing about it."

Futurists from the University of Massachusetts asked a group of preschool children to draw pictures of yesterday, today, and tomorrow. Their pictures of tomorrow were much more colorful and active than those of the past and present. When high school students were asked to do the same thing, their pictures of tomorrow were dull in comparison to those of the past and present.

This may say less about school than about age. We seem to enjoy deciding less as more and more decisions have to be made. Futurism's major goal may be finding ways to help people start deciding about their own lives again. Many futurist methods are geared to making group decisions about world and national issues. But some are just as good for making the kinds of choices one person must make.

Decisions: Less and More   A *decision* is a knowing choice among two or more possibilities of what a person wants.

What we may need as people today, alone and together, are fewer and better decisions. A good start might be cutting down on the use of the word "decision" itself. Suppose you're really hungry. There is one cookie on the plate. You eat it. You don't decide to eat it. Suppose there are two cookies on the plate and you want one. You *know* they're just alike. You take one. You aren't deciding which one you'll take.

It's often said that all of us have to make dozens, even hundreds of decisions every day. You decide whether or not to get up in the morning. You decide whether to take a shower or a bath. You decide what to have for breakfast. You decide what to wear. You decide how you'll get to work and when.

If all these were active decisions, you might never get outdoors at all. You'd have to spend all day, every day, thinking how to start the day. Perhaps these are better called routine or low-thought choices. (Toffler calls them *programmed decisions,* as compared to *novel decisions.* Our "inner computer" is set to make these choices over and over again in pretty much the same way.)

Sometimes a low-thought choice can be raised to a higher decision level. Take Jack, who has had juice and toast every morning for the past 13 years. He decides to decide on something different. This could suddenly involve a study of all the different breakfasts that might be made (see Figure 6-1). It might also raise many questions of taste, food value, cooking time, and so on. It could be a decision of much worth to Jack. But it would be a trying task if it were often repeated.

Some people do seem to try often to make major decisions out of low-thought choices. Take the person who spends huge amounts of time each day deciding what to wear. Carried too far, too long, in too many ways, this kind of decision-making habit may rattle the mind.

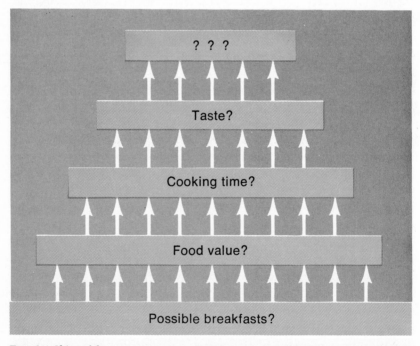

Fig. 6-1 If breakfast were a major decision, you would have to choose from among many different possible foods. Each would have to be considered in terms of food value, cooking time, taste, and other personal preferences.

Some business leaders take pride in making hundreds of decisions in a working day. But many of these decisions are also likely to be low-thought choices. The way of making them is "programmed" from past experience. Each time a certain need for choice comes up, the decision is the same. There may be trouble if a different new problem is mistaken for a familiar old one. But the new problem is likely to get the time and effort it deserves.

A first rule, then, may be to limit decision making to where it matters most. People with clear goals and values have an edge in doing this. They know where they're going. They don't have to make major decisions at every turn. But they also know which forks in the road need serious thought and study.

Decisions should be made in the order of their importance. Say a person is trying to decide on a new kind of breakfast cereal, new carpeting for the living room, and a new job. If the breakfast cereal gets more study than the carpeting and the carpeting more study than the job, the person may have very serious decision-making problems.

Two other kinds of decision-making faults afflict many people. One is the attempt to decide between two things that are, in fact, just as alike as the cookies on the plate mentioned earlier. The second is trying to decide by process of elimination—finding out which choices are worse rather than which are better.

An old story about a mule illustrates these two problems. At first, the mule is standing between two bales of hay, each bale exactly alike. The mule tramps back and forth between the bales, trying to decide which is better. Finally, the mule happens to walk extra close to one bale and to get a good sniff of it. That bale suddenly seems better, and the mule can't help eating it. A great deal of time has been wasted, but a decision has finally been made.

In another situation, the mule stands among five skunks. The mule wants to decide which are the four worst skunks so that it can walk past the other one and get away. But every time the mule sniffs one of the skunks, the odor prevents close inspection. The mule will never solve the problem. It will keep wandering from one skunk to the other, never getting out of the circle. The skunks smell so bad that it cannot get close enough to find out which one is worst.

The point here is that decisions can't easily be made by cutting the list of choices from the bottom up. Decisions are made by taking the choice the person thinks best. It doesn't matter which choice is worst, second worst, and so on. It doesn't matter, for that matter, which choice is second best, third best, and so on.

Chance and Choice   Every real decision involves risk. It may be simple risk. You order pork chops at a restaurant. You're later told that the lamb chops were much better. You choose to wear blue on a big date. You find out later that your date really likes red. You buy a car for $5,000. Soon afterward, you find that another dealer is selling the same car at $4,500.

In each case, you somehow failed to get enough information for a good decision. It may not have mattered much in the first two cases, but it cost you $500 in the third.

There are many other cases where you may never be able to get sure information. (See Figure 6-2.) Suppose you bet a dollar that a flipped coin would come up heads. You lost. Then you bet a dollar that a pair of dice would come up 12 twice in a row. You won.

Was your first decision a bad one? Was your second decision a good one? Not at all, in either case.

The coin could have come up only heads or tails. Your *probability* of winning or losing was just 1 in 2. But the dice could have come up 1,295 other ways than 12 twice. So your probability of winning was 1 in 1,296. You were lucky once, but your sort of decision making won't be very good in the long run.

You hear that the probability of rain is 1 in 10. You go on a picnic. The sun shines. But your decision is as good as it can be even if it rains. You know your risk.

Should you buy life insurance? The insurance company knows, and you can too, that the probability is that 3 of every 100 people your age will die this year. But no one really knows *which* three people will die. You only know that a hundred people can make payments, most of which will go to those left behind by the three who die. You may decide to take the insurance, hoping you don't "win" the payoff. You don't know what will happen to you, but you know the risk.

Probabilities are not so clearly known in most cases as they are with coin flips, cards, dice, and insurance. Careful study may tell you, however, that you face a 1-in-2 or 1-in-10 risk of losing a job you're thinking about. Careful thought may tell you that you have a

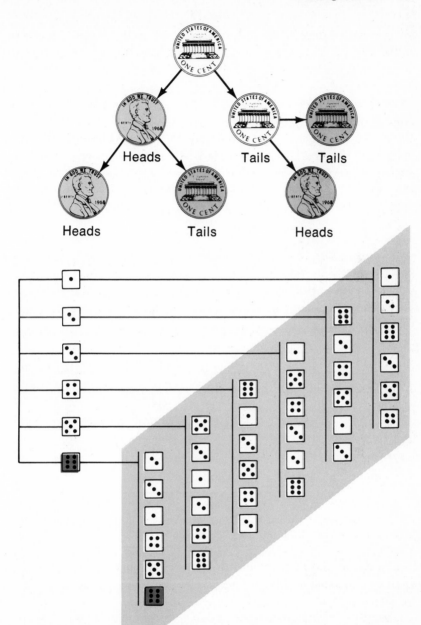

Fig. 6-2 The probability of a tossed coin coming up heads twice in a row is 1 in 4. The probability of a rolled die coming up 6 in a row is 1 in 36. When making a decision, you should consider the probability of it turning out the way you want it to.

9-in-10 chance of losing a certain friend. You don't *know* these things will finally happen. But you know how high or low your risk is. This can help you make a decision.

Charting the Future   Futurists have invented and tried out a number of ways of making decisions better. All start from the idea that each of us has a number of possible futures—*alternative futures*. Each one of those futures is the result of a long chain of decisions. Every choice in the chain is made possible by earlier choices. Every choice is likely to lead to others. This kind of chain can be seen, or foreseen, in several different ways.

Scenarios   Where do you want to be 10 years from now? Who do you want to be? How do you want to be? A *scenario* is an action story about that. You don't make it like a daydream, too wild for you to believe. But you do stretch your real possibilities as far as they can go. Your scenario might take the form of a news story, like this one:

Yourtown, 10 years from today—Vincent Amato announced today the opening of the fifth hobby shop in his successful chain. Since starting out in the hobby business five years ago, Mr. Amato has become one of the nation's best-known experts on model trains. He has also been active in local politics. He is serving his fourth term on the city council. He is married to the former Phyllis Ahlberg. They have three children. . . .

The scenario may form in your mind as a film or play:

The scene is the conference room in the country home of Mary O'Brien. The swimming pool and horse stables can be seen through the large picture window. The men and women around the table represent manufacturers from Japan, Nigeria, and Brazil. "Design by O'Brien," says one, "has encouraged American men by the millions to make their own clothing at home. We need your ideas in our lands too, Mary O'Brien. We believe your patterns can change men's way of dressing abroad, just as they've done here."

Mary O'Brien, a tiny, blue-jeaned figure at the head of the table, smiles thoughtfully. . . .

A scenario is done best by taking the brakes off your ideas and hopes about the future (see Figure 6-3). Done that way, the scenario offers a useful picture of many possible goals put together into a life-style. The story may not hold up. It is made to be tested. It raises questions about how to get from here to there. What decisions have to be made now and all along the way to make the story come true? It may be, as the old Maine farmer said when asked for directions to the city, that you can't get there from here. In that case, other scenarios need to be made up and tested. They may prove to be better than the first.

Future Wheel   An important decision may cause many things to happen. Some are not expected and may not at first have seemed to be connected. Building a *future wheel* like the one shown in Figure 6-4 can help a person to think about such results. Some of these results may seem good to a person. Others may seem bad. This is a personal matter.

Suppose that a person decides to build a fancier wardrobe. The person expects that better clothes will bring more attention from bosses at work. This kind of attention may lead to better work and higher pay. But what will happen to spending needs for other things when more money is spent on clothing? If the new clothes need more time for care, where will this time come from? How will fellow workers feel about the person's new look? Is it possible they might become harder to work with? This might hurt the person's job picture, rather than helping it. The future wheel can help a person think about the many outcomes of a decision.

Decision Tree   One important decision often leads to another. Even a decision to change breakfast habits (see Figure 6-1) may demand many other kinds of choices. But it does not follow that a decision made now must lead to one certain path for the whole future. That is a favorite idea in folklore. "For want of a nail," an old saying tells us, "the shoe was lost. For want of a shoe, the horse was lost. For want of a horse, the rider was lost. For want of a rider, the

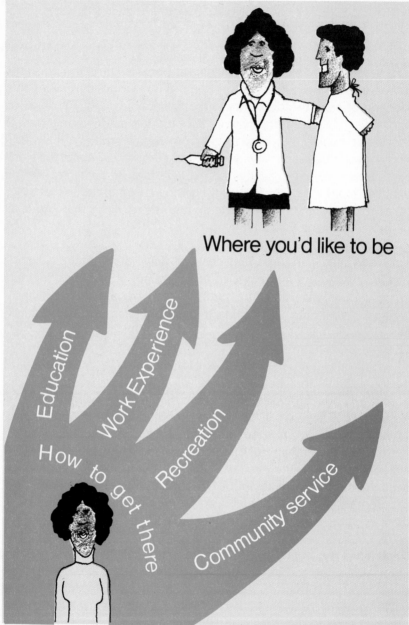

Fig. 6-3 Imagine a scenario depicting your future. Who and where do you want to be? A doctor? What kind of experiences—educational, work, recreational—will help you get there?

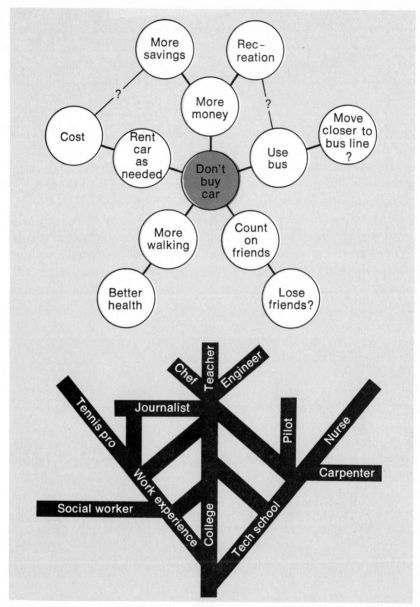

Fig. 6-4 When you are faced with a decision, a future wheel (top) can help you think out all the possible choices and consider carefully the results of each. A decision tree (bottom) shows you that there are many possible ways to reach each of these goals. Usually, each decision you make now will lead you to many other decisions in the future.

message was lost. For want of a message, the war was lost." If you want to win a war, in other words, you can't make one careless decision about nails. You'd better choose A now if you want to reach Z years from now.

This is the case sometimes. More often, there are several paths to a goal. A decision tree like the one shown in Figure 6-4 may help you find them. Unlike the scenario, the decision tree starts with a present choice. Then it follows the many branches of that choice into the future. For example, a student may choose to take part in school sports or not. The choice may be made in favor of team sports. This choice can be made several more times at different branches in the future. The team-sport choice finally runs out for most people when they reach a certain age. They must then choose non-team sports or none at all. These same non-team sports have been there to be chosen all along by others. Some people, in fact, have started to ski or play tennis or jog only when they were into their sixties.

Though sports are a simple example, they show there may be many ways of reaching goals. The decision tree can show these ways of getting to a known goal. It may also reveal possible goals to people who may not have thought of them.

Cross-Impact   A final outlook that can be borrowed from the futurist for personal use is the cross-impact idea. Most of us think of conflicts as occurring between our good habits and our bad habits. We want to watch television less and get more exercise. We think we ought to give less time to parties and more time to helping others in the community. We hope to spend less time spending and more time saving money. We may set these goals one at a time, each for its own sake.

Futurists try to study all sorts of decisions to see how they may work upon each other as time goes on. For example, both improved communications and personal privacy have been thought of as good. But better communications—the telephone most of all—have tended to cut into people's privacy.

The cross-impact idea can be borrowed for one person's use. Cathy has just been named a department manager. She has more "homework" and she travels on company business more often. She has also been named an officer of the local United Fund. This means more meetings every month. She has also been asked to join the local Big Sisters group. Finally, she has taken up weaving. She's ready to invest in weaving tools. Cathy may need to think about cross-impacts. She may then foresee all her good goals bumping together by the end of the year—perhaps with bad results.

Decision making and forecasting are ways of thinking. They never give the same sure answers as simple arithmetic. Used well, however, they offer a better chance for self-direction and independent living.

THINKING IT THROUGH

1. Abraham Maslow says that a person who cannot think about the future is helpless and is stuck with having other people making her/his decisions. Do you agree or disagree? Why?

2. What is the biggest change that will take place in your life within the next year? How have you planned for this change? What is the biggest change that you would like to have take place? What can you do to make it happen?

3. Ask your teacher or the librarian to help you find a recent book or magazine article in which the writer makes predictions about life in the next century. Which prediction makes you most look forward to the future? Which one makes you dread it the most? Share these predictions with the class.

Decision Making
(Finding All the Facts)

Making decisions can be painful. If they're important, they almost have to be hard to make. Any major decision involves risk. It is often a very personal kind of risk. The decision maker has needs, values, and goals at stake. (This is likely to be true even when a group makes the final decision.) A bad decision can bring unhappiness and self-blame.

The odds being what they are, some of us try to escape decision making entirely. Does that work? Think about these two well-known sayings of the 1960s:

"Not to decide is to decide."

"If you're not part of the solution, you're part of the problem."

In other words, if you don't make your own decisions, someone else will make them for you.

If we *must* decide, then, many of us would like a few easy rules for doing it right (see Figure 7-1). Here are five:

1. Think broadly about what you really want.
2. Think about your possible choices of ways to get what you want. Cover as many choices as you reasonably can.
3. Get as much information as you can about each possible choice.
4. Weigh the risks, costs, and returns to you for each possible choice.
5. Make the choice that seems to be in your best interest.

There, in a nutshell, are the past six chapters. The summing-up could be made to look even simpler. Top business leaders often make decision making sound easier. Many say they decide by "hunch," or "the feel of things," or "the seat of my pants." Most often, it's the seat of the pants plus about 20 years or more of know-how. They simply have all their choices in mind or at hand for high-speed comparing and selecting.

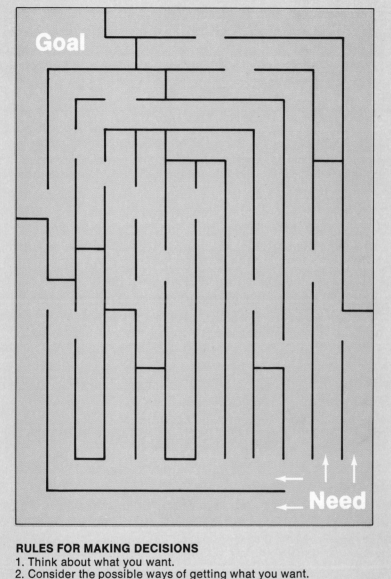

RULES FOR MAKING DECISIONS
1. Think about what you want.
2. Consider the possible ways of getting what you want.
3. Gather information about each choice.
4. Weigh the risks, costs, and returns of each choice.
5. Make the decision.

Fig. 7-1 Decision making may look like a maze—how do you get from your need to your goal? As you decide which path to take, keep in mind these few basic rules for making good decisions.

For the rest of us, hunches can be dangerous to the health of any decision. When we really want to make the best choices among many possibilities, we have to get our information the hard way. The facts aren't come by easily. Yet they are often available in huge amounts.

Facts: Scarcity and Plenty

A person *could* apply all the rules of decision making to the purchase of a pair of socks or a pad of writing paper. This could let loose a flood of facts about socks or writing paper that would drown most of us. Whole books have been written, in fact, about lesser subjects than those. Few of us want to read them. Risking the flood of facts may seem more important when the goals are larger. Most of us will never know all that can be known about cooking a meal, buying a major appliance, or choosing a college. But we'll try harder. How do we know when we've got *enough* facts? That is one of the toughest decision-making questions of all. It may never be surely answered.

Facts may be hard to handle even when they are right before our eyes. Money is a major fact of our lives. We live with it daily. We know the shape and feel of it. We are trained from earliest childhood to count it and make it count. Yet strange things often happen in simple decision-making cases like these:

The oranges on the supermarket counter are marked:

12¢ EACH—8 FOR $1

The 12-ounce box of detergent on the shelf costs 75 cents. The 2-pound size costs $2.15.

Auto Dealer A offers a trade-in of $3,700 on a two-year-old car toward a new $5,300 car. Auto Dealer B offers a trade-in of $3,500 on the same old car toward the same new car, which he prices at $5,000.

What's strange, of course, is that many people bite readily for the *more* expensive choice in all three cases:

1. We're used to paying a slight amount less when we buy more than one thing of the same kind. A typical "twofer" would be

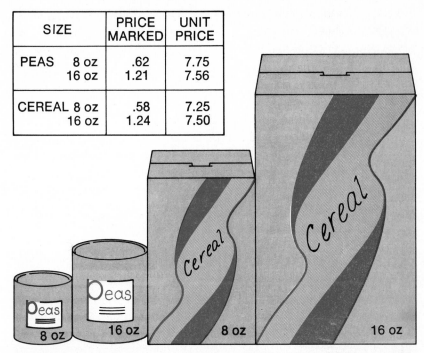

SIZE		PRICE MARKED	UNIT PRICE
PEAS	8 oz	.62	7.75
	16 oz	1.21	7.56
CEREAL	8 oz	.58	7.25
	16 oz	1.24	7.50

Fig. 7-2 To get the best buy, be sure to compare unit prices when you are shopping. The price per ounce of the large can of peas, for example, is slightly lower than that of the small can. The price per ounce of the large box of cereal, however, is slightly higher than that of the small box. (Some unit prices may be given for metric quantities. For example, the 8-ounce can of peas equals 227 grams.)

two cans of dog food for 59 cents. If we bought just one, it would cost 30 cents. We save a penny. But the deal on oranges doesn't work that way. The eight oranges together cost 4 cents more than the eight oranges bought one at a time. Yet some people do buy the eight for the "saving."

2. We're also used to the idea that the larger size costs less per unit. For example, a 2-ounce tube of toothpaste may cost 40 cents—or 20 cents an ounce. The 7-ounce family size costs $1.33—or 19 cents an ounce. We seem to save 7 cents. But the detergent in this case isn't priced that way. Yet some people do buy the 2-pound size for the "saving."

3. Cases like the first two are often just marking mistakes made by store workers. Auto dealers say, however, that the size of the

trade-in price means the most to some buyers. This is so *no matter what* the price of the new car. So Dealer A would rather raise the trade-in offer than lower the new car price. And many buyers *would* buy from Dealer A because that trade-in price is higher.

Facts can be clear and confusing at the same time (see Figure 7-2). Money facts can seem clearest of all and most hopelessly mixed up. That may be why financial decisions—like those in the following case studies—bear great interest and lots of ground for second-guessing.

Annabelle: Out of Balance

Annabelle has been on her own for four years, since her college graduation. She studied to be a teacher. All during college, she was told how wise she was to pick a field where jobs were sure things. But somehow there were far too many teachers and too few jobs as soon as she started looking for work. She got along with part-time and fill-in work for three years. Then she finally won a full-time classroom position. That seemed to start, rather than finish, her money troubles:

Annabelle "At last I could count on a steady paycheck. So I found a bank I liked the looks of and started a checking account. It was a special account. You paid a dime for every check you wrote and a dollar service charge each month. The regular checking account didn't have any charges, but you had to leave at least $500 in it. Having my own checks made me feel like a solid citizen. For a while. Before long, I felt like part of an old joke—the dumb woman who couldn't keep her checkbook straight. You know, I think it's true that young girls are practically forced to be afraid of math and things like that. Because arithmetic isn't 'feminine.' We shouldn't stand for that.

"Anyway, it's been less than a year and I'm giving up my checking account. I'm sticking to cash whenever possible. Why? Because I made almost *every* mistake anyone could think of. I started out by writing a couple of checks and forgetting to fill in the stub. It was a whole month before I could tell how much money I had. The monthly statement from the bank cleared that up. Then I made a really dumb mistake. I made out a check for $7 to 'Cash' and then I lost it. Someone else found it. Not only was it cashed, but it was 'kited.' That means the amount was raised. To $70. They never could find the person who did it. Of course, that meant I had $63 less than I thought I had. I didn't know about it until the statement came.

"That was pretty bad, but the worst was yet to come. I got careless about checking the monthly statement. I'm sure I forgot to keep track of the little service charges for quite a while. I forgot to take them away from my balance. And then I had to get tricky. I was cutting my budget very thin. I was making car payments and installment payments on a few things. I knew my account was low by the end of the month. On the morning before payday, I needed gas

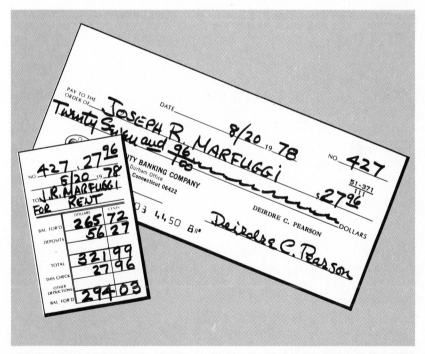

Fig. 7-3 This is the correct way to make out a check and stub. Notice how every space on the check is filled out, how the amount in numbers and the amount in writing agree, and how the balance and check amount are fully recorded on the stub.

for the car and I had to buy some things at the drugstore. So I wrote checks. I'd heard you could get by with that. I expected to get my paycheck to the bank before the gas station and the drugstore brought the checks in. But they must have just *run* to the bank with them. A few days later, I got a notice that I'd overdrawn. That meant a penalty charge of $5. The bank paid the station and the druggist anyway. I didn't have to explain to them why the checks bounced.

"By the end of the next month, I knew I was running low in the account again. But I *thought* I had enough to write a check for $40 for my auto insurance. Then payday came again. I deposited my pay and felt safe again. But sure enough, about a week later I got an angry letter from my insurance company. My $40 check had been returned to them marked 'insufficient funds.' In other words, it did bounce. What I'd done, of course, was to forget to subtract the $5 the bank charged me for overdrawing the first time. I had to fill out forms for the insurance company. And this time I had to send them a *certified* check. That meant the bank had to write a special message on it saying it was good. That cost extra. And of course I had to pay *another* $5 penalty for the check that bounced.

"Well, to make a long story shorter, I just gave up. On payday I buy money orders at the bank or post office for the things I have to pay by mail. I travel around to other stores and pay as many bills as I can in cash. The rest of the money—if I've got any left—goes under the mattress or into the cookie jar. I've got a number of hiding places for it. And that's about it. If I run out of cash, I know I'm broke. I may start another checking account sometime. But I think I'll study the way it works for quite a while first. Until then, I'll take my chances on cash."

Rating the Decision   Is Annabelle's decision reasonable? Now she has to spend a good deal of time paying bills in cash and buying money orders. She may be taking some risk by carrying large amounts of cash or leaving cash in her apartment. A checking account does away with these problems. It also serves as a good record of spending. Annabelle may manage nicely, on the other hand, if she has to buy only a small number of money orders. And if she manages to keep her supply of cash low.

On the other hand again, the "school of hard knocks" may have taught her most of what she needs to know about checking:

1. Fill out the stub *before* you make out the check.
2. Fill out the check in ink, not pencil. Make sure that the amount in numbers and the amount in writing agree. Write the amount as close to the left edge as you can. Fill any leftover space with a wavy line, as shown in Figure 7-3.
3. Never make out a check to "Cash" or "Bearer" until you're at the place where you're going to cash it. If a check is made out to you, don't sign (endorse) it until you are at the place where you're going to cash it. Refer to Figure 7-4 for examples of correct endorsements.
4. Examine your monthly bank statement as soon as possible. Put canceled checks in order by number. Make sure your figuring also includes (a) amounts of your checks that haven't gotten to the bank yet, (b) amounts of your deposits that may not have

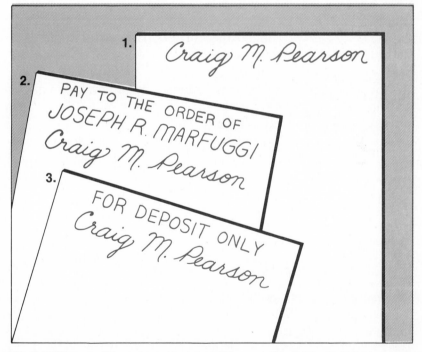

Fig. 7-4 There are three correct ways to endorse a check. Example 1 is a blank endorsement and makes the check payable to any holder. Example 2 is a full endorsement and makes the check payable only to the person named. Example 3 is a restrictive endorsement, which limits the use of the check.

gotten to the bank before the statement was made up, and (c) all service charges and penalties.

Mark: Credit Crunch

Mark has fought for independence in his life-style and in his work as well. He has lived on his own for 14 years. Almost half of those years, on and off, have been spent in his own small business efforts. Starting up a business is risky. Mark's first try was a company making heavy plastic tags and key rings. It went well for several years, but a fire wiped it out. There was not enough insurance to permit rebuilding. After that, Mark worked two years for an advertising agency. Now he's back on his own in his one-person industrial design studio. He has had more than his share of problems with credit:

Mark "Credit, used right, is a great thing. It makes it easier to manage money. You can pay most of your bills once a month. With fewer checks. It's easier to make a budget. And you don't have to carry a lot of cash around. But you have to be careful.

"Getting started with credit is a funny kind of problem. I have a friend now who's having trouble. She's twenty-nine. She's been working at a fairly good job for several years. She just got a good raise in pay and wanted to borrow money for a vacation trip. The bank turned her down. She didn't have a credit rating. In other words, she couldn't borrow money because she'd never borrowed money before. How could she have a record of paying back money if she never borrowed money? She finally had to have her *mother* sign the loan with her. And she's twenty-nine!

"I was turned down myself some years ago. I went around town for a while looking for a store—any store—that would let me charge something. No go. Finally I had my own idea. I went into a bank and started a savings account. As soon as it got up to a couple of hundred dollars, I went in and took out a passbook loan. That is the greatest way to borrow. It's like borrowing your own money. You can borrow as much as you have saved. Your money stays in the bank and keeps drawing interest—say 5 percent a year. For borrowing the money, you pay a little more—say 8 percent. All together, you can see, it costs you about 3 percent.

"I really didn't even need the money I borrowed. So I took it over to a second bank and started another savings account there. Of course, it was drawing about 5 percent interest there too. It almost sounds as though I were *making* money. I wasn't, but the loan was costing me very, very little. Anyway, at the end of a couple of months, I took my money out of the second bank and paid back my passbook loan at the first bank. That gave me the start of a credit rating. Then they let me have a new-car loan. After I kept up my payments on that, I applied for a bank credit card and got it.

"Since then, I've had a dozen or so kinds of credit cards at one time or another. The gasoline credit card is the most sensible, I think. It covers things you have to buy. You don't do much impulse buying at the gas station. You don't say, 'Hey, that's a great looking can of oil, guess I'll take some home.' Instead of paying cash five or

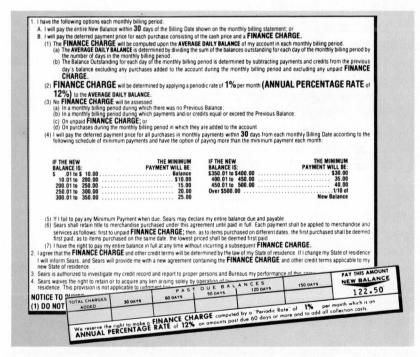

Fig. 7-5 Before you buy something on credit, find out how much that credit plan is going to cost you. The truth-in-lending law requires stores, banks, and finance companies to provide clear statements on what credit costs. Be sure you read and compare all the credit plans.

six times a month, you pay one check. If you do have to have a big car repair, you can put it on your bill and pay it off in time payments. You pay a little interest to spread it out over several months.

"You can get pretty clever with credit-card buying. Banks and stores often don't charge any interest if you charge something and pay back in 30 days. But *watch* that. Some of them charge interest *from the day you buy* something on the account. When you've got 30 days to pay without interest, it's like getting a free loan for that much time. Sometimes you can stretch it even more. You look at the 'billing date' shown on your monthly bill. If you have something big to charge, you do it that day. Say your billing date is the tenth of the month. So you charge something on July 10. It isn't billed to you until August 10. And you may have until September 9 to pay without interest. But don't take my word for it. *Read* what the credit plan says. Shop around. You have to be told in clear words what the rules are.

"Do I sound like I know a lot about credit? Don't believe it. After all these years, I've gotten in over my head. My trouble was with my bank credit card. They tell you what your credit limit is. You feel easy about charging up to that limit. But then they send you a letter increasing your limit.

"My limit went from $400 all the way to $1,200. It was too tempting. I was having problems about pay, so I used the card to tide me over. I suddenly realized I was paying $15 a month in interest. So I put all my credit cards away except the gas card. Paying cash every time you buy something is really a pain. Maybe pain is what you need to keep your senses about credit."

Rating the Decision   Mark seems to know more about credit than most people. Yet he has put his credit "on hold." Is his decision reasonable? Or should he use credit to help him out of the troubles credit caused?

Mark mentions two good rules for anyone who wants to use credit as wisely as possible:

1. **Read!** The federal truth-in-lending law requires full information on what credit costs (see Figure 7-5). It must be given in a way that can be compared easily. This makes credit one of the easiest things to shop for. A person can go to the bank, store,

credit union, finance company, and other sources of credit. Each source must say clearly how much the amount of borrowing will cost. Nothing can be hidden—unless the buyer's eyes are closed.

2.   **Use credit only when you need it.**   Clear goals and a good budget help a person use credit wisely. Credit can lull people into buying what they don't need at costs higher than they really ought to pay. On the other hand, credit can help save plans and goals. It can do this by spreading unexpected costs over a longer time. It can turn such costs into mere bumps, rather than big roadblocks, on the way to what you want.

Charlie: Diet Decision

About 80 million Americans weigh at least 10 pounds more than doctors think they ought to. At any one time, about 20 million of them are trying to lose weight. Charlie has joined that group. In the two years he's lived in his own apartment, Charlie's weight has jumped from his normal 170 pounds to 190 pounds:

Charlie   "Yep, I really do make a meal out of potato chips and candy bars every now and then. But not *that* often. Some days I don't eat enough to feed a fly. However you cut it, I've got a lot of flab on me. I'm getting so I puff up the stairs. It's not good.

"How do you take the weight off? When you live by yourself, you've got many choices. It's not like you have to make anybody else change the way they cook or eat for your sake. You can take your pick of diets. That's just the trouble. Everywhere you look there's a diet. There a grapefruit diet and a cottage cheese diet. There's a lemon juice diet and a beer diet. Et cetera.

"I decided to study up. It turns out to be simple and scientific. Every food has so many calories—which are measures of heat and energy. You take so much fuel into your furnace. If you burn it up with exercise, you don't gain weight. If you don't burn up calories, though, they turn to fat. A man my size ought to burn up about 3200 calories a day. If I take in less, I lose weight. It's that simple.

"I thought about eating nothing at all for a few days. They say you lose a pound if you burn up 3500 calories. If I don't eat anything at all, then I lose almost a pound a day. I've read that fasting like that is OK for a healthy person. But the thought of no food at all scares me.

"I decided I would cut down to 2200 calories a day. That is 1000 less a day than I burn. That means I should lose two pounds a week. I bought a couple of little calorie-counter books. I made a pretty good game out of it. I kept eating until I got to 2200 calories, and then I quit. I'd start out with orange juice, 118 calories, and cereal with milk, which is about 320. Then I'd have a hamburger, about 400 calories, and a glass of milk, about 160. And then I'd have a handful of potato chips, about 1000 calories, and have to go without dinner.

"I didn't mind that so much until somebody reminded me I had to have balance too. You've got to have so much protein, minerals, and vitamins. That made the figuring harder and sort of spoiled the game. I tried it for a while, but it meant a lot of planning.

"Finally, I saw a diet in a doctor's column in the paper. It said you didn't have to measure or count. You had to give up desserts, milk products, bread, and potatoes. You had fruit juice for breakfast, a salad with diet dressing for lunch. For dinner you had a good-sized piece of lean meat, fish, or chicken and another salad. You had to drink plenty of water.

"Do I like it? Not much. But I'm losing weight. When I get back to normal, I'm going to enjoy real meals again—but no potato chips ever again."

Rating the Decision   Charlie has decided to take someone else's word for it. Is his decision reasonable? It works for him. But could he do better?

The wonder of dieting is its treatment of plain facts in so many different ways. Weight losing has become a big business in the United States. There are diet books, clubs, pills, plans, and packages sold by the millions. Most are based on the same simple arithmetic of dieting. The arithmetic facts, however, are clouded by the many different values of many people. These people want to lose weight fast, or to be with other people when they are losing, or to lose weight without giving up favorite foods. All of them are doing much the same thing: taking in fewer calories. But the facts often get lost in the effort.

People making decisions about factual matters such as prices, money management, or calories *should* try to let the facts come first. At other times, values must be foremost.

THINKING IT THROUGH

1. "If you don't make your own decisions, someone else will make them for you." Do you agree or disagree with that statement? Why? How often do you "decide not to decide"? Do you want that situation to change? Why or why not?
2. What kind of questions would be important enough for use of the full five-step decision-making process described in Chapter 7? List as many as you can.
3. Have you ever been fooled by the "facts" in making a store purchase or other decision? How did it happen?
4. Do you agree or disagree with Annabelle's decision to give up her checking account? Use the facts in explaining your position. In what ways could her decision be improved?
5. Do you agree or disagree with Mark's decision about his use of credit cards? Why? Use the facts of the situation to explain your position. In what ways could his decision have been improved?

PART TWO

A Place of Your Own

Getting Your Own Place

"Should I get my own place or not?" This is a question that almost everyone asks sooner or later. It's a big step toward independence—real independence.

Maybe some of your friends already have their own places. Do they seem happy? Having your own place and inviting friends over can be very exciting. Does it seem like a great idea—being able to come and go as you please, playing any kind of music you want, cleaning up when you feel like it, having your own mailbox and telephone, picking out the kind of furniture you want? You can probably think of lots of other good reasons for being on your own.

It's fun just to think about living independently. But are you a little unsure, maybe scared because it would be such a giant change? It's natural to have doubts about such a big decision. After all, there are many questions to answer. Things like: "What if I find a place and start to live there and I don't like it? How can I get out of it? How much money does it take? Where can I get enough furniture that I can afford?" Do you wonder, also, if it might be too lonely without anyone else around?

Maybe you've already changed your mind a couple of times about going ahead. It's hard to know if you're ready to take this step. Some days, you may be in the mood to do it, but there are so many unanswered questions you just put it off. Or, did you all of a sudden decide that there is no time like the present for going full speed ahead? Well, where do you start? What's the first step?

Where to Start

The first thing that probably comes to mind when you are thinking about getting your own place is—you guessed it—money. Even

92

when you have made up your mind that you really want your own place, it's wise to figure out a *budget* (a plan for spending)—even a rough one—before going ahead.

Add It All Up   Start by figuring out how much money you can count on having each month. That's your monthly salary after taxes and union dues (if any) are taken out. This is referred to as *take-home pay*. If you are paid once a week, your total monthly income equals about four paychecks. To be more exact, you can multiply your weekly take-home pay by 52 (number of weeks in a year). Then divide by 12 (number of months in a year). This will be your average monthly income.

Now add up all your monthly expenses. It might be easier first to figure out the ones you have each week: transportation (gas and parking, or bus and train expenses), food (including lunches you eat out, as well as food you use for cooking), entertainment (like movies), laundry and cleaning, drugstore items, and any others.

Next, add up all the bills that have to be paid every month: payments for things you bought on installments, charge accounts, savings account deposits. You should figure on depositing money in a savings account for such yearly expenses as insurance or a vacation. Now think about where else your money goes—clothes, records, hobbies, charities, gifts, and so on. Make the list as complete as you can. Now subtract these expenses from your monthly take-home pay. What's left over is about how much you can count on for rent and *utilities* (services such as gas, electricity, water, and telephone). Even then, you will want to keep some additional money for emergencies and little things that come up. Remember that your list of expenses is your *usual* expenses. Your car may need repair; the winter coat you thought you'd put off purchasing till next year may go on sale—for cash only; your friend may go into the hospital and you'd like to send some flowers. Do you have as much left over as you thought you would? Is it enough to think about getting your own place?

Rent and Other Charges   As a general rule, the amount you pay for rent each month should be no more than one-fourth (25 percent) of your total income. If you are paid once a week, this would be equal to your weekly take-home pay.

Actually, you will need quite a bit more than one month's rent to start. You'll probably have to pay two months' rent before moving in—the first and the last month's rent. A *security deposit* (usually one month's rent) may also be required. The security deposit is held by the *landlord* (the owner of the building) as a guarantee that the place will be in the same condition when you leave as when you moved in. This deposit will be returned to you when you move out, except for the cost of anything you break or damage.

In many apartments (and other rental places), you must also pay for utilities, including your own phone bill. Also, there is usually a fee charged to the *tenant* (renter) to turn on or hook up a utility. You can be sure the phone company will charge to put in your phone. A deposit may also be required for persons who have never before had a phone in their own names.

In some areas, you may have to pay a cleaning fee when you move in. That's to cover the cost of cleaning the apartment after you leave. You do not get this fee back. There may be other charges too, such as a key deposit or an extra charge if you have a pet.

There's a good way to remember the difference between a fee and a deposit. A *fee* is a charge usually not given back. A *deposit* is usually returned, in full or in part, if terms of an agreement are met.

Do you think you can take care of all those expenses and have some money left over for the furniture you may have to buy? If the answer is yes, you're ready to look for your own place.

The Great Apartment Hunt

Sometimes it takes a lot of looking to find the place you want, at the right price. So don't get discouraged or take something you really don't like. That can be very disappointing. Did you ever buy a pair of shoes and, after one wearing, decide you hated them, or they didn't fit right? Getting the right place is much more important, so it's wise to take your time.

Where to Look   Maybe you already have a good idea where you want to live. Finding a place is a lot easier, of course, when you're not moving out of town. In a strange area, just knowing where to look is hard. But you can get some good clues by asking people at work, reading the "for rent" part of the newspaper, and spending some time riding or walking around the neighborhoods. In some apartment houses, the available rentals appear on a sign outside the building. Other apartment houses may have a sign on which the landlord's name and phone number appear. You can call and find out what is available, or what is expected to be available soon. In some towns, drugstores, supermarkets, and the library have copies of rental guides. Neighborhood stores may also have bulletin boards where rental notices are posted. You can try calling the Chamber of Commerce and ask about rentals. Real estate agencies (listed in the telephone book's Yellow Pages) offer house and apartment rentals. Looking at what they have to rent can give you a good idea of prices and different locations. (Before you rent through a real estate agency, be sure and find out if there is a fee for their service.) You can put an ad in a newspaper, or on a bulletin board, describing what kind of place you want.

After looking at a number of apartments you'll learn what kind and size of place you can afford. Then, you can answer only those rental ads that seem to fit your budget. After answering a few rental ads you'll begin to learn how to read and understand them.

What to Look For   There are many reasons why people pick one place over another when they are looking around. The amount of rent can make a big difference, of course. Sometimes, too, people choose a place that is close to work or to transportation that gets them there. This can be very important to people who do not have cars. People with cars may look for apartments with good off-street parking.

To some people it's important to live in a place that's as nice looking and clean outside the building as it is inside the apartment. If you feel that's important, then an apartment building that faces a parking lot, or is above a grocery store, is not for you. Or maybe you want to be able to walk almost every place you go. If so, take a good look at the whole neighborhood to make sure everything you need is close at hand, like a drugstore, a dry cleaner, a grocery store, and so on.

If the neighborhood is new to you, it may be necessary to visit it more than once, at different times of the day. This will give you a better idea of what the neighborhood is really like.

Furn Apt for Rent	Apt Wanted	Unfurn Apt for Rent
DAWES ST — Small, a/c studio apt, separate modern kitchenette & bath. Attractively furnished top floor of a beautifully renovated bldg. Available immediately. Call for appointment 555-1234	**2 YOUNG TEACHERS** need 4 rooms (2 BR) within walk. distance of Centerfield high school. Prefer modern kitchen and bath. Max rent $300. Call 555-8826	**HALES FERRY** — BEAUTIFUL 1 & 2 BDRM GARDEN APTS — COUNTRY SETTING Featuring: • Spacious Rms • Air conditioning' • Indiv thermos • Parking on premises • Free gas & elec Write to: Box 432

Fig. 8-1 There are many ways to find a new apartment: visit a real estate agency, read the "for rent" part of the newspaper or place an "apartment wanted" ad in the paper; visit apartment houses with a rental agent on the premises; look for apartment houses with "for rent" signs out front. (J.I. Sopher)

A Place to Fit Your Life-Style   Big is not always better. The big apartments are likely to be very expensive. Besides, you may not need that much space. First decide how much space you need to suit your *life-style* (the way you live), and your wallet. There are some questions that may help you understand your life-style. Will you have a lot of company? Will a hobby or collections take up a lot of space? How many closets will you need to store your belongings? Do you like a large or small kitchen? Do you need any extra room for overnight guests?

Getting a larger place than you need is not a good idea. Try to imagine how your belongings will look in each place you see. It's a good idea to take along a yardstick to measure the rooms. Empty rooms may look larger or smaller than they really are.

What's Right/Wrong with It?   Check out each apartment with care as you look at it. Keep a list of the good and bad things you see. After you've seen a few places, it's hard to remember one from the other. Your notes will be helpful.

As You Go In   Consider the following as you enter each place:

- Is the neighborhood quiet, especially at night? You don't want to feel it's deserted, but, on the other hand, if the building is on a busy street you will hear traffic all the time.
- Do you get the feeling that, in general, the building is well cared for?
- Do the hallways and steps have good lighting, as well as being clean?
- Is the apartment in the back of the building (maybe you want the front)?
- Is the apartment on the ground floor (maybe you wanted the second floor or higher)?
- Can you hear everyone talking inside and walking around (maybe the walls aren't thick enough)?

Inside the Apartment   As you look around inside an apartment, ask yourself these questions:

- Is it clean?
- Do you like the *layout* (the way the rooms are arranged)?

Fig. 8-2 Each of these rentals offers you different advantages. Which one suits your life-style? Which one can you afford?

- Is the amount of space just about right?
- Do the windows open well? In older buildings, where the apartments have been painted many times, the windows sometimes stick or are impossible to open.
- Are there enough windows to let in light and air? Enough light and air makes any apartment cheerier. The right light is especially important if you plan to have lots of plants.
- Is the view from the windows pleasant?
- Do the range, refrigerator, and other appliances work? If they are very dirty, find out whether or not they'll be cleaned by the landlord. You may have to do this yourself.
- Turn on the water faucets in the kitchen and the bathroom. Is the water hot? Does the water run freely?
- Do any of the faucets leak? Sinks may be stained from water dripping.
- Are there enough electrical outlets to plug in lamps, TV, radio, and other appliances?
- Are there enough cabinets in the kitchen for dishes, food, and supplies?
- Is there a broom closet or other storage space for cleaning supplies?
- Are there enough closets for your clothes, storage, linens, and space for visitors' coats?
- Are the floors in good condition? If not, will the landlord repair or recover them?
- Are there screens and shades on all the windows? (The landlord should supply these.)
- Are there locks on the doors and windows and is there an easy escape route in case of fire?

Before Leaving   After you've seen the apartment, you may want to find out more about the building. Ask the manager or rental agent questions such as:

- Is there a safe place to park your car (if you have one)?
- Where do you pick up the mail? Is there a lock on the mailbox that works?
- Is there a laundry room in the apartment? (If not, check for one nearby.) Is it well lighted and in a safe location? (You wouldn't

feel safe, for example, if a door from the laundry room led to a back alley.)
- How do visitors get into the building? Do they just buzz your apartment or can they buzz and talk to you? It's better if they can talk to you too so you know who's buzzing.
- How well do the heating and air conditioning (if it's included) work? This may be difficult to find out. The best thing to do is ask other tenants if they have any problems with heat in the winter or air conditioning in the summer.
- Where do you have to go to throw out your trash and garbage?

Some of these questions may be less important to you than to other people. Again, it depends on your life-style. You may find that it's depressing to have your bedroom window face a brick wall. Someone else, whose hobby is photography and who plans to use the bedroom as a darkroom, would be delighted. The questions about safety should be important to everyone.

The Lease or Rental Agreement

Just as the looks of each apartment will be different, so will the rules—what you can and cannot do. The rules are usually found in a *lease*. This is a formal contract which both the landlord and the tenant must agree to and sign. It includes each person's rights and responsibilities.

Leases are often hard to read because of all the legal words. The person renting the apartment, for example, is called the *lessee,* and the landlord is the *lessor.*

The lease's main purpose is to tell how long the lease runs and how much the apartment costs. Most leases are drawn up for a year. This means that you, the lessee, are legally responsible for paying a certain monthly rent for a period of a year and the landlord cannot raise the monthly rent during that year. After a year, your rent could be raised, but the landlord is required to let you know about the change ahead of time. And, a new lease must be signed.

You may be asked to sign a *rental agreement* instead of a lease. A rental agreement continues on a month-to-month basis as long as landlord and tenant agree. Some advance notice (usually 30 days) is required to end the agreement. This makes it easier to move on

Fig. 8-3 Everybody has different needs and values when it comes to choosing an apartment. What delights you may not satisfy others.

short notice if you decide you want to. But, the landlord can also ask you to move within 30 days.

Leases as well as rental agreements will tell you when the rent is due. It's usually on the first day of every month. They also tell what things your rent includes. Electricity, for example, may be included in the rent. Most of the lease is taken up with listing rules and regulations that you (and others in the building) must follow. There may even be some other rules that are not shown in the lease. Be sure to ask the landlord or *building manager* (the person who takes care of the building and usually lives there, too) about any such rules.

Don't feel that you can sign the lease and *then* read it carefully. Understand it first. There's nothing wrong with asking for a copy to take with you to read at your leisure. You may want to have someone who has had some experience with leases or legal language go over it. It is as important to be sure you understand the terms of your lease or rental agreement as it is to like the apartment.

What to Look For   Reading the lease and finding out about any unwritten rules and regulations may convince you to find another place. Or, you may decide to go ahead and move in.

You've already learned about some of the common terms in a lease. The lease also tells what happens when a tenant *defaults* or does not follow what has been agreed to in the lease. A tenant who fails to pay the rent, for example, has defaulted on the lease. While reading the lease, make sure you understand the following:

- Do you have to pay a security deposit? How much? Will it be returned when you move out? Will it earn you interest while the landlord's bank holds it?
- Who pays for the utilities?
- Can the lessor enter your apartment and take possession of it and your personal property if you default? Can your lease be canceled if you default? Does the lessor have to warn you?
- What happens if you decide to share the apartment with someone else at a later time?
- Can you have pets? If the lease says you can have pets, then remember that other people in the building may have them.

Would this bother you even though you don't wish to have any of your own?

- What happens if you want to move out before the lease is up? Are you still responsible for paying the rent for the length of the lease?
- When do you have to tell the landlord you are moving? Do you have to give written notice of this?
- Can you *sublet* (rent the apartment to someone else before your lease is up)? Subletting gives you a chance to move out before your lease is up; however, it also means that you are responsible for the apartment even though you no longer live there.
- Under what conditions can the lessor, or building manager, enter the apartment? If the lease says the lessor can enter at a "reasonable time," what does that mean?
- Will the apartment be painted by the landlord before you move in?
- Can you paint or paper the walls if you want to? Most landlords want to make sure that when you leave the apartment it looks like it did when you came. If you can put up wallpaper, make sure it's the kind that can be easily removed. (You may love the little fish design on the wallpaper in the bathroom but the next tenant may not.) The same idea goes for painting too. The landlord may tell you it's okay to paint one wall in your bedroom canary yellow. Still, when you move you may have to paint that wall the original color or pay the landlord to do it. (That money would probably come from your security deposit.)
- Can you hang pictures? If this is allowed, you will have to remove the nails and plaster up the hole in the wall before you move out.
- When you move, will you have to leave those things you've paid for and put up (like curtain rods, towel racks, hanging planters, extra door locks)? Or, if you take them, are you required to remove the hardware (nails or screws) and plaster up the holes?
- Can you install your own air conditioner or dishwasher?
- Can you store equipment (maybe your bike) in another area of the building?
- Are there any rules about loud noises that would make it hard for you to entertain your friends?

It's also wise to check on rules for parking, trash collection, and the laundry room. Don't wait to move in to get the answers to any questions you may have.

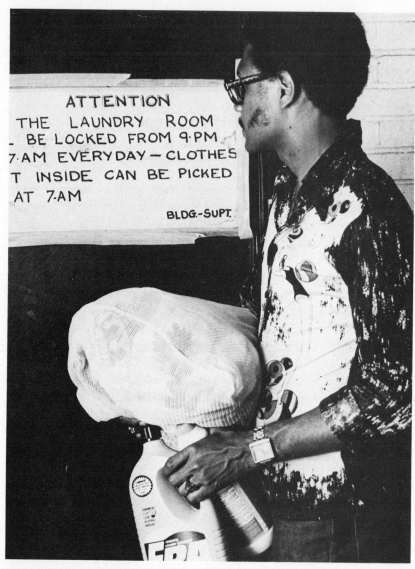

Fig. 8-4 Before you sign the lease, ask about all the building's rules. Don't wait until you move in to find out if the laundry room is open at convenient hours. (Susan Berkowitz)

Signing the Lease or Rental Agreement You have read the lease, understood it, and are now ready to sign. Wait! One more thing. You and the landlord may have agreed on something that is not in the lease. Be sure it's added so there's a written record of your agreement. Most lease forms have extra space at the bottom for such additions. You'll probably be given more than one copy of the lease to sign. The landlord will also sign each copy and will give you one to keep. Don't throw it away. Store it in a safe place where you can find it when needed.

Renting a Furnished Apartment People who rent a place that is furnished may have to sign an extra form. It is usually called an *inventory agreement.* It will list the furniture and equipment that comes with the apartment. It's wise to describe the condition of any item that is damaged or dirty. Put the description right on the form. Otherwise, you could be held responsible for the condition, and charged for it, when the lease is up. Keep your copy of the agreement with your copy of the lease.

Moving In

You'll get off to a good start by spending a little time getting ready to move. It's wise not to put everything off until the day of the big move.

Getting Ready to Move Before moving, take one more look at your new place to make sure it is as clean as you'd like. You can take care of most jobs easier and faster when it's empty. You can also measure windows (if it's necessary to buy curtains or shades). Take careful room measurements too. They'll come in handy when looking around for furniture.

Find out who is responsible for telling the utility companies when you want their services to begin. In some places, this will be your responsibility. In others, the landlord will take care of it. Usually, you are responsible for calling the phone company to ask to have your phone connected.

Hire a Mover or Do It Yourself? How much stuff do you have to move? Do you have enough time to do it yourself? How much money are you willing to put out? Answering all these questions will help you to decide if you would rather hire a mover or move yourself. It's a good idea to compare different ways and costs of moving.

Hiring a Professional Mover   Moving companies will give you free estimates of their charges for moving you. This will be based on what you have to move and the distance you are moving. This estimate is only a guide. You will be charged for what is actually moved. The best way to select a moving company is through someone who has had a good experience with one. Otherwise, you could call your local Consumer Affairs office and the Better Business Bureau for information.

After selecting a mover, it is wise to get written agreement covering the move. Will you box your own things? Will they do some? Is the company *liable* (responsible) for any breakage or loss? If so, for how much? Usually the full purchase price is not covered unless, of course, you wish to buy some additional insurance. Hiring professionally trained movers with just the right equipment may be worth any added expense.

Moving Yourself   If you don't have a great deal to move, you may wish to move yourself. With the help of a couple of your friends, you may enjoy this do-it-yourself experience. Even if you have a suitable car for moving, such as a pickup or van, you still may wish to look into the cost of renting a trailer. You may locate a dealer by looking in the telephone book's Yellow Pages. Make a list of the things you have to move, so you can estimate the size of trailer you'll need. It may cost less to rent a small trailer and make more than one trip. If you have heavy or large pieces to move, it may be worthwhile to rent a hand truck or a *dolly* (a platform on rollers) or both.

Packing for the Move   There are many small things you can do ahead of time to make sure your belongings get to the new place with nothing broken, torn, or scratched.

Boxes will come in handy for packing and carrying everything from books and records to dishes and pans. Supermarkets are a good place to find cartons. Liquor stores have boxes with compartments—great for protecting many things. Make sure they're sturdy and clean. You can also buy or rent packing boxes

Fig. 8-5 When you pack up to move, wrap all fragile things in old newspapers. Then, mark each box to show its contents or the room in which it belongs. (Susan Berkowitz)

from a moving company. It's possible to get special ones for clothes and objects of almost any size.

Books need to be packed in strong boxes that are not too large. Otherwise, the boxes will be too heavy to lift. Dishes and other things that break can be wrapped in newspaper. Put the large pieces in the bottom of the box. Plates can be wrapped and then placed on their sides in the box. Do not put them flat.

Put smaller items inside large ones to protect them. Each piece should be wrapped to protect it from moving around. Mark each box to show its contents or the room in which they belong. That will make the job of unpacking easier.

Some large things, such as mattresses, will have to be moved in one piece. Other large items, like tables, can be moved more easily and with less danger of damage if the legs are removed.

Clothes can be left on their hangers or folded in a box. If you are moving a long distance, a clothes rack for the car will be a big help. Or, you can get a special clothes box from a moving company.

Houseplants can be carried by hand or set inside a box so they won't tip over. For a plant like a fern that spreads out, cut off the bottom of a grocery bag. Slip the pot down through the top of the bottomless bag. This will protect the plant.

And Now, On to the New Place

You may be wondering as you are getting ready to move whether it's really worth it. Lots of decisions have had to be made, but making decisions is a big, and a good, part of being independent. There are lots of different decisions to be made and ideas to think about in the next chapter on decorating your place.

THINKING IT THROUGH

1. Consider this statement: "I don't really need a budget. I have the same bills every month, and I know where my money's going even before I make it." Is this a common attitude? In what specific ways, if any, could it lead to serious financial problems?
2. How would you rank, in order of importance to you, the considerations listed in Chapter 8 under each of the following headings: "As You Go In," "Inside the Apartment," and "Before Leaving"?
3. In your opinion, who gets the most protection or benefits the most from a lease, the landlord, the tenant, or both?
4. Do you know of any landlords or tenants who have taken legal action concerning a lease? What were the circumstances? What was the outcome?

Decorating on Your Own

Next time you go to a restaurant or a movie, look around at the clothes people are wearing. Chances are you will see a lot of different looks—from casual jeans to more formal dress shirts and ties, the latest fads and classic styles, bright colors and basic black. Clothes tell a lot about the people wearing them. You may see a terrific outfit, but you know you wouldn't feel comfortable in it because it's not you. Well, the furniture and all the other objects *(furnishings)* in a room are like a wardrobe for that room. The way some rooms are furnished will seem all right to you. Others will look uncomfortable.

The furnishings you pick and how you arrange them are important decisions in decorating your apartment. The way you decorate, like your clothes, tells a lot about you. And the way you decorate also can make your apartment more comfortable to be in, a place you want to come home to. A little know-how can make decorating easier. That's what this chapter is about.

Preliminary Steps to Decorating

The most important rule to follow in decorating your place boils down to two words: Know yourself. The furnishings, the colors, the atmosphere should fit you. You don't want to have to fit them. That means decorating to fit your life-stlye. Will it be busy or quiet? Will many hours be spent in your new dwelling or just a few? Will your place be home base for a lot of your friends as well as yourself? If so, furnishings will get more wear and tear, so they should be chosen with this in mind.

What kinds of things will occupy your hours at home? Sleeping, eating, having company, cooking, listening to music, studying, read-

Fig. 9-1 What are your interests? The apartment you choose should fit your hobbies, interests, and life-style.

ing, working at a hobby or craft, watching television? What do you need for each of these activities? If you like sports, you'll need enough room to store necessary equipment. Taking classes in addition to working could call for a quiet place for studying or finishing projects. Should it be in the living room or in a corner of the bedroom? How about meals for guests? They can be served formally at a table, informally on a coffee table, or even with your friends sitting on the floor. Thinking about your own personality and what makes you tick will help in selecting furnishings.

To find out more about yourself, a good idea is to make two lists. One could be labeled "My Personal Activity Choices." The second list, used to describe your personality, could be called "My Personal Likes and Dislikes." You might list that you are outgoing, that you like quiet sometimes, that you are sentimental, or that you hate gaudy colors.

Another idea is to start collecting pictures of furnishings you like, from magazines, advertisements, or newspapers. Your best finds can be put in a scrapbook or in a manila folder. In either case, it's a good idea to go through the scrapbook or folder regularly, keeping only the best ideas.

Picking Colors   Our everyday life is filled with different colors—thousands of them. Trying to pick the best ones for your place can be discouraging or fun. The best guides are your own good taste and common sense. If a certain color is in style, but you don't like it, why use it? Bold colors, like dark purple, are sometimes used by professional decorators because they attract attention. Before choosing them for yourself, try to imagine how it would feel to live with them everyday.

Some colors affect almost everyone the same way. What do you wear, for example, when you feel happy? How about when you are under the weather? Do you think of pink as being only for females and its cousin, red, as more suited to males? How do you feel when you see someone in blue or yellow? Would you feel at ease in wearing any shade or tint of these colors? The same kinds of questions can be asked in picking colors for rooms.

Some colors may remind you of something that happened in the past. If the experience was bad, the color may make you feel uneasy. So you need to know the effect different colors have on you.

Then it's easier to pick the colors you can live with day after day, month after month.

There are also some hints about using colors that may be helpful in making decisions. Did you know, for example, that:

- In small apartments, the use of white or colors from the cool family (the blues, greens, and violets) will make rooms seem larger.
- Colors from the cool family also help tone down rooms that get a lot of sun.
- A dark room, one that gets little sun, can be perked up by using warm colors: reds, oranges, and yellows.
- Generally, no more than three colors should be used in one room, not counting the neutrals (white, beige, gray, black).
- Colors should be used in unequal amounts. The main color may be used in two-thirds of the room.

Getting the Feel of Things   When you can't resist touching something because of the way it looks, you've stepped into the world of textures. Like the world of color, it's a big one. Again, you are the best judge of how textures affect you and how much attention you want to give them in decorating.

Textures are usually chosen for one of two reasons: the way they look (their visual effect) or they way they feel to the touch (their kinesthetic effect). Think about whether you like the look of chrome as well as the touch. Does it look and feel cold to you, or shiny and attractive? How about something made of corduroy, plastic, rattan, or leather?

Materials with smooth textures (silver, glass, polished woods, velvet) make a room look formal. For a more casual look, think about using materials and items that are rough textured or that have coarse surfaces. Keep in mind that texture must work in harmony with color and that one can influence the other. For example, do you like a red plastic chair as well as a white one? Or is a black metal frame with a yellow canvas sling seat the best choice?

Colors and textures should be tried to make sure they go together. Sometimes, stores let customers take swatches of fabric home to try out. On the other hand, customers can take samples of colors to the store to match them to fabrics.

Fig. 9-2 The use of rough textures can give a room a casual look. Here, the nubbly-textured sofa and pillows macrame wall-hanging, and the baskets full of plants all give this room a warm, comfortable, casual feeling. (Ginger Chih)

If furnishings will receive a lot of use, it's a good idea to find out what it takes to keep them clean. Both color and texture must be considered. Surfaces that are slick, for example, are usually the easiest to keep clean.

Planning Living Space

Many of the pitfalls of decorating can be avoided by studying each room. How big is it? What are its good and bad points? How can it be improved? Planning should be done before moving in. If furnishings are purchased and moved into a place in haphazard fashion, that's how it will look.

Plan on Paper First Good decorating depends on a four-letter word: a *plan*, one that is put down on paper. To plan a room or a whole apartment, the basic supplies needed are simple: a measuring tape, some graph paper, a clear plastic ruler, a pencil, and an eraser.

The first thing to do is to measure the length and width of each room. *Draw it to scale* (sized to a proportion) on the graph paper.

Allow each square on the paper—¼-inch (in) [0.625 centimeter (cm)] or ½-in [1.25 cm] squares—to equal 1 foot (ft) [30 cm] of floor space. Don't forget to measure and draw to scale all doors, windows, and closets. If the way doors and windows open means that furniture cannot be placed in front of them, mark this on the plan. Also mark any ledges, counters, and heating and cooling units that limit how furniture can be placed. Your plan, whether it's for one room or the whole apartment, is called a *layout*.

Consider the Beaten Path   Have you even noticed carpets being worn in certain areas or paths? These paths mark the *traffic patterns* people take to get from one place to another. You may see some that go around pieces of furniture. This may mean that placement of furniture was decided without enough thought to traffic patterns.

A basic rule in arranging furniture is to figure out what will happen in a room and what paths will be used. No one wants to stumble over a chair, for example, while on the way to raid the refrigerator. In addition, furniture should not block entrances or exits. The layout in Figure 9-3 includes the paths likely to be used in each room. Against which living room walls could you place a sofa so as not to block the path to the balcony? Now picture a coffee table in front of that sofa. Does this sofa/coffee table combination change the possibilities? Where would it be best to put a table in the kitchen?

Furniture Cutouts   Several uses can be made of paper cutouts (*templates*) of each piece of furniture drawn to scale. They help you arrange furniture without straining your back or losing your temper. If you want to, you can change your mind many times about where to put something. Before buying new pieces of furniture, you may want to draw them to scale and put them in your layout, trying them out for size and fit. So it's a good idea to hang onto the layout and furniture cutouts for rearrangements or future purchases.

Furniture cutouts are scaled to two measurements: width and length. (Height is not considered for furniture placement on a layout, although it should be kept in mind when placement is in front of a window.) Each piece of furniture must be measured accurately to determine how much floor space it takes. Each is then drawn to scale on a piece of paper. Say, for example, you are making a

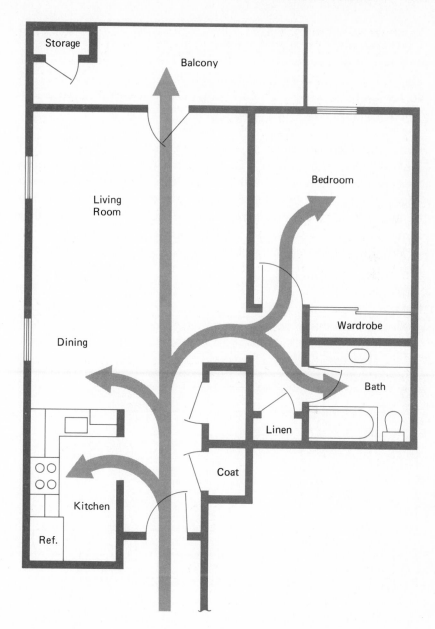

Fig. 9-3 The arrows show the likely traffic patterns for this apartment. Furniture should be arranged so that it does not block these paths.

cutout of a sofa. It measures 30 in [75 cm] wide by 72 in [180 cm] long. You may have already determined that each ¼-in [0.625 cm] square of graph paper equals 1 ft [30 cm] of floor space. The paper cutout for the sofa, then, should look like a rectangle, ⅝ in [1.56 cm] wide by 1½ in [3.75 cm] long. This is shown in Figure 9-4 along with a cutout of a chest.

Look to the Focal Point   In each room, there should be one part that attracts attention. This is called the room's *focal point*. A room may have more than one focal point, but too many waters down the effect. Just as there can be only one or two stars in a football game or in a movie, the same idea holds in decorating. All the other furnishings in a room should support the focal points.

What kinds of things can be used as a focal point? Practically anything, depending on what you like. You might have one large

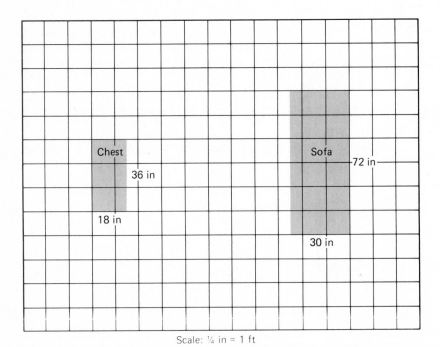

Scale: ¼ in = 1 ft

Fig. 9-4 Cut a scale model of each piece of furniture using a scale of ¼ in = 1 ft. Then, draw a room layout on ¼-in graph paper. Arrange (and rearrange) the furniture cutouts on the room layout, until you find the best plan.

wall hanging, poster, or antique vase that you want to show off. Another idea is to group different-sized pictures or other favorite objects together. Items that are collected or that are made as a hobby are often the most fun to use. Anything used as a focal point can become a *conversation piece* (an object, or the way an object is displayed, which catches the eye and stirs up conversation about it).

Avoid Tight Squeezes In addition to thinking about the focal point in each room, it's good to consider how each item of furniture is used. Chairs are not always neatly tucked in under the table. Space must be allowed to get in and out without squeezing. Things that open, like refrigerators and other doors, need swing space. Similarly, it takes room to make a bed, serve meals, even to sit down without hitting your leg on a coffee table placed too close to a sofa. Table 9-1 serves as a guide in showing how much space to allow for various activities.

Making Small Places Grow Living in a cramped apartment can be nerve-racking to some people. There are ways, however, to make a place look more spacious than it really is. The best way to open up a room and not feel cramped is to avoid clutter. There are two ways of doing this. One is to put away the things not in use and organize the others. The second way is to resist buying more furnishings than needed. It is better to have too few pieces of furniture than too many.

Furniture Placement and Color The scale (size in relation to something else) and placement of furniture and the use of color can also make a room seem smaller or larger. Figure 9-5 shows a room in which the furniture is in proper scale and one in which it is not. Generally, small- to medium-size furniture fits better and looks more attractive in smaller apartments.

The furnishings in a room must be in good proportion to it and to each other. How do you think a tiny, fragile-looking chair would look next to a huge. overstuffed sofa? Probably no more effective than the 3-ft rug in front of the 6-ft sofa, shown in Figure 9-6.

Where and how furniture is placed is also important. Placing furniture across the corners of a room takes more space than putting

Table 9-1   HOW MUCH SPACE TO ALLOW

Room	Area	m	ft/in
Living room	Space between coffee table and sofa or chair	.45	1 ft 6 in
	Space in front of chair or sofa (leg room)	.45–.75	1 ft 6 in–2 ft 6 in
	Chair or bench space in front of desk or piano	.9	3 ft
	Space for grouping chair, average-size sofa, coffee table, end table	1.95 × 2.7	6 ft 6 in × 9 ft
	Space for grouping long sofa, end tables, two lounge chairs, coffee table	1.95 × 4.2	6 ft 6 in × 14 ft
	Bookcase with flanking chairs	.6 × 2.1	2 ft × 7 ft
	Space for card table and four chairs	2.4 × 2.4	8 × 8 ft
	Study area with desk, chair, lounge chair, ottoman	1.5 × 2.4	5 × 8 ft
	Corner grouping with two lounge chairs and corner table	1.8 × 1.8	6 × 6 ft
	Fireplace grouping: two lounge chairs, love seat, two lamp tables	1.6 × 2.7	5 ft 3 in × 9 ft
Dining room	Space between table and wall or buffet	.8–.9	2 ft 8 in–3 ft
	Space around chairs at table for serving	.45–.6	1 ft 6 in–2 ft
Bedroom	Space at each side of bed for making bed	.45–.6	1 ft 6 in–2 ft
	Space between twin beds	.45–.9	1 ft 6 in–3 ft
	Space between chest of drawers and bed	.9	3 ft

Source: Hazel Thomson Craig, *Homes with Character*, D. C. Heath and Company, 1970. [*Metrics added to original chart*]

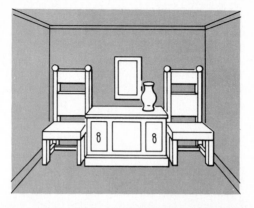

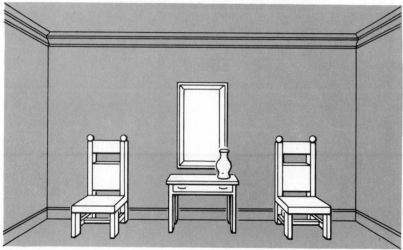

Fig. 9-5 Choose furniture that is in proper proportion to the size of the apartment. In the room shown above, the chairs are too big in scale. They make the room look small. In the room shown below, the chairs are in proper scale.

it parallel to or at right angles to walls. This doesn't mean that all pieces of furniture must be lined up with the wall or shoved against it. Study Figure 9-7 and experiment with your own furniture cutouts for the best arrangement.

Trickery will fool the eye about a room's size. For instance, a room can be made to look larger through the effective use of color. A room with light-colored walls, carpeting, and furniture looks larger than one done in a darker shade.

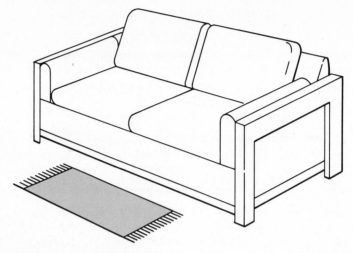

Fig. 9-6 Choose furnishings that are the same relative size. This small rug is in poor proportion to the large sofa.

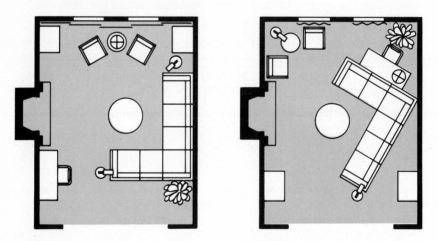

Fig. 9-7 Placing furniture at right angles and parallel to the wall (left) uses less space than placing it across the corners of a room (right).

A problem for some apartment dwellers is how to deal with a long narrow room. Sometimes this room is a combination living room/ dining room. Come nighttime, it doubles as a bedroom. One way to make the room look wider and more interesting is to paint the end wall a bold shade and the side walls a light neutral. Before doing so, however, check with the landlord.

Using Mirrors   Another way to make a room look larger is to place mirrors in strategic locations. Putting mirrors on one wall usually doubles the size of the room. But, good mirrors are expensive, so the view they reflect must be worth seeing. And the landlord's okay may be needed. A table with a glass top, instead of a mirror, may give the look of space you want.

Double-Duty Furniture   In a small apartment, each piece of furniture should be put to as many uses as possible. With *double-duty furniture* (furniture that can be put to more than one use) fewer pieces will be needed. Consider using a coffee table for dining or for playing games. Or a low wicker chest which has many uses: a lamp table, a coffee table, a bench, or a storage bin for extra linens.

Inexpensive squares of *polyurethane* (a man-made foam) serve as seats. Just add covers made from fabric remnants and you've added color and interest to a room. They can be stacked in a corner when not in use or made into a bed for an overnight guest.

Collapsible furniture (furniture that can be made smaller) can be a good buy, especially for cramped quarters. Some types of collapsible furniture, like snack trays or folding chairs, are stored until needed. Other types are free-standing and become part of the furniture arrangement. One example is the collapsible table shown in Figure 9-8. It is a buffet that becomes a table when you pull out the legs and insert an extension.

Selecting Furniture

Almost anything goes nowadays in decorating. In fact, this do-whatever-you-want way of decorating has a name. It's called *eclectic*. All that really matters is that you are pleased and comfortable with the results.

In buying furniture, whether your plan is eclectic or not, think about how it will be used. A small apartment may not have room for do-nothing furniture. A piece of furniture that fills up space and is not *functional* (serves a definite purpose) may not be really needed. On the other hand, some pieces of furniture, like large beanbag chairs, may be functional but take up too much floor space.

Consider the design of furniture before buying it. Try it out! Does

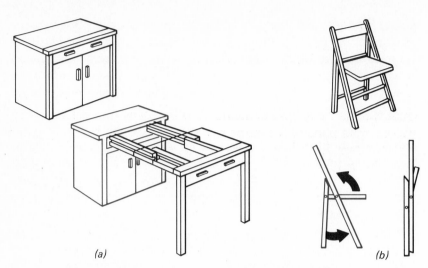

(a)   *(b)*

Fig. 9-8 Collapsible furniture is a practical choice for a small apartment. This buffet (a) can be extended to become a dining table. These chairs (b) can be folded up and stored in a closet when no longer needed.

the chair you like fit the shape of your body? Sit on it! Is the bed comfortable? Lie on it!

Making Good Furniture Buys   What makes for a good buy in furniture? This depends on how much it is worth to you, whether it is needed or not, and how long it will last. Antiques must be considered separately because their value depends on their scarcity and on how much people want them.

Better quality furniture will cost more when you buy it, but probably less in the long run. Cheap, poorly constructed furniture, on the other hand, will break or wear out sooner and have to be replaced sooner. Better furniture may last you through more than one apartment. You may consider using it in your own house someday. A good quality end table, for example, may be used eventually as a bedroom lamp table. And a convertible sofa bed could be used later in a den.

Checking Out Construction   Check the construction of each item you buy, whether new or used. The condition is less important than the construction. A piece of furniture can be recovered, but redoing the basic structure or *frame* may be impractical. Make sure the construction of wooden furniture is solid, and that there are no cracks or defects in the frame. Following are tips on checking the two types of furniture: *case goods* (wooden, without upholstery) and upholstered furniture.

Case Goods   Pay special attention to the *joints* (the places where two or more parts of the frame meet) in wooden furniture. In good wooden furniture, screws rather than nails are used at the joints. Glue is often added at the joints to strengthen them. Dowel joints may be used to connect table or chair legs, as shown in Figure 9-9a. And dovetailed joints, like those in Figure 9-9b, are often used in a good quality chest of drawers.

Check to see that the corners underneath tables and chairs are reinforced with corner pieces of wood or metal. In Figure 9-10a, screws are used to hold the corner block in place.

A drawer will not get off the track if it has a center guide underneath. (See Figure 9-10b.) Another sign of quality is dust panels between the drawers, as shown in Figure 9-10c. Check the hardware, such as drawer pulls. If any of it is broken, find out if replacement is easy.

Upholstered Furniture   The construction of upholstered furniture is mostly hidden so it's hard to determine how good it is. In buying a new piece, you can ask to see samples of the materials and of the

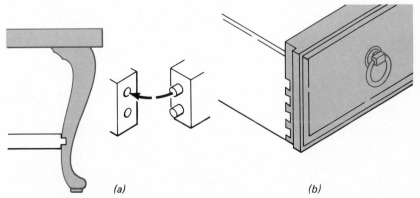

(a)   *(b)*

Fig. 9-9 When you buy wooden furniture, check for these signs of good-quality construction: (a) dowel joints in chair or table legs, (b) dovetail joints in drawers.

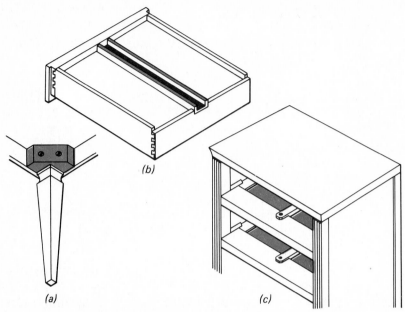

Fig. 9-10 Some other signs of good-quality furniture construction are: (a) the use of corner blocks to reinforce chair and table legs; (b) the addition of a center guide to keep drawers on track; (c) the presence of dust panels between drawers in a chest.

inside works. Often, stores display cross sections of pillows, mattresses, or whole chairs and sofas. (See Figure 9-11.) Check the inside frame, *webbing,* (or crisscross straps used in upholstery), springs (which should be tied), filling, and outside covering. You may want to compare the quality, workmanship, and materials used in furniture available from several different stores. Your time and research will pay off in better buys.

When buying used upholstered furniture, don't worry about the condition of the upholstery. That's less important than the basic structure. The cover can be replaced if worn or grimy, the springs can be retied and new padding added. You may be able to do it yourself especially with the help offered in an adult education course in upholstery.

Where/When to Buy Furniture   One way to save money in buying new furniture is to find out when your local stores normally hold

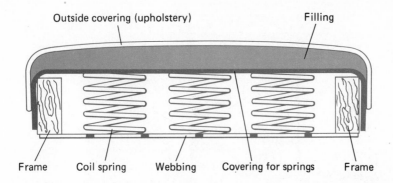

Cross-section of upholstered seat

Fig. 9-11 This cross-section shows you the construction of good-quality upholstered furniture. When you buy a new chair or sofa, ask to see a sample cross-section.

furniture sales. Furniture ordered from a catalog may save money, but don't forget to add shipping charges. Another possible money-saver is to visit one or more walk-in warehouses. Go armed with solid ideas about what you want in order to avoid being completely puzzled by the large number of choices. Beware of being pressured into buying something that doesn't really fit your decorating plans. These warehouses almost always operate on a cash-and-carry basis. This means that you cannot charge the cost on a credit card and that you must pick up the furniture. Delivery is not provided by the store.

Buying raw or unpainted furniture may offer some advantages. For one thing, imperfections in materials and workmanship are easy to spot. And you can paint or stain it any color you want. But don't forget there will be added costs for the materials used as well as the time involved.

Used Furniture　When buying used furniture, check the classified section of the newspaper and watch for garage or patio sales. Those held in the better residential areas are prime hunting grounds for good usable "junk." Frequently, churches and similar groups have permanent sales rooms or shops that are worth browsing in.

Newspapers often carry notices of swap meets, flea markets, and furniture auctions. Moving and storage companies, freight shippers, police departments, and the U.S. Bureau of Customs also hold auctions and sales from time to time.

Fig. 9-12 You can find good used furniture at auctions, flea markets, garage sales, and second-hand furniture stores. When you buy used furniture, check its condition carefully. Is the structure sound? Are the joints tight? Is the hardware missing? (Michael Wheatcroft)

Renting Furniture   When is it a good idea to rent furniture rather than buy it? When renting furniture, you will probably have more pieces to use than if the same amount of money were used for making payments on bought furniture. However, making rental payments could go on forever. When you buy furniture, you own it once payments are finished. Sometimes, though, the rental agency will let you apply the rent toward the later purchase of the furniture. Another reason for renting is that it gives you the opportunity to try out different sets and styles of furniture before buying.

Furniture can usually be rented by the piece or by the room. For a list of furniture rental agencies, look in the telephone book's Yellow Pages. The customer generally must pay at least a minimum amount per month. And a pickup and delivery fee will be required if the customer wants to exchange one set of rented furniture for another. However, it may cost less to rent furniture and an unfurnished apartment, than to rent a furnished apartment. Also, unfurnished rentals may be easier to find.

Accessories Make the Difference

Adding the little extras that spark up rooms—the accessories—can be fun and rewarding. They can cost little but make the big difference in a place's look. Because they are personal touches, they make a place seem like home. Whether functional or not, they can give a lot of pleasure for a little money.

Before Adding Accessories Renters are bound by leases, and leases limit what accessories can be added to walls, cabinets, windows, and other surfaces. So, it is always a good idea to read your lease thoroughly and to talk with the landlord before adding something the lease doesn't allow. The landlord may okay worthwhile changes that add to the value of the property. One example could be your offer to paint a room. The landlord may not only give approval but also pay for the supplies.

Types of Accessories Accessories can hide unattractive or unsightly things, such as minor cracks in walls. They can dress up bare and uninteresting walls. Although there are many, many things that are called accessories, five major classes will be described here: wall accessories, table and shelf accessories, room dividers, lighting, and houseplants.

Wall Accessories These accessories go beyond the usual pictures, photographs, and posters. Consider also one or more of the following: mirrors, tapestries, macrame or fabric hangings, sports equipment, needlework, wallpaper, candelabra, and shelves. It is not necessary to group together only similar items (such as all pictures), but care is required in mixing different objects.

Pictures and mirrors, probably the most common wall accessories, may be mixed. They are more interesting if hung in a random pattern. If used in a row, they'll look best when they are all lined up with the largest piece in the middle. Choose pictures and posters, whether cheap or expensive, because you like them, not just to fill up space.

The size of pictures or mirrors should relate well to that of the furniture under them. Not every piece of furniture that is against the wall, however, needs a picture or mirror over it. A group of objects, like pictures, should look balanced. Imagine a line in the middle of the group: half of the visual weight should fall to the left of the line, half to the right. Almost always, pictures and mirrors should be hung at eye level. Not too many mirrors should be used. What is reflected should be nice to look at and any light that hits the mirror should not cause glare.

Table and Shelf Accessories   Items such as lamps, clocks, vases, bowls and baskets, books, bookends, paperweights, candles, and candlesticks are functional accessories. Other items may be placed on a table or shelf simply because they are pleasant reminders of friends or family, hobbies, places visited, or accomplishments. They can be pictures, trophies, glass ornaments, or souvenirs.

Table lamps, useful accessories, should be bought with care. They should be heavy enough so as not to tip over easily. The base, which can be used for many years, should be sturdy. For good looks, the shade should be simple in design and have good proportion (between one-third and one-half the base's height). See Figure 9-13. The shade should be made of a material that light can pass through. Finally, lamps should be safe to use as shown by the Underwriters Laboratories (UL) symbol attached to them.

Room Dividers   Two rooms can be made out of one by a change in color, carpeting, or furniture, or by adding a room divider. First, figure out if the purpose is to give more usable area or to make your place look more interesting. Folding screens, curtains, cabinets, fabric or bamboo panels, beads, shutters, or plants are a few things that function as room dividers.

The one thing to remember is that room dividers should look like they go with the other furnishings. For example, a casual-looking room divider would look best with informal furniture. Dividers that

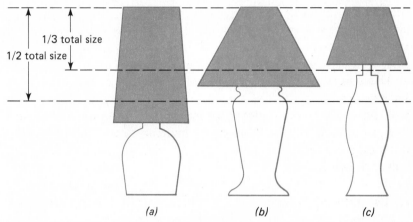

Fig. 9-13 When you buy a lamp, choose one whose shade is in good proportion to the base. The shade and base of lamp (b) are considered in good proportion.

are horizontal in appearance will widen a room; those that are vertical will add height.

Lighting   Natural light—sunlight—can't be beat, but where there is not enough, artificial lighting is a necessity. It can be turned as low and soft as candlelight or so bright that midnight seems like noon. Artificial lighting is often used in decorating to set a mood or to make the objects in a room look better.

Artificial lighting comes in two types: *incandescent* and *fluorescent.* Incandescent light bulbs range from the 7-watt (W) size used as night-lights to the high wattage sizes used in spotlights. Fluorescent lighting, provided by long tubelike bulbs, however, comes closest to resembling daylight. A fluorescent tube provides 2½ times as much light as an incandescent bulb of the same wattage. Fluorescent tubes are also less expensive to operate.

Some rooms will appear dark unless there is overall lighting in addition to the spotlighting provided by lamps. When painting ceilings, remember that light-colored, dull or *matte* (not shiny) paint reflects light best, that is, without glare. Two other tips: Avoid shadows that interfere with reading or other activities; and, place TV sets so they do not reflect light from lamps or windows.

Houseplants   Plants probably add more to a room than any other accessory. They make a place look lived in and alive. They fit into any room and blend with any color combination. Besides being a restful color, the greenery of plants also brings inside a little of the outdoors.

How many plants to use is a matter of personal taste. Little space may be available, thereby limiting what can be done without creat-

Fig. 9-14 Before you buy a plant, find out how big it gets and how much care it requires, and if it adds to rather than detracts from your apartment. (3M Company)

ing a jungle look. On the other hand, you'll find that using plants is an inexpensive way to fill space. A large plant can fill a corner with greenery. It shouldn't block traffic, however. Nor should a hanging plant cause people to bump their heads or bend to get by.

When used as room dividers, plants can separate living areas without blocking much light. They can be used also to divide an entrance from the living areas.

Many people who like plants give clippings to their friends. Otherwise, when you have a choice of plants to buy, pick them with care. The main thing you need to know is whether the plant you want will get enough light in your place. When in doubt, choose another plant. Some like a great deal of sunlight, others will grow in darker areas. Find out how big the plant gets and how much care it requires. If you are away a lot, you may not have the time required to care for plants. At any rate, it's safe to stick with the strong varieties, such as philodendron, that grow well with minimum care.

Now That It Looks Homey

Remember that decorating has many angles. It can be fun and a challenge. And the results can make all the effort seem worthwhile.

So that the time spent in decorating is not time spent in vain, Chapter 10 focuses on keeping order and caring for your place.

THINKING IT THROUGH

1. If you were about to redecorate this classroom in a way that made you feel more comfortable, what decorating changes would you make if you were limited to color, fabric, and lighting? If there were no limitations?
2. A friend describes her apartment as "small and depressing." What questions would you ask her (without visiting the apartment) in order to help with some decorating suggestions?
3. Individuals and families often have "favorite" pieces of furniture in their houses or apartments. Think of the examples that you know. How does a piece of furniture become a "favorite"? Is the piece of furniture usually expensive? Old? Comfortable? Useful? What can these "favorites" teach us about furnishing our own places?

Caring for Your Place 10

When you think about the things you like to do, what comes to mind? Eating, watching TV, taking care of your car, shopping for something new? How about doing dishes, straightening up the living room, or doing the laundry? Believe it or not, some people really enjoy the nitty-gritty things that keep a place clean and in order. It is a big part of their life-style, and they put a lot of time and energy into it.

Other people feel just the opposite. They enjoy the freedom of coming and going as they please, like spending Saturday doing fun things—not housework. They may put off housekeeping chores until there are no more clean dishes or clothes. The only time they clean could be when they are giving a party. Most people fall into the middle category. They don't have every little thing in exact order all the time, but neither do they live in an impossible mess. How about you?

There is no question about it—keeping a place clean and neat can be the greatest test of real independence. It means mastering a plan that makes the best use of your time, money, and energy. But in the end, you'll be proud of yourself. Your friends will wonder how you can keep everything under control and still have plenty of time for your real interests.

This chapter gives helpful hints on housekeeping, but pretty soon you'll discover your own shortcuts and cleaning methods.

Setting Up a Plan

Remember the plan you used for decorating your place? Well, the same thing goes for cleaning. The best way to go about it is to have

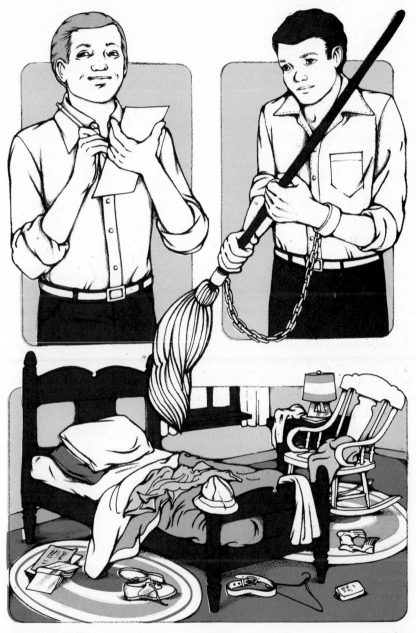

Fig. 10-1 What is your attitude toward housecleaning? Do you make a list of things to be done, then plan the quickest way to do them? Or do you just slave away endlessly?

a plan that will put you in command of your household. After all, it's not fun to be a slave to your place.

Actually, you've probably already succeeded in carrying out lots of your plans. Just think about how many plans you made before going to your first dance. Did you figure out what to say and what to wear? Where would you have been without a plan to guide you? Or, how about when you went to get your driver's license? Didn't you spend a great deal of time learning the laws and practicing your driving? This was all part of your plan to get a license. Although taking care of your place may not be as exciting as going to a dance or getting your driver's license, it still takes careful planning.

In your plan, there are three things to consider: money, energy, and time. Only you can figure out how to put each one of these to the best use.

Use of Money   People often spend a lot of money buying gadgets and products that are not really very useful. Planning can save you money by knowing what you want a product to do and by finding out as much as you can about that product before buying it. Reading labels and instruction booklets can help. Have you ever bought spot remover just because it worked well in a demonstration? Then you used it and, even though you put on the whole bottle, you could still see the spot. Maybe a careful reading of the label would have told you it wouldn't work on some fabrics, that it works on only certain kinds of stains, or that the directions called for several applications. Comparing labels on different brands might have showed you that another brand could have been returned if you weren't satisfied with the results.

Money can also be saved by looking for things that can be used for more than one job. Liquids that clean and polish, metal cleaners that can be used on several different kinds of metals, vacuums that work on rugs and floors are some examples.

When a particular item—such as a vacuum—gets a lot of use, remember also to consider quality before you buy.

Use of Energy   Caring for your place can be as easy as ABC. Or it can be so exhausting that you'll flop into bed and hate the thought of going through it again. It's all a matter of making the best use of your energy. Think about how you found shortcuts on the way to school or to the movies. There are also shortcuts in doing house-work. Sometimes two tasks can be combined—like folding the laundry and separating it into like items at the same time. Having the right tools can also cut down on the amount of energy you use in getting a job done.

Use of Time   Before you moved into your own place, did you seem to have lots of time on your hands? Now is there too much to do and too little time? More and more, you'll find that time is the most precious thing you have. Figure 10-2 shows an example of how one person spends 24 hours (hr). How do you spend a day?

How much of your day is used for cooking and caring for your place? To find out, make a list of all the jobs needed to keep your place in shape. Next to each job estimate how much time it takes.

In making the list, you'll see that some jobs have to be done much more often than others. Making the bed, for example, will be done daily. Other tasks will be done once a week. The monthly jobs can be called "occasional." Twice-a-year jobs can be listed as "seasonal." How different is your list from the one in Table 10-1? Do you see any ways to save time?

Making Your Plan Work

Putting your plan in operation can be a big challenge. For one thing, there will be different problems in each room. Some people will do all the dusting at once, then all the vacuuming, finally ending with the kitchen and the bathroom. Others prefer a reverse order. Below are hints for making your plan work in each room.

The Kitchen Plan   One way to reduce kitchen work is to save steps. This may be hard, depending on how your kitchen is ar-ranged. Usually, the range, sink, and refrigerator—which are your work stations in the kitchen—are spaced several feet apart, so as to provide some counter space. Notice the work stations shown in Figure 10-3a form a triangle.

If these work stations are too close, your steps are fewer but you may feel cramped. There's another reason for not wanting the range too close to the refrigerator. The heat from the range would

Bay Area Rapid Transit

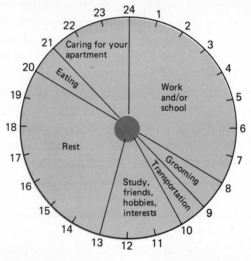

Ginger Chih

Fig. 10-2 Are you spending your time on what you really want to do? To find out, make up a 24-hour time clock, like the one shown above. How many hours a day do you spend on school, grooming, transportation, hobbies, rest, eating, caring for your apartment?

Table 10-1   JOBS TO KEEP THE PLACE IN SHAPE

Job	Time needed to do the job (to the nearest ¼ hr)
Daily	
Make bed, tidy bedroom and bathroom	¼ hr
Straighten up living and eating area	¼ hr
Prepare meals	1 hr
Wash dishes, clean sink	½ hr
Empty wastebaskets, ashtrays, etc.	¼ hr
Sweep kitchen floor	¼ hr
Weekly	
Change bed sheets and other linens	¼ hr
Do laundry and mending	2 hr
Wash garbage pail or change liner	¼ hr
Wash kitchen floor	¼ hr
Clean bathroom fixtures (sink, tub, and toilet)	¼ hr
Wash bathroom floor	¼ hr
Dust pictures and wall accessories	¼ hr
Dust and polish furniture	½ hr
Vacuum lampshades	¼ hr
Vacuum carpet, shake small rugs	½ hr
Shop for, and put away, groceries	2 hr
Occasionally (monthly)	
Vacuum and turn mattress, wash mattress pad and bedspread	½ hr
Remove old wax and rewax floors in kitchen and bathroom	2 hr
Vacuum drapes, wipe blinds	½ hr
Vacuum upholstered furniture	½ hr
Wash windows and mirrors	1 hr
Clean and wax furniture	1 hr
Clean shelves and reorganize food items, dishes, and linens	1 hr
Clean and defrost refrigerator	1 hr
Wash bathroom wall tiles	¼ hr
Clean range, including oven	½ hr
Seasonally (twice a year)	
Clean closets, air clothes	2 hr
Take coats, seasonal clothes, bedding to dry cleaners	1 hr
Clean drapes thoroughly	2 hr
Wash dishes, glassware (not normally used)	1 hr
Replace shelf paper	1 hr
Clean silverware	1 hr
Clean woodwork	1–2 hr

make the refrigerator work overtime. It can ruin the motor too. If your kitchen is arranged this way, place an asbestos board between the two appliances. The asbestos will stop the heat of the range from reaching the refrigerator. Your landlord may supply it for you.

If these work stations are too far apart, you may be putting too much time and energy into preparing a meal. What you can do to cut down steps and save time is to arrange the little things conveniently. You may find it handy, for example, to keep the cereal bowls with the cereal. It is generally a good idea to put the cups with the coffee, tea, and cocoa. Buy two of things that are often used, but in different parts of the kitchen. For example, salt and pepper shakers. How about a set near the range and one near the table? Put paring knives near the sink, where they are used. If you have no drawer close by, try putting them on a shelf or in a knife holder. You can also save steps by using a tray when you have to move a lot of items from one place to another.

Items used most frequently should be placed near the front of shelves. So should the small items. Put bigger things in the back, with labels showing. Things like vases, which may not be used too often, can be put in the hard-to-reach cupboards.

Saving Time and Energy   Get used to working from right to left (counterclockwise) especially when setting the table and doing dishes. Rinse and stack dishes on the right side of the sink. Dry and put them away from the left. The arrows in Figure 10-3b show the flow of work which is done from right to left. People who are left-handed may find it easier to work from left to right (clockwise).

Do you get a clean dish each time you measure something or mix it? Try reusing both bowls and utensils to save time. It may be easier, too, to wash the dishes as you use them. Otherwise, the food may dry on them, which doubles washing time. Some people wash all the dishes used to prepare the meal as it is cooking to cut down on cleanup time later. It's a good idea to finish the dishes and clean the kitchen before going to bed.

Defrosting and Cleaning the Refrigerator   Have you ever seen a refrigerator with so much ice on the freezer there was no room for food? This can easily happen because *defrosting* (removing the built-up ice) can be a messy, time-consuming job. *Frost-free* re-

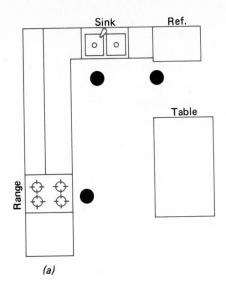

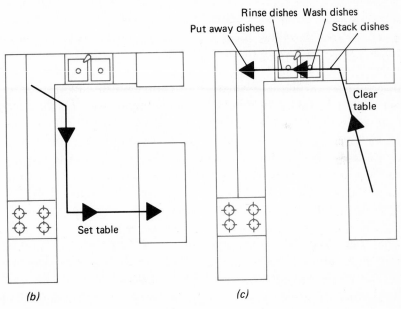

Fig. 10-3 These three diagrams show you how to save steps in the kitchen. The ideal kitchen arrangement would be one in which the refrigerator, sink, and range form a triangle (a). If you are right-handed, it's easier and quicker to work from right to left (b and c) in a counter clockwise direction.

frigerators (ones that defrost themselves) are made but most apartments do not provide them.

Generally, defrosting should be done before the ice is ¼ in thick. If you let the ice get too thick, you'll have to fight to get food or ice trays out of the freezer. You may win the fight but end up with scraped fingers as battle scars! Also, defrosting will take less time if the ice is thinner.

First, turn the control (located inside the refrigerator) to OFF. All frozen food should be removed and wrapped in heavy newspaper or placed in paper bags, two thick. To speed up the melting, pour boiling water from a tea kettle into empty pans placed inside the freezer. Repeat this action until all ice is melted. Also, put some empty containers under the freezer to catch the ice and water. Do not use a knife or other instrument to chisel away at the ice. It's dangerous and it could ruin the freezer. When the ice is all gone, the job is done. The refrigerator control is ready to be turned to ON again, and the food put back.

While you're waiting for the ice to melt, clean the inside of the refrigerator. Use a cloth dipped in water and detergent or water and baking soda (about ¼ cup [60 milliliters (mL)] baking soda to ½ gallon (gal) [1.8 liter (L)] water). Rinse and wipe dry. Plan to defrost and clean the refrigerator before a big shopping trip. The less food to move out, then back in, the faster you can do the job.

To keep the motor from overheating, it's important to remove the dirt and dust from the *condenser* (mechanical part of the refrigerator where gas changes to liquid) occasionally. Use the vacuum, with a long attachment, for this job. The condenser is usually at the bottom, or at the back, of the refrigerator.

Cleaning the Oven   Few apartments have self-cleaning ranges. Cleaning the oven should be done before the grease and boiled-over food have a chance to build up. This will also prevent the oven from smoking. How often you need to clean the oven depends on how often you use it. The more grease and food you allow to build up, the more time-consuming this job will be. There are lots of products you can buy to clean the oven. Follow the directions on the container carefully as most of these products contain an acid. Note the warning on the container about inhaling the fumes and remember always to use rubber gloves to protect your skin.

The Laundry Plan   A good way to save laundry time is to buy only clothing and other articles that require minimum care. This is fairly easy to do nowadays with so many wash-and-wear and permanent-press fabrics.

Another time-saver is to pick the best time to go to the laundry. Have you ever shot a Saturday morning because you arrived at the laundry 10 minutes (min) after all the machines were taken? After that experience, did you start to do your laundry at a different time—when other people were eating dinner or very early in the morning? If so, you probably could use more than one machine at a time, a great time-saver.

If you have to go outside of your apartment to do the laundry, you should have everything in a basket or other container that's easy to carry. Is the place where you do your laundry safe and comfortable? Instead of running back and forth, you may want to take along something to do. It's a good time to catch up on letter writing, or reading. While waiting, you'll also be able to fold and sort your clothes and hang up the drip-drys (to prevent wrinkles).

A Plan for the Rest of Your Place   Outside of the kitchen, many of your cleaning problems will be the same. Your biggest enemies will be dust and clutter. Start by picking up and putting away everything that is out of place. That's a big improvement already, right? Empty ashtrays and wastebaskets as you go. This is a good time to change the sheets, shake the covers, and air the pillows. That way, the extra lint, dust, and feathers can all be vacuumed up at one time.

Work from high to low, starting with any cobwebs clinging to corners at ceiling level. Reaching them is easy by putting a large cloth over a broom. Next, dust venetian blinds, picture frames, window sills, and then furniture. A slightly damp cloth helps pick up the dust, instead of scattering it. Your good friend, the vacuum, can be used on lampshades, drapes, and upholstered furniture. Or, you can use a soft brush for lampshades and a sturdy one for drapes and upholstered furniture. Shake or vacuum all small rugs.

The last step is doing the floors. On bare floors, use a dry, clean mop. Or you may want to dampen it with a special spray that's made to help collect dust. The last step, vacuuming the carpeting or rugs, is the final chore.

Fig. 10-4 Work from high to low when cleaning a room, starting at the ceiling and working down. The last step is vacuuming the carpeting or rugs. (The Hoover Company)

Bedroom Cleaning Some people give extra attention to the bedroom because it seems to collect the most dust and lint. Do you have allergies or breathing problems? Or are you just bothered by the sight of that layer of dust on everything? You may want to try the following:

- Dust and vacuum the bedroom more frequently than the rest of your place.
- Buy lint-free bedding.
- Fold clothing in the laundry room.
- Use *casters* (removable wheels) on the bed so it can be rolled out and cleaned under. Casters are not expensive and can be bought in most hardware stores.

• Put all dirty clothes in a hamper when they are taken off. (If they're damp, let them dry first.) Return others to drawers or closet.

Some Special Problems

At times, there will be extra jobs that have to be done in addition to the weekly cleaning—things like cleaning venetian blinds, waxing furniture, caring for the bedding, maybe even getting rid of some unwanted little creatures.

Cleaning Venetian Blinds For some reason, venetian blinds seem to attract dirt like a magnet. Dusting or vacuuming them keeps you slightly ahead of the dirt. But sooner or later, you may decide to wash them. A vacuum should be used to go over them first. Or you can use an inexpensive brush which is designed for venetian blinds.

Blinds can be washed in three ways: while hanging at the window, in a bathtub (if they are not wooden), or while hung outdoors.

If you are able to wash the blinds while they are still hanging, you will save time. Towels or newspaper should be placed on the floor under the blinds. Using soapy water, start at the top slat and work down. You may wish to try wearing a pair of cotton work gloves in place of using the usual sponge or cloth. Simply dip your gloved hands in the soapy water, wring out excess, and run the blind slats between your fingers. Be careful of cuts from sharp edges of the slats. Tapes can be washed with a small brush, such as a toothbrush. Rinse both slats and tape and wipe dry. Waxing the slats after the blinds are thoroughly dry will keep them cleaner longer.

To wash blinds in the bathtub, protect the bottom by covering it with an older shower curtain or piece of plastic. Use warm detergent water, but do not get the cord mechanism wet. Make sure the slats are in an open position so as to expose them. Rinse and wipe slats dry. Hang in an open position until cords are dry.

When washing blinds outside, either while flat or on a clothesline, you don't have to worry about getting anything wet. You can also finish by rinsing them with a hose.

Cleaning and Preserving Wooden Furniture From time to time, you may want to put wax or oil on your wooden furniture. Use wax if your furniture has a *varnish* (a hard shiny coating) finish. Use oil if your furniture has a satiny, dull look. The oil will emphasize the natural wood grain.

Some preparations for cleaning furniture should only be used on one type of finish, so it is necessary to read the labels. Sprays are more expensive than other types of containers. Care should be taken that rugs don't get sprayed too.

Cleaning Chrome and Stainless Steel Furniture   Glass or window cleaner can be used to clean dirt and fingerprints from chrome and stainless steel furniture. Do not use scouring powder or steel wool as this will scratch the surface. Leftover club soda that has lost its fizz is excellent for cleaning this type of furniture.

Cleaning Lampshades   If your lampshade is sewn, instead of glued, and made of fabric, it is probably washable. First, remove any trim. Then, vacuum the loose dirt. Add enough warm water to any basin large enough to cover the shade. Use a mild detergent. Swish the shade up and down. Rinse in the same way. Use towels to pat dry or hang it up while it drips dry.

Caring for a Mattress and Pillows   A mattress should be vacuumed on all sides occasionally. It also will stay cleaner and be more comfortable if covered with a mattress pad. The best pads cover the sides as well as the top of the mattress. It's easy, however, to substitute an old quilt by adding elastic at the corners to keep it in place. Turn the mattress monthly.

All pillows can be washed except those filled with *kapok* (a stuffing made from the flossy fiber found in the pod of a kapok plant), but some require extra care in drying. Read the label to find out what stuffing is used. Pillows containing down or feathers should be put inside a pillow case before washing in case of weak seams. After all, who wants a washer full of feathers? Pillows will stay cleaner, too, with zippered covers that go under the pillow cases.

Controlling Pests   Mice and bugs are not necessarily signs of a dirty house. They'll come to live with you for other reasons, and once they do, getting rid of them can become a major project.

Mice   They can be cute when they're running around in a cage, but no one wants them popping in and out of cupboards. To avoid them, it's necessary to know a little about their likes and dislikes. They don't like cold so they may appear indoors about the time of the first cold spell in the fall. They like to nibble at food and to collect materials for making a nest. One way to get rid of mice is to get a cat. Another way is to set a mousetrap or two right in the path of their usual runs. These can be identified by mouse droppings. With a little luck, you'll catch the creature before you have 16 or 60 of its relatives to worry about, too.

Cockroaches   One of the most troublesome types of bugs that apartment dwellers have to cope with is the cockroach. It can be brought home from the supermarket in grocery bags or may come to live with you from a nearby apartment. Like mice, the cockroach multiplies quickly. They come out most often at night when the lights have been turned off, and may have their home around the sink. They get into food so jars and boxes should be kept tightly covered and the trash emptied often. Small food scraps left in the sink and crumbs on the floor can attract cockroaches. Get in the habit of scouring the sink and sweeping the floor after your last meal or snack of the day.

The best way to get rid of roaches is to put boric acid powder (available in drugstores) around baseboards, in cracks, and under kitchen and bathroom sinks. In a couple of weeks, the powder should be vacuumed up and more put in its place. (Don't try this if you own a cat or dog. They could eat the powder and get sick.) If this doesn't work, you may have to call an exterminator. Some apartment houses have exterminators come in once or twice a month. Cockroaches are so common in apartments that someone always has them. Ask your landlord to add your name to the exterminator's list.

Crickets   These little creatures can bring in the sound of the great outdoors, but they also can ruin fabrics. To get rid of them, spread boric acid powder where the sound comes from—probably the kitchen or basement. It'll help if some of the powder is put into the cracks and crevices that make good hiding places.

Moths When you move into an apartment, it's wise to go over closets—even cracks and crevices—with a good insect spray. The purpose is to get rid of any possibility of moths. There are also steps that can be taken when clothing, bedding, or other woolens are put away for the year. Dirty garments or blankets should be sent to the cleaners or washed, if possible. The seams and pockets of clean garments should be brushed. Then everything can be stored in tightly sealed plastic bags with some moth balls or crystals.

Silverfish These fast-moving, little silver creatures like to travel along water pipes to get where they are going. They'll eat paper, including books, and starchy fabrics. Since they like moisture, it is wise to keep things dry. Keep the cupboard doors ajar if pipes seem to sweat. Also make it a habit to dry out the tub or shower after you use it. This will also prevent the bathroom from collecting mildew. To get rid of silverfish, boric acid powder or an insect spray may help.

Necessary Tools and Supplies

Some basic tools (Figure 10-5) are necessary to make cleaning simpler and less time-consuming. The tools all can be kept in one place or one can be put near the place where it will be used most.
most.

It may not be necessary to purchase the most expensive of these tools—the vacuum cleaner. Sometimes, the resident manager or landlord will lend a vacuum to tenants. If your place is not carpeted, you could get by with a smaller hand vacuum for such things as upholstered furniture. A toilet bowl plunger, on the other hand, may be a necessity. The manager may not be able to come to your rescue at the time the toilet is flooding. So it's wise to be prepared to handle this little emergency yourself.

As far as cleaning supplies go, so many are on the market that it could take days to read the labels. Trying all of them out can take even longer, and cost a small fortune. Unless you are careful, what you thought was a large sack of groceries may turn out to be mostly cleaning aids. One thing you can do is ask friends and relatives what products they like. Or test a new product yourself by buying the smallest size.

Fig. 10-5 Here are some basic tools that are necessary to make housecleaning simple and efficient.

CATHY   by Cathy Guisewite

Fig. 10-6 There is a huge variety of cleaning supplies on the market and buying them all can be very expensive. Remember that many cleaning tasks can be done with the same basic supplies. (Copyright, 1976, Universal Press Syndicate)

An important thing to remember is that many cleaning tasks can be done with basic supplies. Ammonia, baking soda, and borax—all *alkalies*—can be used to remove grease from china, windows, walls, and woodwork. Read the directions on each one to find out how much to use. Note, too, that some of these chemicals react when mixed together. Chlorine bleach should not be used with ammonia or with acid cleaners, such as toilet bowl cleaners. It causes a dangerous gas to be formed.

Lemon juice and vinegar—two acids found in the kitchen—can be used for jobs such as removing tarnish from brass and copper. For the sake of convenience, however, many people like ready-mixed products.

Storage Space

Having a place to put things can make it much easier to keep an apartment clean and neat. But, when you have more things than you have storage space, trying to clean up could seem hopeless. So what do you do? There are three ideas that work for many people. One is tossing out unused articles. The second is to organize your belongings better. Third is to add on to your storage space.

Tossing Out   Did you move some things into your new place even though they hadn't been used for years? Maybe souvenirs, scrapbooks, old sports equipment, clothes that are out of fashion? When you buy new things, like sports equipment and clothes, do you hang on to the old ones?

It's easy to become a pack rat—saving everything that comes along for use someday. The only problem is that pack rats gather more things than there's space to store. Then, it's a matter of moving or tossing things out. The message here is simple: Save only what will be helpful instead of everything that comes along. Another idea is to go through your belongings from time to time. Give away what isn't used or worn. When you haven't worn something for a year, you probably won't wear it again.

Better Organization   Opening a closet door and having everything fall out is an old joke. But it happens. Tossing out what isn't used will help. So will taking the time to organize your belongings better.

Some things may have to be moved around. For example, where do you keep belts, knitwear, shirts, or blouses? In the closet? Is there more space in your drawers? Somehow, drawers with empty spaces get messed up. One way to get around this is to make partitions for them. Even boxes with the lids taken off will do, as long as they fit the drawer. Some people find it easier to keep small items like jewelry and pencils neat by putting them in plastic or rubber trays.

Closets   The main idea in organizing a closet is to put the things you use in front and the others in the back. Never put so much stuff in a closet that it takes you three times as long as it should to find something.

You can buy all kinds of items to help organize closets, like shoe bags, clothes covers, adjustable shelves, and plastic or cardboard boxes. You can also build all kinds of shelves and drawers in closets to get some extra space to put things. But there are many things you can do without spending a great deal of money. Clear plastic drawers, stacked on top of one another, will store a lot of small items. And you'll be able to see what's in them without taking everything out. Shoe boxes or used gift boxes are handy. Just write what's in them on the outside or on a label and you won't have to go through them each time you're hunting for one thing.

Adding Storage Space   Some people get around the problem of having enough storage space by buying furniture with shelves and

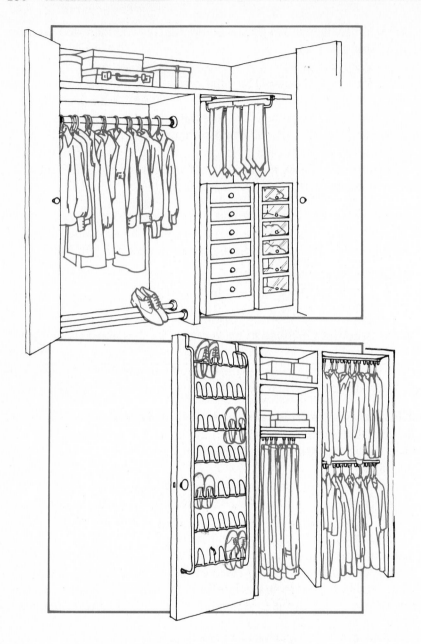

Fig. 10-7 You can organize your closets by adding shelves and drawers and by using shoe bags and garment bags.

Fig. 10-8 Think storage! This room makes use of many double-duty furniture ideas. The headboard has concealed shelves for books; the trunk can hold linens or out-of-season clothes; the lamp table can double as a desk; sweater boxes can be stored under the bed; and the small bureau can hold your clock, telephone, stationery and other writing supplies, and so on.

drawers. Others simply shove everything under the bed since it's hidden by the bedspread.

When planning your room, think storage! You can find extra storage in many parts of a room, like the bedroom in Figure 10-8. The headboard also provides shelves. Books can be stored on top of the shelves too. (This is the kind of double-duty furniture we mentioned in Chapter 9.) Another example is the foot-of-the-bed trunk. Towels, linens, out-of-season blankets, and so on can be stored in the trunk. The top provides storage space too. Maybe for the bedspread when you're sleeping. Doesn't that seem better than heaped on the floor? By putting a cloth over a table, you'll not only have a small desk but can use the space under the table to store boxes, phone books, etc. Little things under the bed attract dust but you can store large boxes there. Long, low, heavy cardboard boxes can be bought in variety stores. Or, save the box when you buy a bulky item, like a coat. Bathing suits can be kept there in the winter, winter boots in the summer, little-used things (maybe dress shoes or evening bags) all year round. A table next to the bed is a smart buy. It can hold a lamp, box of tissues, a phone, a clock. One with drawers is a better idea. Small items can be kept there.

Adding shelves and bookcases is a very neat and popular idea for extra storage. And they're not hard to make yourself. Sound like a good idea? In Chapter 11, you'll learn how to build and put up shelves.

THINKING IT THROUGH

1. Certain household workers now refer to themselves as "household technicians." How would you define a household technician? Is the word "technician" appropriate? Why?
2. Despite a deluge of new gadgets and appliances, some household tasks are best done "the old-fashioned" way. What are some of these tasks? In what significant ways has household work changed since your parents were your age?
3. What steps are involved in accomplishing the following household tasks: defrosting the refrigerator; cleaning the oven; cleaning venetian blinds. Have modern appliances eliminated the need for any of these tasks? If so, what are some of the other major tasks in today's modern household?

Repairs and Improvements

11

Would the drip, drip, drip of a leaky faucet keep you awake all night? Could you learn to live with it—maybe for days—until the landlord or resident manager fixed it? Or, could you fix it yourself? If your apartment needed shelves for storage, would that mean months of saving before you could afford a carpenter? Will you keep your favorite picture in a closet until you meet a handy friend who can hang it on the wall? For many people, learning to make *repairs* (or fixing something) and *improvements* (changes for the better) starts when they get their own apartment. Learning to be a do-it-yourselfer is fun for some people. For others, it's a chore. But

Fig. 11-1 Anyone can learn to do simple repairs and improvements. With a few tools, you can save yourself money, time, and trouble. (Skil Corporation)

for everyone, simple do-it-yourself repairs and improvements can save money, time, and even a sleepless night.

It's not possible to include remedies for all problems in this chapter. And real disasters need the help of an expert. Some safe, simple repairs and improvements that anyone can learn to do are suggested in this chapter.

Repairs

Keeping plumbing, electrical equipment, furniture, and appliances in good working condition takes time. It may require daily care, but it pays off in the long run. Remembering to pour drain cleaner down the drain regularly, for example, will mean there's less chance of clogging. Sometimes, in spite of this attention, things will need repair and you'll have to get out the tool box.

A Necessity: Some Basic Tools   Before you run into an emergency or try to make repairs, it's necessary to get some basic tools. Not all of them have to be bought at one time. Tools are kept for a long time, so buying the cheapest ones is not really a good idea. After all, who wants a tool to break in the middle of making a repair? Sometimes it's possible to buy tools secondhand at garage sales. Check the local newspapers or bulletin boards in supermarkets for possible leads. What do you need? Figure 11-2 shows some basic tools and equipment that may come in handy in taking care of your place.

What to Do about Plumbing Problems   No one can get by without having a plumbing problem from time to time. The most common ones are dripping faucets, clogged drains, and clogged toilets.

Dripping Faucets   Besides staining the sink and causing some people to lose sleep, a dripping faucet wastes an awful lot of water. Most drips are caused by a worn-out stem washer. Fortunately, it is easy to replace—you can get one at any hardware store. Figure 11-3 shows you how.

Clogged Drains   The best way to avoid getting a clogged drain is to be careful what goes down it. Hair or grease will clog up any

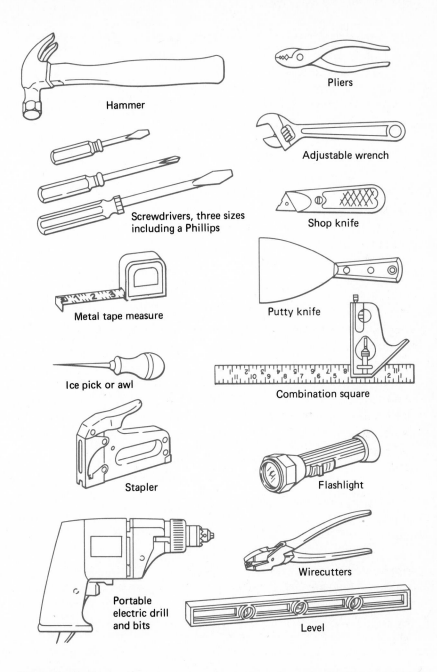

Fig. 11-2 Here are some basic tools and equipment you should have to take care of your place

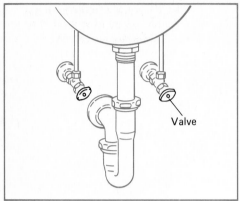

Fig. 11-3 Follow these steps to fix a leaky faucet.

Step 1: Shut off the hot and cold water supply by closing the valves under the sink. Make sure you turn the valves all the way.

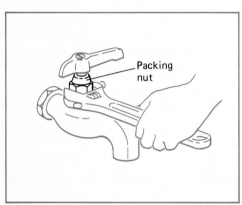

Step 2: Loosen the hexagon-shaped packing nut with pliers or a wrench. Be careful not to scratch the faucet.

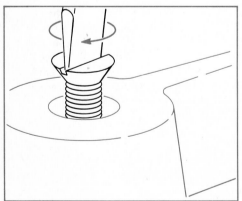

Step 3: Remove the top screw. This will allow you to take apart the faucet.

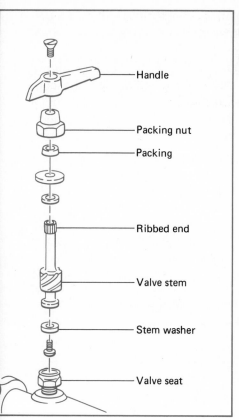

Handle

Packing nut

Packing

Ribbed end

Valve stem

Stem washer

Valve seat

Step 4: As each piece is removed, put it down in the order you took it off. Putting everything back together will then be easier.

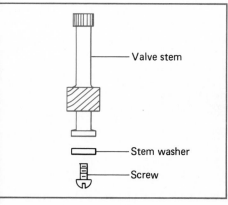

Valve stem

Stem washer

Screw

Step 5: Remove the screw from the end of the valve stem and replace the worn stem washer. Replace the screw and tighten securely. Now put the valve stem, packing nut, and handle back. Tighten the packing nut. Open the water valves under the sink.

drain. So will some food, like potato peelings, unless there's a garbage disposer. Another way to keep drains open is to use a drain cleaner on a regular basis.

If the drain does become clogged, the first thing to try is dry or liquid chemical drain cleaner. Follow the directions on the container. It must be allowed to stand in the drain for some time, but it should solve the problem. Chemical drain cleaners can be dangerous (many contain lye) and should be used with great care. Always use rubber gloves.

If drain cleaner doesn't work, try the *plunger,* also called the plumber's friend. Remove the strainer from the drain. Partially fill the sink with water and cover the drain hole with a damp cloth. Work the plunger up and down over the drain hole as hard as you can, 15 to 20 times. (See Figure 11-4.) If this works, the water will drain out quickly, and your problem's over.

If the plunger doesn't open the drain, try an *auger* (or plumber's snake). (See Figure 11-5.) Feed the auger into the drain line and rotate or turn it as you push. Keep doing this until the obstruction is cleared. If the auger fails, you need a plumber. Let the landlord know so he can call one.

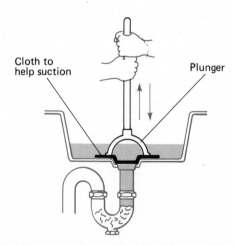

Cloth to
help suction

Plunger

Fig. 11-4 If a drain cleaner won't unclog your sink, try a plunger. Follow these steps: (1) Remove the strainer from the sink. (2) Cover the drain with a damp cloth. (3) Run some water into the sink. (4) Work the plunger up and down over the drain.

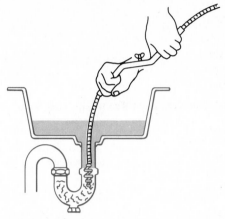

Fig. 11-5 If a plunger doesn't clean your drain, try an auger. Feed the auger into the drain line, as shown here. Rotate the auger as you push.

Clogged Toilets   Is there anything worse than having a toilet that won't work? Somehow, they always seem to break down at the worst time, as when company is coming.

The easiest way to keep toilets working is *never* to use them for getting rid of such things as sanitary napkins or paper towels. These are likely to clog up the toilet.

To stop a clogged toilet from overflowing, first remove the cover from the tank and reach inside. By pushing down on the tank ball (shown in Figure 11-6), you can close the opening at the bottom of

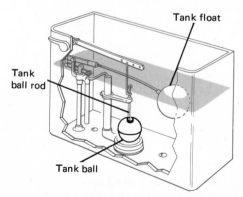

Tank float

Tank ball rod

Tank ball

Fig. 11-6 To stop a clogged toilet from overflowing, push down on the tank ball. This will close the opening on the bottom of the tank and prevent any more water from going into the toilet bowl.

the tank. This will stop the water from going into the toilet bowl. Next, use the plunger. Put it over the drainage hole and plunge it up and down. This should work. If it does not, try using the auger, being careful not to scratch the porcelain. The last hope is to call the landlord for a plumber.

Electrical Repairs   Fooling with electricity is just asking for trouble when you're not too sure of what you're doing. The big jobs should be left to electricians. But there are some repairs that are safe to do. It's easy to replace a fuse, reset a circuit breaker, and repair a plug.

Fuses and Circuit Breakers   *Fuses* and *circuit breakers* are both electrical safety devices that "break" or cut off the flow of electricity before wires get too hot. This can happen when too many appliances are turned on at one time (overload), or there's a short in one of them, or the apartment wiring is faulty. Cutting off the flow of electricity prevents electric shocks and the possibility of fire.

If you suddenly find yourself in the dark or your appliances have stopped working (or both), the fuse or circuit breaker has done its job. The first thing to do is to disconnect all lamps and appliances and turn off all *fixtures* (ceiling lights). A flashlight, with batteries that work, can come in handy now. To be on the safe side, keep a couple of extra batteries on hand.

Find the *entrance panel* where the fuses or circuit breakers are located. If a fuse has blown, it will be cloudy or blackened, like a used flashbulb on a camera. If your apartment has circuit breakers, one of them will be in the OFF position. Both types of entrance panels are shown in Figure 11-7*a* and *b*.

Take out the burnt fuse by unscrewing it as you would a light bulb. Now, screw in the new fuse. For a circuit breaker, just flip it to the ON position.

Safety rules   You can't be too careful when dealing with electricity. Here's a few rules to follow:

1.   Each fuse is marked with a number. This tells you its capacity in *amperes* (units for measuring electricity). Note this number in Figure 11-8. Be sure the new fuse has the same amp (ampere) number as the one that blew. Do not, for example, put in a

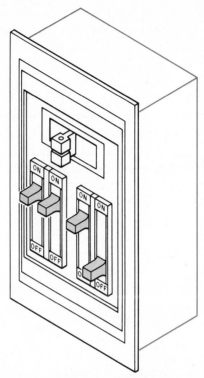

Fig. 11-7 Circuit breakers are located in the entrance panel. Each circuit breaker covers one circuit. When a circuit breaker has been tripped it will be in the "off" position. To reset, you simply push the switch up to the "on" position.

Fig. 11-8 A fuse is a safety device that will cut off electricity before wires get too hot. All fuses are labeled with their capacity. This one is a 15-amp fuse. Use it only to replace another 15-amp fuse.

20-amp fuse when a 15-amp one blew. That would allow the wires to build up too much heat before cutting off the electric current.

2. *Never* try to replace a blown fuse with a penny or other metal object. A fire or severe electric shock could be the result.

3. Make sure your hands are dry and that you are not standing on a wet spot, or damp floor, when you are touching anything in the entrance panel. For added protection, wear rubber gloves.

4. If any wires are showing in the entrance panel, *don't touch anything*. All wires should be covered by a metal plate, but sometimes it is left off. Call the landlord to have the plate put on and to change the fuse.

You can prepare yourself for this emergency and make the job easier if you follow these two suggestions:

1. Have a couple of extra fuses on hand for each amp number needed. You may want to tape a reminder to the entrance panel so you don't forget where you stored them. (See Figure 11-9.)

2. Know where the entrance panel is located. Many people make a diagram of the outlets and fixtures covered by each fuse or circuit breaker and tape it to the entrance panel. (See again Figure 11-9). You can find this out by removing all fuses except one, or flipping all circuit breakers to OFF except one. Now, turn on each fixture, one by one. If one goes on, make a note of it and which fuse was screwed in, or which circuit breaker was ON. Now, test each outlet. Do this for each fuse or circuit breaker in the entrance panel. Don't try to make the diagram while you're replacing a fuse.

Locating the trouble   Once the fuse has been replaced, or the circuit breaker has been flipped ON, you're ready to find out what caused the trouble in the first place.

If the new fuse blows out again right away, or the circuit breaker flips back to OFF right away, the house wiring is faulty. Call the landlord and let him know you need an electrician.

If the new fuse does not blow out then, one by one, turn on then

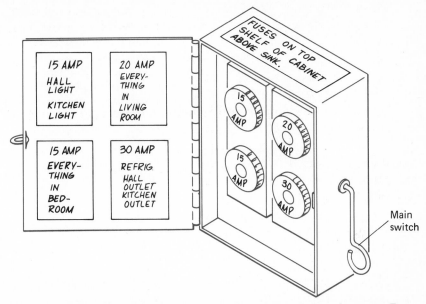

Fig. 11-9 Make a list of the fixtures and outlets that are on each circuit. Tape this list to the inside of your fuse box. When you overload the circuit and blow a fuse, you'll know which one to replace.

turn off every light fixture covered by that fuse. If you don't have a diagram (as in Figure 11-9), you'll have to do this with all the fixtures in the apartment. Check the new fuse after doing this to each fixture. If the new fuse blows, the fixture has faulty wiring. The landlord should be alerted and the fixture fixed by an electrician.

If the new fuse is still good, check every outlet. One by one, plug in and then unplug each appliance or lamp. It should be switched on before you plug it in. If one of them blows the new fuse, there's a short in that lamp or appliance. (You'll learn how to replace a plug later on in this chapter.)

If it's not the house wiring, a short in a fixture, or a short in an appliance, you can be pretty sure an overload caused the original fuse to blow. Think back to what was on when the fuse blew and don't use all these together again. A general rule is not to use more than one heating appliance at one time on the same circuit.

Repairing Plugs   There are two reasons why you would want to replace the plug on a lamp or an appliance. A fuse may have blown

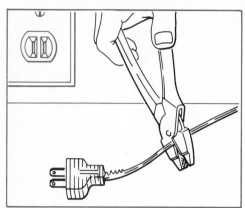

Fig. 11-10 1. The first step is to disconnect the plug from the outlet. (Once it's disconnected there's no electrical current to worry about.) Next, use wire cutters to cut the frayed wire several inches below the break. If there's a short you can't see, cut the wire several inches below the plug.

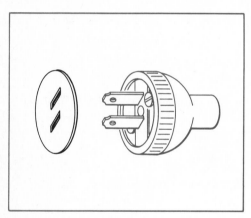

2. Remove the top disk from the replacement plug.

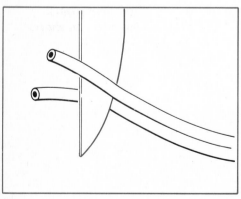

3. Look closely at the wire. It's really two wires, each wrapped in its own insulation. With a knife, separate the two wires by a short cut. Now pull the two wires apart for about an inch.

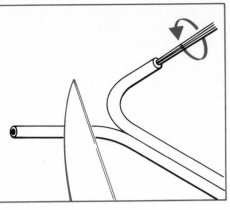

4. Remove ½ in or more of insulation from each wire. Using your knife again, carefully cut through the insulation *only*. Then gently pull it off. Notice that the wire is actually made up of numerous very thin wires. Gently twist them together tightly.

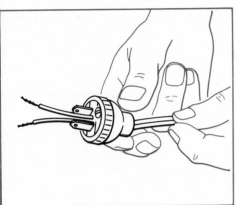

5. Push the wires through the new plug.

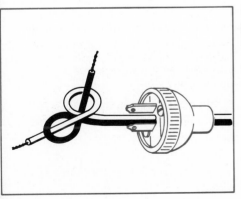

6. Tie an *Underwriter's knot.* This knot protects the connection if you should happen to yank on the cord.

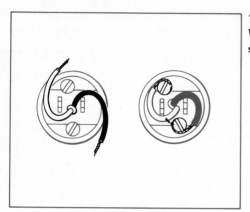

7. Wrap each wire around a prong. Wrap each twisted end around the screw and tighten the screw.

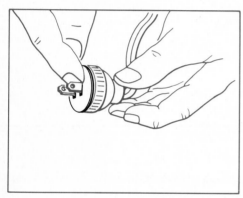

8. Snap the top disk back over the prongs. Now, reconnect the plug in the outlet.

and you traced the trouble to the appliance. Or, you notice frayed wires near the plug. Fixing the frayed wires now will prevent a short later. It only takes 5 or 10 min time and the proper equipment. All you need are a screw driver, wire cutters, pocket knife, and a re-placement plug. You can buy a new plug in any hardware store and in most variety stores. They are inexpensive.

Sticking Doors and Windows   When it rains a lot and the air feels damp, it's a safe bet that some wooden doors and windows will stick. Minor sticking can be fixed by rubbing sandpaper along the edge that sticks. If this damages the paint, a little retrouching with paint will be needed. Then, rub candle wax along the sanded (and retouched) edges to make them smooth. Do any retouching before using the wax. Otherwise paint won't stick. On double-hung windows, rub candle wax in the tracks where the window slides up and down.

Furniture Repairs   Use these tips to repair your own furniture. Or, save yourself some money by buying secondhand things and repairing them yourself.

Replacing Drawer Knobs   Most drawers have knobs that are held in place by screws inserted from inside the drawer. Sometimes a screw loosens up. You go to open a drawer and the knob ends up in your hand. The first problem is to get the drawer open. If you can't pry it out easily, try using a wire coat hanger. Bend the hooked part so that only the end is curved. Pliers help do this easily. Feed the wire into the screw hole until the curved part is inside the drawer. Now gently tug on the wire. The curved end should pull the drawer out. If this doesn't work, try using a rubber plunger. Wet the rim of the plunger and push it tightly against the drawer. The suction should enable you to pull the drawer out. To replace the knob try one of these tips:

1. Dip the screw in white glue. Wait a few minutes until the glue gets *tacky* (sticky). Screw in the knob and wait until completely dry before pulling on it.
2. Fill the hole almost full with wood putty (available in hardware stores). Wait until the putty starts to harden. Screw in the knob and wait until it hardens completely before pulling on it.
3. Fill the hole with steel wool or pieces of a matchstick dipped in white glue. Then screw in the knob.
4. Wrap aluminum foil around the threads of the screw. Then screw the knob into the drawer.

Loose Table and Chair Joints   First, heat some white glue by putting the container in a pan of hot water. Pull the loose joint away from its socket and insert some glue. You can use an eyedropper filled with glue or, if the opening is very small, try applying it with a toothpick. Wait a few minutes until the glue gets tacky, then push the joint firmly into its socket. Wipe off any glue that oozes out with a damp cloth. Depending on where the loose joint is, lay a heavy book on top or tie the joint and socket together with cord or wire while the glue dries. Wait until the glue is completely dry before testing it.

Scratches or Blemishes   Scratches that are not very deep are easy to hide by rubbing them with nut meats. Use pecans for light-colored woods, walnut meats for darker woods. For scratches in mahogany furniture, put on a little iodine with a cotton swab. Or, rub on the same color shoe polish followed by a little car wax. For deep scratches or other marks, you may have to refinish the whole thing.

Improvements

The most needed improvement in small apartments is added storage space. Even if there are plenty of closets, what about those books and mementos that you don't want to hide away? Wall shelves may be an answer. In the bathroom they can store towels and toilet articles. In the kitchen, a long narrow shelf can hold all your spices and gives you more cabinet space for pans or for dishes. By using shelves in the living room, books, trophies, collections, and souvenirs are kept in full view. In the dining area, treasured pieces can please the eye and still be ready for use.

Like shelves, pictures on the wall can be functional as well as ornamental. Pictures, posters, mirrors, wall hangings, and the like can hide a cracked wall, or a water stain from the apartment above yours. And, of course, these items make your apartment more personal.

Wall-hung Shelves   To add shelves to just about any room you'll need this equipment:

1. *The shelves themselves.* Precut shelves, in various sizes and colors, can be bought in hardware and variety stores. If you can't find the size you need, go to a lumberyard and have the shelves cut to the size you need. If you plan to put a TV or stereo speakers on a shelf, you'll need one deeper than the precut ones available. Shelves cut at a lumberyard will not be

stained so you'll have to do that (or paint them) yourself. You can also get shelves made of plate glass. Any glass company will cut them to size. Glass shelves will cost more than wooden ones and, of course, are breakable.

2. *Wall brackets.* The brackets hold up the shelf. They can be bought in stained wood or metal and are available in hardware stores. You'll need to know how deep the shelf is so you get the right length bracket. You'll need two brackets for each shelf.

3. *Shelf supports.* The shelf support is attached to the wall and the brackets hook onto them. Figure 11-11 shows you what the shelf looks like when the bracket and support are in place. You'll need two supports for each shelf.

4. *Electric drill.* If you've never used an electric drill, you may be surprised to find out this is not an expensive, complicated piece of equipment. It is safe, fast, and easy to use.

5. *Screws and anchors.* These are needed to hold the wall support to the wall.

6. *A screwdriver.* Match the size of the screwdriver to the diameter of the screw head.

7. *A level.* This piece of equipment (see Figure 11-12) will help you make sure the shelf supports are perfectly straight.

Before You Do the Job   You need to know what material your wall is made of before you can get the proper hardware. Don't skip this important step. If you do, your wall shelf may look great for only

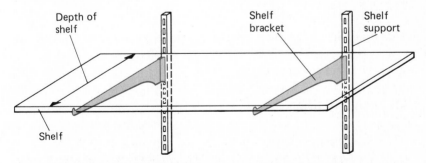

Depth of shelf

Shelf bracket

Shelf support

Shelf

Fig. 11-11 You'll need these supplies to put up wall-hung shelves. (1) Lumber or glass cut to the exact length and depth you need. (2) Brackets (wood or metal) that are as long as the shelf is deep. You'll need two brackets for each shelf. (3) Shelf supports which are attached to the wall to hold up the shelves. You'll need two supports for each shelf.

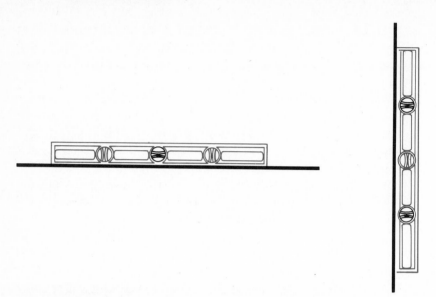

Fig. 11-12 A level will help you make sure that everything is perfectly straight. Place the level against the line you want to check. When it is perfectly straight, the air bubble will appear exactly between the two marks.

a short time. The supports may start to pull away from the wall as soon as anything heavy is put on the shelf. Walls that are made of plaster (or wallboard) can crumble and will not hold the screw tightly. You'll need to insert an anchor (see Figure 11-13) to hold the screw.

Putting Up the Wall-hung Shelf   Figure 11-14 shows you how to put up a single shelf, but the same procedure can be used for any shelf arrangement.

Free-Standing Shelves   If you're in a hurry, are a constant rearranger, or the landlord doesn't want you to drill any holes in the wall, free-standing shelves are for you. The free-standing shelves in Figure 11-15 don't need any tools. Simply support the boards with bricks. If a long shelf is used, add brick supports in the middle too. This kind of shelf arrangement can be placed against a wall or used as a low room divider. You can change the shelves around and take the whole thing with you when you move.

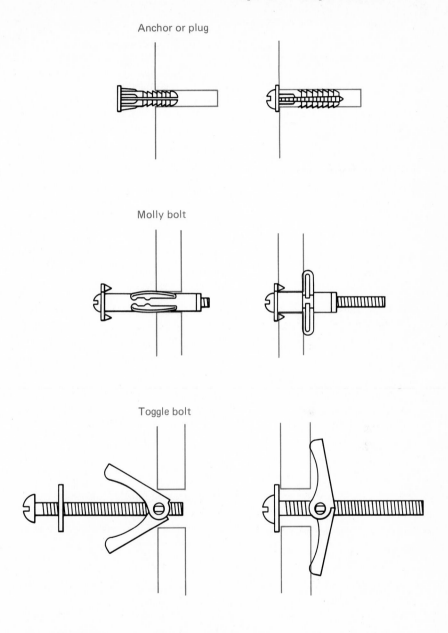

Anchor or plug

Molly bolt

Toggle bolt

Fig. 11-13 Before you hang shelves, make sure you have the proper hardware. With brick or concrete walls, use a lead anchor. For plaster or plasterboard walls, use the molly or toggle bolt.

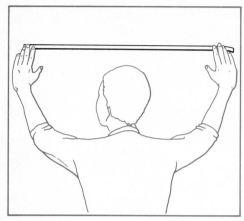

Fig. 11-14 Follow these steps for putting up wall-hung shelves.

Step 1. Decide where, how long, and how deep you want the shelf to be. Buy two brackets, two shelf supports, and the shelf.

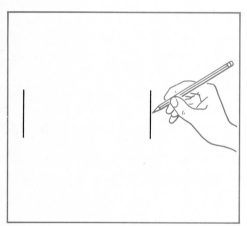

Step 2. With a pencil, lightly mark the wall where the wall supports should be placed.

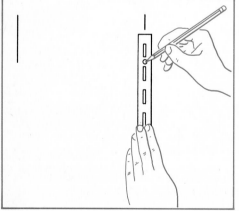

Step 3. Hold up the wall support so it looks straight, and with a pencil, mark where one screw should go. Make the mark through the screw opening. Put the support aside.

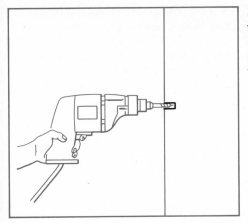

Step 4. Drill a hole where you marked the wall in step 3. The booklet that comes with the drill will tell you how to use the drill safely and how large a hole to make.

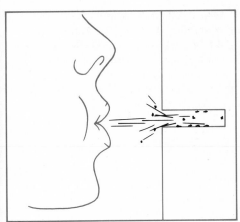

Step 5. Blow into the hole to remove the crumbled plaster. Be sure to close your eyes when doing this so that no plaster dust ends up there.

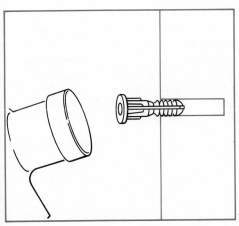

Step 6. Insert fastener into the hole and tap in gently with a hammer. The fastener should fit in the hole snugly. If it swims around you've drilled too large a hole. In that case, plaster up the hole with a putty knife and start again by drilling a hole along the same vertical line. The shelf support will cover up the plastered hole.

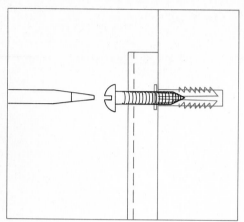

Step 7. Line up the shelf support over the hole. Place a screw through the support and into the hole. Use a screwdriver to tighten up the screw.

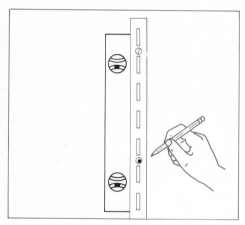

Step 8. When the screw is fairly tight, straighten the support with a level. When the support is perfectly straight, mark where the second screw should go.

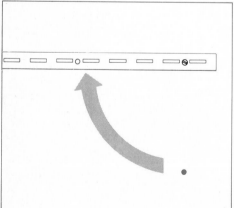

Step 9. Loosen the first screw and turn the shelf support so it's horizontal. Tighten the screw just enough for the support to remain there. This gives you room to drill the second hole. Repeat steps 4-6 for drilling the second hole and inserting the second anchor.

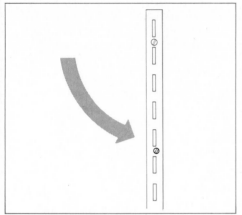

Step 10. Loosen the first screw and swing down the shelf support until it's vertical. Insert the second screw. Tighten both screws as much as you can.

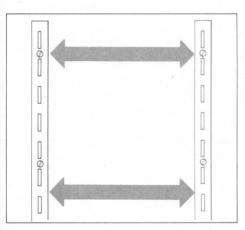

Step 11. Repeat this procedure for the second shelf support. Make sure the second shelf support is straight and that the distance between the two is the same along the length of the support.

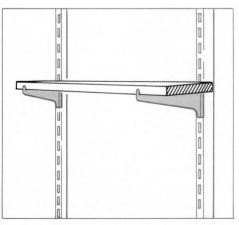

Step 12. Hook the brackets onto the supports and place the shelf into position.

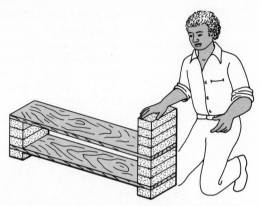

Fig. 11-15 To build free-standing shelves you simply need some boards and bricks. Stack the bricks to the height of the shelves you want, then place a board across them.

Using Boxes as Shelves Several boxes, stacked on top of one another, or placed in a row, are a good way to add storage space and make the place look better at the same time. Boxes made of plastic, wood, or other materials come in all sizes and colors. Or, you can build your own. Have the lumberyard cut four pieces of

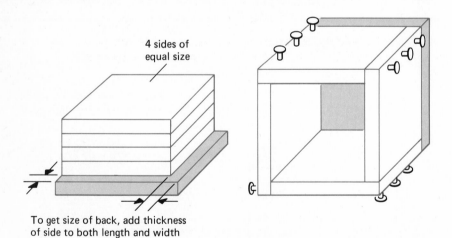

4 sides of
equal size

To get size of back, add thickness
of side to both length and width

Fig. 11-16 Follow these steps to build stackable storage cubes. (1) Have the lumberyard cut plywood to the dimensions you want. (2) Nail the pieces together along the edges that meet. (3) Paint, stain, or cover the boxes with paper.

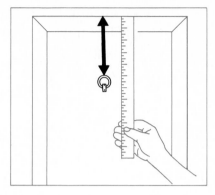

Fig. 11-17 Follow these steps for hanging a picture.

Step 1. Some frames have hooks on the back where the nail rests. Measure how far down the hook is from the top of the frame.

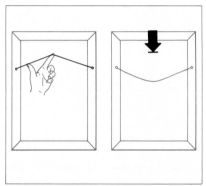

Step 2. Some frames have wires across the back of the frame. Hook the wire on your finger and mark this point with a pencil. Now measure the distance from the top of the frame to your pencil mark.

Step 3. Hold the picture up where you want it and lightly mark the top of the frame on the wall. Then put the picture down for now.

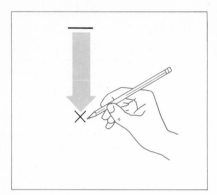

Step 4. Make a second mark on the wall directly below the first. How far down? Use the measurement you got from step 1 or 2. This is where the nail goes.

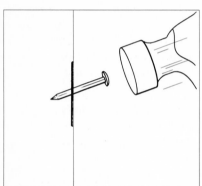

Step 5. Put a small piece of masking tape over the second, or nail, mark. The masking tape will help keep the plaster from crumbling when you put in the nail. Gently tap the nail into the wall with a hammer. Leave enough of the nail out of the wall for the picture to hook onto.

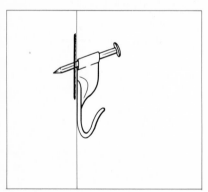

Step 6. An angle-drive is often used to hang things on the wall. It's inexpensive and comes in different sizes; which size you use depends on how heavy your picture frame is. The procedure for inserting an angle-drive is the same as for a nail. However, when you use an angle-drive, your picture will hook on slightly below the nail mark.

¾-in plywood. Figure out the dimensions yourself. Four equal pieces will make a square box. Two sets of equal pieces will make a rectangular box. Nail the pieces along the edges that meet. Add a back if desired. You can paint it or cover it with paper. Stand it against the wall or arrange several as a room divider. Figure 11-16 shows you the "before" and "after" boxes.

Hanging Pictures   Figure 11-17 shows how to hang one picture. The same procedure is used for hanging mirrors, framed posters, and so on.

Large or heavy pictures should be hung over a *stud* (the framework, or vertical strips of wood, beneath the wall). Studs are generally 16 in [40 cm] apart and begin at the corner of the room. To locate a stud, gently tap along the wall with your knuckle until you find a spot where there is no hollow sound. There's the stud. Insert the nail into the wall at this point.

All Finished

Do-it-yourself repairs and improvements help contribute to the satisfaction that independence brings. And, it can save you money. If you want to learn more, there are lots of books available. Look in the home repair section of your library or bookstore.

THINKING IT THROUGH

1. What basic tools would you choose if you were limited to ten? Five? Three? Explain your choices.
2. What kitchen repairs do you think are most frequent? What bathroom repairs? What appliance repairs? Can you think of any reason why certain repairs seem more frequent than others?
3. What common repairs do you think give people the most trouble? Make a list of repairs that require a professional repair person. Are there reasons, other than cost, that keep people from calling a professional when one is needed?

PART THREE

Food and You

Nutrition: Balancing a Diet

Food can be a blessing, a bore, or a bother. It may be all these things and more at the same time. Take the case of the fellow who's become a sort of hero in TV ads. He stuffs himself with a big, rich, spicy meal. He *knows* that he will suffer for it. But never fear; the sponsor's pill or tonic will take care of him.

In this kind of story, food becomes a good-bad custom. It pleases us so much that it makes us sick. (The TV writers call this "overindulgence.") But then we have the pleasure of getting well again.

Strange. We need to eat. Most of us like to eat. Some of us love to eat. Yet we're often troubled—even frightened—by what we do with food and what food can do to us. People who live alone reflect some of the difficult diet problems of today's living:

Marty "I eat very, very little. Really. But I swear every bit of it turns to fat. Sometimes I'll skip a meal a day for a week or more. It's weakening, believe me. But it doesn't matter. All I do is gain weight."

Sally "I'm a finicky eater. I was brought up on a very limited menu. Now I can't bring myself to try new things. That's no problem when I'm alone. When I'm asked out to dinner, though, things can become very uncomfortable. You have to feel a little foolish when you push away food that *everyone else* seems to like. And you feel ungrateful to the people who asked you. But I can't seem to change. It's just the way I am. I'm worried, though, that some people I know may think I'm really dull."

Lucy "I seem to keep cutting down on the number of things on my shopping list. Between the high prices and the health warnings, I feel less and less like eating meat. I've cut out a lot of other things since I started reading labels. All those mile-long chemical words

Fig. 12-1 Food and nutrition make daily headlines. Some of the news makes people more uncertain, even frightened, about what they eat.

scare me. I decided I wasn't going to eat anything I couldn't pro-
nounce.''

Joe   "Yes, I know that certain foods are supposed to be better for
me than others. Like protein. Like vitamins and iron. I know I'm
supposed to have a balanced diet. I've never had time to figure it all
out. You could make a career out of that. I just try to eat different
things. If you mix them up, you're bound to do something right.
Right?"

At the simplest level, most people live with mixed feelings about
food. They think they know what they like. And they think that
some of what they like is "good for you" and some is "bad for
you." They also admit they dislike some things that are "good for
you." Such feelings often cause confusion—even guilt—about
food choices. The feelings often start when people are very young.

Yet no food is likely to be good for you or bad for you in itself.
The value of any food depends on a whole set of conditions. Who is
eating the food? When? How much of it? What other foods are
being eaten with it? Those are all questions about *nutrition*.

What Is Nutrition?

Nutrition is the way that a living thing takes in food and uses it to
keep working, growing, and repairing damage or wear. Any food is
nutritious when it serves these purposes. At different times, almost
any food can work for better or worse in the body.

Food's first task is simply keeping the body alive and moving.
Fairly small amounts permit bare survival. Properly used in the right
amounts and mixtures, food adds up to good health, vigor, and
basic good looks.

This balance is impossible to make when people have too little
food. But it can also be difficult when people have too much.
American stores today offer more than 32,000 different food items,
fresh or packaged.

A shocking number of the poorest Americans simply cannot afford to buy enough nutriment from this huge variety. Millions of
others can buy a nutritious diet only by the most careful skimping
and planning.

But those are not the typical American problems. The great

majority of food buyers have some range of choice, often very wide. A great many in this majority may be choosing far more of what's "good" than of what's "good for them." The average shopping list may include too much fat, too much sugar, or just too much. Because of that, millions of people are said to be overfed and undernourished.

Colorful food advertising and packaging can tip the scales heavily toward pleasure and away from real bodily needs. Fancy foods can fight good nutrition—and very often win. "A good deal of the art of cookery," nutritionist Ancel Keys observed, "goes into . . . persuading people to eat more than they need or want."

By contrast, nutritional science may look dull and hard to understand. Most of us have heard the belittling (but accurate) saying that the human body is made up of a few dollars' worth of common chemicals. Nutrition is concerned with how those chemicals work together.

But nutrition is hardly a gloomy science. It studies the thousands of wonderful ways that chemicals in our bodies and in our food combine. What is the chemistry of a bright smile, clear skin, a good figure? By what chemistry can food help to make strong muscles

Fig. 12-2 One nutritionist has observed that "A good deal of the art of cookery goes into . . . persuading people to eat more than they need or want." (The Sheraton Corporation)

and minds? Those are questions that make the major ideas of nutrition worth knowing.

Calories   All food can be used as fuel. Like gasoline in an automobile or wood in a fireplace, it can be burned to give power or warmth. Different foods have different fuel power. The *calorie* is an exact measure of the energy in food. In the nutritionist's terms, it is the amount of a food burned to raise the temperature of 1 kilogram of water (about 2.2 pounds) by 1° Celsius (C) [about 1.8° Fahrenheit (F)].

Up to a certain point, *all* food taken into the body is mixed with oxygen and burned for energy. A mildly active person who weighs 150 pounds may use about 3,200 food calories a day. The person may burn almost 100 calories an hour just sitting at rest. A brisk walk burns more than 300 calories an hour. A long run burns almost 650 an hour. Too much work and too little food can clearly be dangerous. A starving body will burn up any food eaten and then actually "feed" on itself. An overfed body, on the other hand, can grow fat with unburned fuel.

Fig. 12-3 The body needs energy for all its activities—running, walking, even sitting. (Susan Berkowitz)

Fig. 12-4 Children's bodies need protein—found in meat, fish, milk, eggs, and cheese— in order to grow and develop. Of course, adults' bodies also need protein for the proper maintenance and replacement of tissues. (David S. Strickler, Monkmeyer Press Photo Service)

When the amount of food increases to a proper level and beyond, the body sorts it out in different ways. The major nutrients are *protein, fat,* and *carbohydrate.* Some foods, like vegetables, fruits, milk, and shellfish, contain all three. The main animal foods—meat, fish, and poultry—provide protein and fat but no carbohydrate. The body sorts out these nutrients for important uses.

Protein Almost two-thirds of the human body is made up of water. Almost half of the rest is made up of chemicals combined in various ways into proteins. These proteins make up the whole living framework of the body. They are the essential parts of all tissues, the skin, the hair, the muscles, and the living part of the bones. Proteins are very important to growth in young people. But you never outgrow the need for proteins. They must also be in steady supply for the maintenance and replacement of tissues and body parts that "wear out" in adults at the rate of an ounce or more a day. Proteins also are the building blocks of substances that control important workings of the body. Among these is hemoglobin, the red coloring in the blood that carries oxygen from the lungs to other parts of the body. Proteins are also used to build antibodies, which fight disease-carrying germs and viruses.

Proteins are formed from smaller chemical combinations called *amino acids*. There are 22 amino acids that the body mixes in different ways to make protein. Eight of these are not made by the body. They must be provided by food. And they must be supplied in the right amounts, at the same time, to be useful.

All eight of these food-supplied amino acids are supplied in the protein of animal foods—meat, fish, and poultry. Such *complete proteins* also come from animal products, such as milk, cheese, and eggs. Beans, peas, nuts, seeds, and grains are also rich in proteins. They are called *incomplete proteins,* however, because no one food supplies all the needed amino acids. These foods, then, may have to be eaten in carefully planned mixtures if they are to equal the protein in animal foods.

The body cannot store these amino acids, and so protein foods should be eaten at every meal.

Fat   About 15 percent of the normal human body is made up of fat. Certain small amounts of fat are thought to be essential to the healthy working of the body. In cold weather, for example, body fat prevents the loss of too much body heat. The main nutritional use of fat, however, is to supply energy. Since fats are high in calories, they provide a large amount of energy in a small amount of food. One gram of fat counts for nine calories. The same weight of protein provides four calories. Taken as food, fat is burned off in work or else stored in the body until needed. Fat can provide a useful hoard of energy for people doing long hours of very hard work. But it can be bad news for people who do light work and get little exercise. Fat makes up a big part in some of the most tempting foods—ice cream and whipped cream, choice steaks, butter, and salad dressings. In addition to the part stored fat plays in being overweight, doctors have warned against too much fat as a possible factor in heart disease and other health problems. Most now say that people should cut down on animal fats by such measures as eating less beef, butter, and whole milk. These animal fats are usually solid at room temperature (or *saturated*). Vegetable fats, such as corn oil and soybean oil, are proposed as substitutes. These fats are usually found in liquid form at room temperature (*unsaturated* or *polyunsaturated*).

Carbohydrate   Sugars and starches come almost entirely from non-animal foods, mostly grains, vegetables, and fruits. These car-

Fig. 12-5 Fats are high in calories and are a good source of energy. However, if you eat more fat than you need for your regular daily activities, your body will simply store the extra fat. You can cut down on stored fat by exercising more and eating less. (Ginger Chih)

bohydrates provide energy for most people of the world, who eat far less meat than Americans. Carbohydrates are burned off quickly by a body at work. If they are not burned, however, the body turns them into fat. This is another problem for people who enjoy tempting foods without exercise. Sugars, which have come to play a bigger and bigger part in our diets, are a special part of the problem. As found in such foods as candy and soft drinks, sugar is almost pure carbohydrate without other nutritional benefits. That is why such foods are called "empty-calorie" foods. Breads, vegetables, and fruits also include large amounts of carbohydrates in the form of starch and sugars, but offer other benefits to make up for it.

Minerals   About three percent of the normal body is made up of minerals. The largest part of this amount is found in parts of the body, like bones and teeth, which are rigid and slow-changing in

Fig. 12-6 A healthful diet will include some carbohydrates, which are usually burned off quickly by the body. Fruits and vegetables are good sources of carbohydrates. (Ginger Chih)

adults. Other minerals work constantly in very important body functions.

Calcium and phosphorus are needed to build strong bones and teeth and to keep them hard. Calcium also helps in the clotting of blood when a person is wounded. It also helps in the proper working of the nerves and muscles. Milk is by far the best source of calcium. This mineral can also be found in dark-green leafy vegetables, such as spinach.

Iron combines with protein to make hemoglobin, the red coloring of the blood which carries oxygen throughout the body. Important food sources of iron are liver, lean meat, oysters, eggs, dry beans, leafy dark-green vegetables, breads, and cereals.

Iodine is essential for proper function of the thyroid gland. This gland controls the rate at which the body uses energy. When the thyroid is not working properly, a person may be terribly sluggish or wildly active and nervous. Iodine is found naturally in seafood and in vegetables grown in parts of the country near bodies of salt water. The main source for many people is the iodine added to table salt (called *iodized* salt).

Many other minerals are important in the working of the body, even though scientific knowledge about some of them is still limited. Most are involved in keeping body fluids in proper movement and balance. These minerals include magnesium, zinc, copper, fluorine, potassium, manganese, cobalt, and sulfur. Fortunately, these minerals are widely available in many foods. Most of them are called *trace elements* because they appear in such small amounts in food and in the body.

Sodium, or salt, is another mineral that deserves mention. The problem here is not shortage but possible overuse. Most nutritionists agree that the body gets plenty of salt from unseasoned foods. As a matter of taste, however, many people load table salt (sodium chloride) or other sodium flavorings onto their food. Too much salt causes the body to hold bigger amounts of water. This is bad for anyone, and very bad for people with heart problems and other ailments. Pouring salt on any food without tasting it first is a poor habit.

Vitamins   The vitamin content of the human body at any one time is never likely to be more than a quarter of an ounce. Yet these

Fig. 12-7 Some people load salt onto everything they eat, even before they taste it. It's a bad habit and can be harmful because too much salt causes the body to hold more water. Natural foods contain most of the salt needed for good health.

chemical combinations, very different from each other, must be present for good health. The body makes too little of them, or none at all. Vitamins have to come from food or food supplements, such as vitamin pills.

The *water-soluble* vitamins demand most attention in the diet. Since they dissolve in water, they are rapidly used up and moved out by the body. Because of this, they must be replaced daily. (They may, in fact, be lost during cooking. To prevent this, use small amounts of water when cooking, cook a short amount of time, and save the cooking water for gravies, soups, etc.) The water-soluble vitamins include:

- *Thiamine* (vitamin B_1). The vitamin that helps to give us normal appetite and digestion is thiamine. It also helps the body to take energy from food and keeps the nervous system operating properly. A person who goes without thiamine for even a few days may suffer loss of appetite, nausea, jumpiness, and bad temper. Thiamine is provided by meat (especially pork), fish, poultry, eggs, dried beans and peas, whole-grain breads and cereals, and some nuts and green vegetables.

- *Riboflavin* (vitamin B_2). Another vitamin that helps the cells of the body to release energy from food is riboflavin. The health and good appearance of the face are also affected by riboflavin; it prevents the forming of scaly, greasy skin around the mouth and nose. Riboflavin is supplied by skim milk, lean meat, and the "variety meats"—liver, heart, and kidney. It is also supplied by eggs and dark-green leafy vegetables.
- *Niacin* (another B vitamin, not numbered). Niacin, like riboflavin and thiamine, helps the body cells to release energy from food. Niacin also helps to maintain the healthy condition of the skin, tongue, digestive system, and nervous system. Some niacin can be formed in the body, but more is needed from other sources. Niacin is supplied by liver, yeast, lean meat, poultry, fish, peanuts and peanut butter, leafy green vegetables, beans and peas, and whole-grain breads and cereals.
- *Pyridoxine* (vitamin B_6), *cyanocobalamin* (vitamin B_{12}), *and folic acid* (vitamin B_c or vitamin M). These are other B vitamins which come from much the same food sources and help to keep the blood in good condition.
- *Ascorbic acid* (vitamin C). Ascorbic acid helps the body to heal wounds and resist infections. It also helps to make a substance that holds the cells of the body together and to build hard teeth and firm gums, strong muscles and blood vessels. Vitamin C is supplied by all citrus fruits, such as oranges and grapefruit, and by cantaloupe, strawberries, tomatoes, Brussels sprouts, raw cabbage, peppers, some leafy greens, and potatoes.

Some other important vitamins are *fat-soluble*. Because of this, they can be stored in the body for longer periods than the water-soluble vitamins. The fat-soluble vitamins include:

- *Vitamin A*. An important vitamin for keeping the skin smooth and firm is vitamin A. It also helps to build and protect the lining of the mouth, nose, throat, and digestive tract. Vitamin A is needed for the building of strong tooth enamel. Because it also helps build eye tissues, it is well-known for promoting better vision in dim light. Most people know that carrots supply vitamin A. Other sources of this vitamin are liver, most dark-green and deep-yellow vegetables, apricots, cantaloupe, butter, cheese, and whole milk.

- *Vitamin D.* The "sunshine vitamin"—D—helps in the building of strong bones and teeth by drawing calcium and phosphorus from the body's digestive tract. It gets its nickname because it is formed by the action of sunlight on the skin of the body. The only natural food source of vitamin D is fish liver oils.
- *Vitamin K and Vitamin E.* Two vitamins that deserve mention are K and E. Vitamin K helps to clot the blood when the body is wounded. It is made in normal amounts by bacteria in the body's digestive system. It may be needed in extra quantities, laboratory-made, in cases of bad wounds.

Vitamin E has been the subject of sensational claims made for its use in increasing sexual power, preventing aging, and curing many ailments. Most scientists say these claims are untrue. This has not discouraged many people from buying large numbers of vitamin E pills. Vitamin E *does* have some important functions, such as helping the body to use oxygen. But most people get enough vitamin E in ordinary foods.

RDA: Nutrition Guideline

Most basic nutritional ideas are expressed in the listing called the *RDA.* This stands for the *U.S. Recommended Daily Allowances,* drawn up under the sponsorship of the federal Food and Drug Administration. Government nutritional scientists set standards, shown in Figure 12-8, for 20 nutrients. This list is the foundation for a system of nutrition labeling of foods which began on a full scale in 1975.

Two points about the RDA have to be emphasized: First, the standards are set for "most healthy adults." No list of this type could give exact numbers for everyone. Nutritional needs depend on many things, such as the individual's height, weight, age, and activity. Different people may be very different in their rates of *metabolism*—the pace at which their body processes work, and how well they work, through the day. Second, most of the allow-

U.S. Recommended Daily Allowances (U.S. RDA)

Protein
Protein quality equal
to or greater than
milk protein   45 grams

Protein quality less
than milk protein   65 grams

Vitamin A   5,000 International Units

**Vitamin C (ascorbic
acid)**   60 milligrams

Thiamine (vitamin B_1)   1.5 milligrams

Riboflavin (vitamin B_2)   1.7 milligrams

Niacin   20 milligrams

Calcium   1.0 gram

Iron   18 milligrams

Vitamin D   400 International Units

Vitamin E   30 International Units

Vitamin B_6 2.0 milligrams

Folic acid (folacin)   0.4 milligram

Vitamin B_{12} 6 micrograms

Phosphorus   1.0 gram

Iodine   150 micrograms

Magnesium   400 milligrams

Zinc   15 milligrams

Copper   2 milligrams

Biotin   0.3 milligram

Pantothenic acid   10 milligrams

Fig. 12-8 The U.S. Recommended Daily Allowances (RDA) list the amounts of each nutrient that are adequate for the average healthy adult. The nutrients shown in bold type are those that must be listed in nutrient labeling of food package.

ances are set with a margin of safety. The RDA is *not* a list of medium or minimum needs. For example, vitamin A may not really be needed every day. It is stored in body fat. Any day's intake may last for a period of time. For another example, nutritionists are not sure of the daily need for some things like vitamin E and various minerals. The RDA plays it safe by listing amounts thought to be ample by most nutritionists. (Some doctors and nutritionists believe in the use of *megavitamins*—huge doses of vitamins to prevent and cure certain diseases. They, of course, think some of the RDA levels are too low).

Reading Labels for Value   The U.S. Recommended Daily Allowances set the marks for a system of labeling which some food companies have had to follow since 1975. The system is designed to help shoppers compare nutritional values of foods easily. It can help people to buy more nutrition for less money.

The samples in Figure 12-9 show the form these labels take. The label tells the size of an average serving. It gives the number of calories for each serving. It lists the weight of proteins, carbohydrates, and fats in each serving. It *may* list the amount of sodium and cholesterol for each serving. (There is no RDA for any of these items except proteins.)

The bottom section of the label must cover the first eight nutrients for which an RDA has been set (proteins through iron). The label tells what *percentage* of the RDA is provided in each serving. Suppose that the label says "Vitamin C........15." This means that one serving supplies 15 milligrams of vitamin C. This is 25 percent of the RDA (60 milligrams of vitamin C). To get the full RDA, the shopper would buy and serve a day's worth of foods whose labels added up to about 100 percent for each nutrient.

Nutrition labeling must be done on foods that are *fortified.* These are foods to which nutrients have been added in natural or *synthetic* (man-made) form. Milk and white bread are two of the food items most often fortified or "enriched." The vitamin A of whole milk is removed with the fat when skim milk is made. The vitamin is then put back in synthetic form. Synthetic vitamin D is added to most kinds of whole milk and skim milk on the market. The flour for white bread is made in a way that takes almost all the vitamins and minerals out of the whole grain. The result is almost pure carbohydrate—

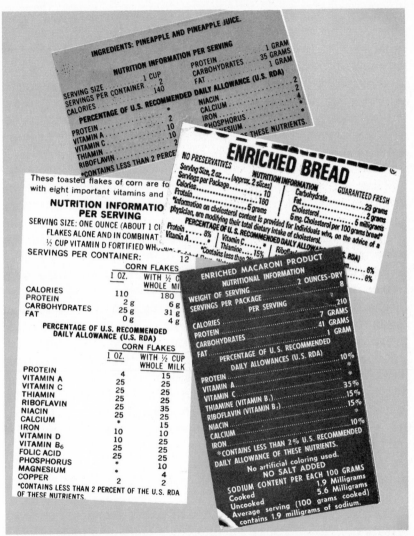

Fig. 12-9 Nutritional labeling is required for any food that is described as "fortified" or advertised as having nutritional benefits. The labels list the percentage supplied of the RDA of each nutrient.

"empty calories." The flour must then be enriched by the addition of a number of vitamins and minerals. Nutrition labeling tells about it.

Nutrition labeling must also be done for foods claimed to have nutritional value. A food company that says that its beans "give you super energy" must put a nutrition label on them. A company that advertises that its hash is "more nutritious than Brand X" must put a nutrition label on it. These foods must have the exact form of labeling required by law.

Other foods *may* be labeled, but don't have to be. Examine a can of peas sold under the label of a supermarket chain. The peas are not fortified or enriched. They are not advertised except by price. They do not have to carry nutrition labeling. Hundreds of other food items, packaged and fresh, fall into this class.

These items make up some very large exceptions from the nutrition labeling rules, of course. How does the shopper compare Brand A peas, which carry a nutrition label, and Brand B peas, which do not? How can the shopper compare mixed foods, like soups or codfish cakes, when some are nutritionally labeled and some are not? Finally, how can the RDA for iron or protein be added up when the bread, milk, and lunch meat are nutritionally labeled and the fresh spinach isn't?

The shopper who wants to know all about nutrition may have to buy one or more handbooks that offer a full nutritional view of many foods. A number of these books may be found in the library or the bookstore. They may even be found, in pocket size, on the nearest magazine stand. A mere calorie-counter is not too useful. The handbook should include information on protein, fats, vitamins, minerals, and fiber as well. Using such tables to "keep score" on diet can be hard work at first. It gets easier with practice, and it can have big payoffs in health and good looks.

Enjoying the Basic Four

Can the average shopper digest the facts of nutritional science? Who can do all the arithmetic involved? Does anyone care? The answer to the third question *ought* to be yes for any person who really wants to live well. The first two questions are more likely to get mixed answers from any group of shoppers. What's to be done, then? It may be enough to know that many years of scientific study have already gone into the problems of making food work best for us. Anyone who wants to take that on faith can profit from the *basic four*. The idea is at least 40 years old. Like most serious attempts to keep things simple, it holds up well through changing times. It says

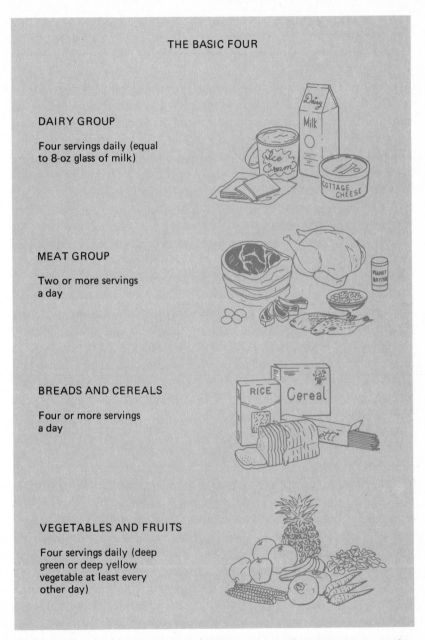

THE BASIC FOUR

DAIRY GROUP

Four servings daily (equal
to 8-oz glass of milk)

MEAT GROUP

Two or more servings
a day

BREADS AND CEREALS

Four or more servings
a day

VEGETABLES AND FRUITS

Four servings daily (deep
green or deep yellow
vegetable at least every
other day)

Fig. 12-10 The average person can still follow a healthful diet without spending
hours studying nutritional labels. Simply eat a variety of foods every day from
each of the basic four food groups.

that a person should eat a variety of foods every day from each of four main groups: milk and dairy products, meats or other protein suppliers, breads and cereals, and vegetables and fruits.

The Dairy Group   Milk in all forms, cheeses, and ice cream or ice milk are included in the dairy group. It is the main supplier of calcium and also supplies protein, riboflavin, vitamin A, and other nutrients.

Two glasses a day are recommended for adults, three or more for children, and four or more for high schoolers. Skim milk (with vitamin A put back) is good for diet-watchers. Non-fat dry milk is cheaper in both calories and cost. The same goes for ice milk as compared to ice cream.

Milk used in cooking (as in soups, sauces, puddings) counts. Two slices of American cheese or a pint of ice milk are about equal to an eight-ounce glass of milk.

The Meat Group   Though "meat" is the label word, this group covers a lot more. It includes all animal meat, fish, shellfish, poultry, and eggs. It also includes dry beans and peas, lentils, nuts, seeds, peanuts, and peanut butter.

Two or more servings a day are recommended. A serving might amount to 3 ounces of lean meat, fish, or chicken, or 1 egg. At least one serving during the week should be one of the "variety meats"—liver, heart, or kidney.

The vegetable items in this group, as mentioned earlier, are "incomplete" proteins. By itself, a serving of cooked dried beans would have to amount to a cup. This is a fairly big amount for most people. But the "incomplete" protein starts rising to meat level (or higher) when beans are mixed with milk, grain, or seeds in many ways. One high-protein mix is that old standby, a peanut butter sandwich on whole-grain or enriched white bread with a glass of milk. Another is beans and rice (a traditional food mixture for many cultures). Still others are pea soup and whole-wheat bread, chick peas (garbanzo beans) with a cheese sauce, or a snack of soybeans or peanuts with sunflower or sesame seeds. The protein-raising trick, remember, is having these things together *at the same time.*

Besides protein, this group supplies iron, thiamine, riboflavin, and niacin in good amounts.

Breads and Cereals   Four or more servings a day from this group are recommended. That level is fairly easy to reach for most people. The group includes all breads (and other baked goods) *if* they are made with enriched or whole-grain flour. This group also includes breakfast cereals (dry or cooked), macaroni, spaghetti, noodles, rice, and hominy grits.

The bread-cereal group supplies iron and B vitamins and also protein (best when taken with milk or beans). A good serving is one slice of bread or one-half to three-quarters of a cup of cereal, spaghetti, or rice.

Vegetables and Fruits   This group supplies vitamins A and C as well as many other vitamins and minerals. Four half-cup servings a day are recommended. One serving a day should supply vitamin C. Oranges, grapefruit, and tomatoes are the best-known sources. The list of substitutes, however, might be surprising: asparagus, lima beans, beet greens, broccoli, Brussels sprouts, cabbage, cauliflower, chard, dandelion greens, kale, mustard greens, green peppers, potatoes, spinach, and turnip, as well as cantaloupe and strawberries.

A deep-green or deep-yellow vegetable should be served at least *every other day* as a source of vitamin A. Possibilities include carrots, of course, and also beet greens, broccoli, dandelion greens, kale, spinach, winter squash, and sweet potato, as well as dried apricots, cantaloupe, and tomatoes.

Other fruits and vegetables too numerous to mention are rich in other vitamins and minerals. Two or three more servings a day should come from this list, which includes beets, corn, cucumber, eggplant, lettuce, onions, peas, string beans, apples, bananas, berries, cherries, dates, peaches, pineapple, plums, and watermelon.

Some people, somehow, think their food choices are limited. And some think that vegetables are dull, or worse. A full look at the vegetable-fruit group gives rise to wonder at their views. It seems to offer the greatest variety and the widest choices of all.

Two Other Basics   Two more items might be added to make a "basic six."

Water   Though it is not a nutrient, water is absolutely vital. A person will indeed survive a great deal longer without food than without water. Water is the main material of the body and should be renewed at the rate of four or more glasses a day. It carries nutrients and removes waste. It helps in digesting and absorbing food. It cools the body.

Exercise   Exercise comes in no recommended daily allowance, but it can be a definite plus to good nutrition and health. Exercise, of course, burns away excess calories and helps to keep muscles and blood circulation working well. Some nutritional scientists believe it can also help cut down the amount of harmful elements such as cholesterol in the body.

Nutrition Issues

Where food is concerned, more and more facts often seem to lead to less and less agreement. The basic four distills more than a century's worth of knowledge in nutritional science. Yet it may often be *too* simple for the many twists of human nature.

Two key words of good nutrition (as in other good ways of life) are *balance* and *moderation*. They go together. *Balance* means the keeping of things in their proper relationship to each other. A balanced diet may deserve the same respect we give a balanced mind or a balanced temper. In eating, balance means thinking about the many foods needed to fill all the body's needs. It means thinking about such things as enjoyment and health, and calories and exercise, as they relate to each other. *Moderation* is knowing when to say "enough." Few foods are "bad" in small amounts. Yet too much of any good thing, whether steak or hot fudge or whole wheat or vitamins, can do harm in some way.

Huge changes have come about only in recent years in the ways food is produced and sold. One of the biggest of these changes is the growth of *food technology*—the use of factory methods to increase the amounts and the kinds of foods available. The modern supermarket itself has made great changes in the ways we live and eat. Hundreds of new and changed food products come to the supermarket shelves each year. Many are "convenience foods," partly or fully prepared for the cook. Many have simply to be warmed and served. A great many new or familiar-looking foods have been *processed*—changed by manufacturing methods to make them tastier, bulkier, smoother, crisper, less chewy, more colorful, etc. They represent more and more unknowns for the person trying to buy a balanced diet.

Many shoppers are further confused by the advertising and packaging of food. Merchandising—presenting food in tempting ways in the store—has become a fine art. It is based on market research, which pinpoints the buyer's strongest wants—and weaknesses. The live-alone person, who has greater freedom to make spur-of-the-moment choices, may have to be especially wary of advertising and merchandising lures.

Changes of this scale put nutrition issues into the headlines almost daily. You have probably read about some of the following "big stories."

Weight-Loss Diets   In all but the rarest cases, losing weight is simply a matter of taking in fewer calories and/or getting more exercise. Yet the weight-loss business has become a billion-dollar American industry. Fancy health clubs, diet books, articles, courses, pills, liquids, and powders are sold to millions of people. Most of the customers want to lose weight in a hurry. Nutritionists feel that many fad diets ought to be labeled as dangerous to the health.

Food Processing and Additives   Our massive national system of food distribution would probably be impossible without some additives. These are chemicals, taken from nature or made in a laboratory, which are added to food for special purposes. Without additives to preserve them, many packaged foods would have to be produced and consumed in a matter of days. Other additives are nutrients. Vitamins, minerals, and even proteins are added to many foods. (Some nutrient additives replace the natural nutrients taken out in processing such foods as white bread.) Still other uses of additives are more controversial. Many chemicals are used to change the color, taste, and texture of foods and to make them easier to handle. Are these needed, critics ask, to benefit the consumer or the producer of the foods? By recent count, more than 5,000 different chemical compounds were being used in food processing. Most seem to be helpful, or at worst harmless. Yet a few have proved, by government scientific standards, to be causes of cancer and other ailments in test animals. Why, critics ask, should we risk harm for the mere sake of prettier, tastier, or smoother food? The battle over additives and the "rebuilding" of foods is likely to gain in heat in the years ahead. Meanwhile, the consumer would probably be wise to use a fair share of old-fashioned, unprocessed foods.

Fat and Fiber   Suppliers in a free market system try to give people what they want. What people seem to want, most nutritionists complain, is too much beef and too little fiber. Americans eat far more meat than any other people on earth. Meat alone provides most of us with *twice as much protein* as our bodies need. This extra protein, as you learned, is "wasted"—burned for energy, eliminated, or added to overweight. Meanwhile the meat fats are likely to be causing health problems. Most doctors and nutritionists are convinced that animal fats in the diet help cause heart ailments. Most believe that too much fat can cause clogging of the bloodstream and the blood vessels. Most now believe that fats should make up no more than one-third of the calories we take in. Many say that animals fats—from meat, dairy products, and eggs—should be no more than one-third of the one-third.

Animal fats also contribute to the troublesome problem of too much *cholesterol* in the blood. Cholesterol is a waxy material that makes up an important part of the human brain and nerves. It is also made by the liver to help carry saturated fats (animal fats) through the bloodstream. When a person eats a lot of animal fat, the body may make too much cholesterol. Some people are able to use up this extra amount, apparently because they do a lot of exercise and have enough B vitamins in their diets. In other people, the extra cholesterol may cling to the walls of the arteries that feed blood to the heart. This clogging may cause heart failure and fatal heart attack.

Few doctors say that animal fats should be given up completely. They recognize that fats—creamy butter, a choice steak "marbled" with fat, ice cream—are among our greatest pleasures and provide for our energy needs. But they say we should pay more attention to the connection between too much of these things and heart disease—our leading cause of death.

The choice of meat over vegetables has been a cause of a lack of fiber in our diets. Fibers are the tough, crackly, or chewy parts of vegetables, fruits, grains, and nuts. Fibers pull solid wastes together and help to move them through the body and out of it.

Health Diets Food problems have worried millions of people enough to push them toward health foods and more "natural" diets. But "natural" diets need to be managed with as much care as any other. Any person attracted to purer, unprocessed foods should beware of fads and rip-offs. The terms *organic, natural,* and *health food* are not closely defined by laws and may be used wildly by some sellers. Some health foods have more nutrients than any one body can use in a month. Others promise magic results, but have far less nutritional value than processed foods in the supermarket. It pays to read the labels—the small print most of all.

Issues like these are bound to last. If all the exact details of nutrition are forgotten, however, one key word should be remembered: *balance.*

Any person attracted to purer, unprocessed foods should beware of fads and rip-offs. The terms *organic, natural,* and *health food* are not closely defined by laws and may be used wildly by some sellers. Some health foods have more nutrients than any one body can use in a month. Others promise magic results, but have far less nutritional value than processed foods in the supermarket. It pays to read the labels—the small print most of all.

THINKING IT THROUGH

1. Americans are said to consume too many "empty calorie" foods—foods that have a great deal of sugar, starch, or fat but are low in such nutrients as vitamins, minerals, and protein. What evidence have you found personally that supports or challenges this statement?
2. Food may be a *necessity* or a *luxury.* Where do you draw the line between the two? Give examples of the difference between an essential food and a luxury food.
3. Suppose that you heard a person making this argument: "There are just too many different kinds of food products in the store. People get confused. It's hard for the average shopper to make good choices from the huge number of things available. Besides that, competition causes food sellers to stretch the truth with advertising claims and fancy packages and labels." Would you agree or disagree with his argument? Why?

The Basics:
Tools and Staples

Charlie Chaplin made a banquet out of a shoe. He had the equipment, but no food. The opposite happened in another funny scene from an Oscar-winning film, *The Apartment.* Jack Lemmon played the part of a bachelor entertaining a date with a spaghetti dinner. His cooking went well, but he found he had no tools to drain the boiling water from the spaghetti. Searching through the clutter in his kitchen, he finally found the tool that suited him—an old tennis racquet. He dumped the hot spaghetti onto the tattered strings. The hot water ran off into the sink. Lemmon "served" the spaghetti deftly onto the dinner plates.

People make do with some novel cooking equipment. Scouts and other campers are known for preparing whole meals in a single container. Sometimes it is just a big tin can propped over the campfire. That skill serves well for a day or two of outdoor living. It doesn't go very far in meeting needs for varied, interesting menus. The good day-to-day cook needs many tools—*utensils*—to do the job well.

Even a simple meal may require all the following steps: (1) handling, (2) measuring, (3) cutting, (4) other processing, (5) mixing, (6) cooking atop the stove or in the oven, (7) cleaning up, and (8) storing leftovers. Every step can be eased by the use of special utensils. Some tools *must* be used to get the job done. Others can save time, motion, temper, and money.

Tools for a Start

Few people living on their own for the first time can afford all the cooking utensils they will eventually find useful. A full list, even at lowest prices, would strain the week's paycheck or the month's

Fig. 13-1 In the film *The Apartment*, Jack Lemmon cleverly used an old tennis racquet to drain his spaghetti. Although you can always make do with various odd utensils for occasional cooking, for day-to-day cooking you need a good, basic set of equipment. (Museum of Modern Art)

credit. A beginner should be able to start cooking, however, with the basic equipment shown in Table 13-1.

Remember, this is a list of the *least* that may be needed for one-person cooking. The utensils won't be perfect for some of the uses to which they will have to be put. A utility knife won't do the best job of slicing bread. A 9-inch frypan is a very large utensil for scrambling an egg. The cook will have to make them do for some unusual jobs. Many utensils will have to be called on for at least double duty. The cookie sheet, for example, may have to double as a tray, and the slotted spoon as a masher. The cake pan may have to be used for baking and warming all sorts of things besides cake.

Choosing Utensils   In spite of such problems, it is probably wiser to start out with a few good-quality utensils than with a bigger supply of cheap tools. First-class equipment may actually last a lifetime. Utensils at half the price may survive for only a few months.

Table 13-1 BASIC COOKING UTENSILS

Use	Utensil
Handling	Can opener
	Pancake lifter or spatula
	Wooden cooking spoon
	Metal cooking spoon, slotted
	Cooking fork, two tines
	Potholders or hot mitts
Measuring*	1-quart glass measuring cup
	8-ounce glass measuring cup
	Set of four measuring spoons (¼ teaspoon, ½ teaspoon, teaspoon, and tablespoon)
	Set of dry measuring cups (1 cup, ½ cup, ⅓ cup, ¼ cup)
Cutting	Utility knife, about 5 inches long
	Paring knife
	Parer (peeler)
	Knife sharpener
	Cutting board
	Kitchen shears
Other processing	Large strainer
Mixing	Rotary hand beater
	Set of mixing bowls, 1-quart, 2-quart, and 3-quart
	Small rubber scraper
Cooking atop the stove	Saucepans with covers, 1-quart and 2-quart
	Frypan with cover, 9-inch
	Cookpot with cover, 6-quart
Cooking in the oven	Round roasting pan with rack
	Cake pan, 7-inch
	Small loaf pan
	Pie tin, 9-inch
	Cookie sheet
	Casserole dish with cover, 2-quart
	Custard cups
Cleaning up	Dishpan
	Dish rack
	Dishcloth or sponge
	Dish towels
	Scouring pads or brush
	Garbage pail
Storing leftovers	Plastic freezer boxes, purchased or saved from other foods.
	Screw-top glass jars, saved from other foods.

*Utensils that offer both standard and metric quantities are preferable.

Dollars, unfortunately, make much of the difference. Some commonsense comparing and questioning are needed to get the most for the money:

Fig. 13-2 Here are some of the basic utensils a beginner needs to start cooking: egg beater, strainer, measuring spoons, hot mitts, measuring cup, two-tined fork, peeler, egg/pancake turner, frypan. (Susan Berkowitz)

Will the Utensil Be Strong and Long-Lasting?   Cheap tools are likely to bend, warp, buckle, break, scratch, crack, or chip easily. Utensils may be made of materials such as aluminum, cast iron, stainless steel, and enameled metal. It pays to know the strengths and weaknesses of these different materials when buying utensils. Weight is a good rule-of-thumb guide in comparing utensils made of the same material. (This often applies also in comparing utensils made of different materials.) As a general rule, heavier is better. A frypan made of cast aluminum (made from melted aluminum poured into a form) is likely to be far better than another pan stamped from a thinner sheet of aluminum. A knife blade made from thick steel ground to an edge is likely to be of far higher quality than a blade stamped from a thin sheet of steel. Handles and knobs of heavy plastic, heatproof and waterproof, will stand heavy use. Handles and knobs of soft wood, painted or varnished, may not last long in heat or water.

Is the Utensil Easy to Clean?   Some materials are naturally easier to clean than others. Any utensil should also be free of sharp corners, joints, and ornamentation. These are places where food and grease can collect out of the cleaner's reach. Such hiding places can be easily seen in a commonsense look at any utensil, from a cooking spoon to a roasting pan. Pots and pans, for example, should have smooth edges. They should be rounded wherever surfaces meet. They should have no holes, folds, or decorations that will collect dirt.

Is the Utensil Safe and Comfortable to Use?   Utensils ought to be thought of in terms of the least effort and the least danger possible. Knives and cooking forks need to be sharp to work well; the edges of pans, spoons, and other utensils shouldn't be sharp. Saucepans should sit solidly on the stove, covering the full area of the burner. A pan with a narrow, rounded bottom (or a warped bottom) and a heavy handle is dangerously out of balance. It can easily tip, causing messy spills or burns. A can opener that leaves jagged edges and threads of sharp metal should be discarded. A rotary beater that slips and jams might as well be thrown away, too. Thoughtful buying of utensils can prevent such dangers and discomforts.

Keeping these rules in mind, the cook can go on to build a basic collection of tools which works well for almost every day-to-day need.

To Buy or Not to Buy?

The answer depends on individual differences of need, habit, taste and storage space. The person who never entertains, and never intends to, clearly doesn't need the larger sizes of cookware. The cook who truly masters the electric blender, and truly prefers to use it, may do without a number of hand utensils for mixing, chopping, and mashing. (This should depend on experience, not advertising claims. Many cooks believe that hand tools take less time and trouble than some electrical "time-saver.") The person who never cooks or serves spaghetti or noodles may not need the larger cookpots.

Storage space or the lack of it may affect the buying of utensils. In many small kitchens, pots and pans have to be hung out in the open. For appearance's sake, the cook may shun plain aluminum in

Fig. 13-3 Consider your needs, habits, and storage space before you buy any utensil. Don't let sales or advertising claims convince you to buy something you'll never use.

favor of more colorful enamelware. Attractive design may sway the buyer's choice, in fact, even if there is plenty of room in the cabinets.

Here are some further notes, by purpose, about buying and using utensils.

Handling Some cooks jokingly refer to the can opener as their most important utensil. That may not be true, but the absence of a can opener would be no laughing matter in most kitchens. Can openers may range in price from 30 cents to $30 or more. The old-fashioned hook type, one of the cheapest, is a fairly dangerous weapon. Its sharp point can skitter and catch a hand. It leaves the top of the can with ragged edges, which can also cut a hand. Most can openers today, fortunately, are the type that work by turning a cog against the rim of the can. The result is a smooth cut. A simple version of this opener may be bought for less than a dollar. This is

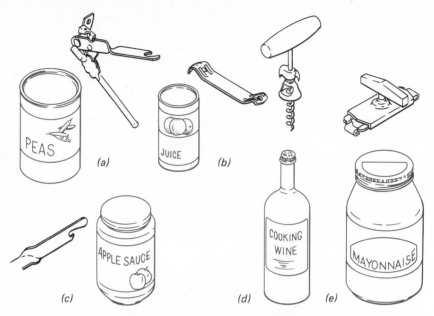

Fig. 13-4 No opener has been invented yet that works on all containers. Shown here are some openers that each have a special use—bottles, cans, or jars.

one case where low cost has benefits. The simple model is sturdy, and it can be carried to the work. Wall-mounted can openers and electric can openers are more costly and sometimes less convenient.

Most kitchens need at least two or three kinds of openers for different jobs. The punch-type opener cuts triangular openings in juice cans. Containers with press-down lids are opened with a key-like lifter. Screw-top containers sometimes resist the strongest hands; a special tool is needed to twist covers loose. A corkscrew comes in handy at times. So does a bottle-cap lifter. Most opening tools combine two or more of these features. No inventor has come up yet with a good utensil to serve all opening purposes.

A good-sized tray can help in preparing meals as well as serving them. Ideally, all foods and utensils should be stored nearest to the spot where they are to be used. Often the design of cabinets and counters won't permit this. A tray helps then by carrying more items in fewer steps to where they're needed.

Cake racks are correctly named, but they also serve to keep hot pots and pans off counter surfaces.

Fig. 13-5 Tongs make it easier to handle spaghetti, corn on the cob and other large vegetables.

Ordinary tableware simply isn't tough enough to use in cooking. Cooking knives and forks should have long handles and good grips, made of heavy plastic or unpainted hard wood. Wooden spoons can be left in a cookpan without getting hot themselves or leaving a stain in the pan. They do need to be rinsed quickly so that they won't hold stains or odors from food. Tongs (see Figure 13-5) are useful for handling foods, like spaghetti or large vegetables, which can't be managed well by other utensils.

Measuring   The success or failure of many cooking projects depends on exact measurement. The wrong amount of garlic salt or baking powder, for example, can turn a great dish into a disaster. A good cook needs several kinds of measuring tools for special jobs. There should also be enough of these tools. Otherwise the cook may wind up washing and drying the measure several times in the course of making a dish.

Liquid measures should be made of clear glass or plastic. Then the cook can set the measuring cup on a flat surface and see—at eye level—when the liquid is at the correct line.

Dry ingredients don't level off by themselves, as liquid will. That is why dry measures come in several exact sizes. The right size—say one-third of a cup—is picked out and filled to heaping. Then it must be leveled off by drawing a spatula (or any flat object) across the top edge.

The length of time a dish is cooked may be as important as the contents of it. Cooking can be timed by wristwatch or the kitchen

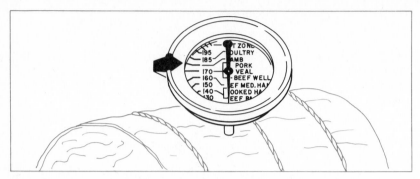

Fig. 13-6 A meat thermometer, inserted into a roast or turkey, reports the temperature inside the piece of meat. You can watch the thermometer and take out the roast when the meat has cooked properly.

clock, of course. But that requires constant attention. The kitchen timer, with its bell signal, is more convenient.

A meat thermometer can help the cook be *sure* that a larger piece of meat or poultry is properly done. This is important to anyone who can't stand beef well done or can't stand it rare. Pork *must* be cooked thoroughly to prevent the possibility of a disease called *trichinosis*. The meat thermometer reports from the center of the roast that the temperature is just right.

Cutting   The total number of special-purpose knives may run into the hundreds. Special knives are designed, for example, for slicing tomatoes, boning meat, sawing frozen food, or preparing fruits and vegetables. Few people would want all of them even if they could afford them.

One rule applies to all knives: However much they cost, they're useless without a good edge. Some lower-cost knives have permanent edges that are *serrated* (saw-toothed) or *scalloped* (formed of a series of rounded-out markings). Such edges may do a fair to good cutting job. They cannot be sharpened any further. The best knife is one that can be sharpened to a fine edge. The sharpest blades are made of high-carbon steel. This is the kind of blade used by many butchers. But high-carbon steel becomes dark and mottled with use. It is not good-looking enough to suit many home cooks. They prefer stainless steel, though it won't hold as good an edge. High-carbon

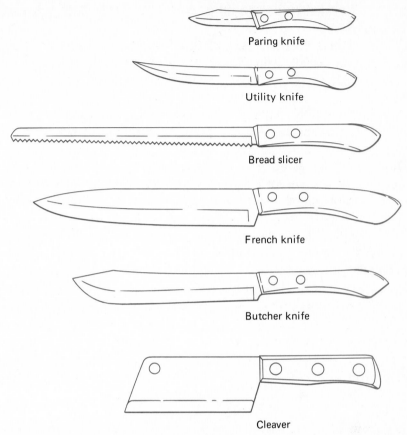

Paring knife

Utility knife

Bread slicer

French knife

Butcher knife

Cleaver

Fig. 13-7 Knives come in all shapes and sizes, each for a specific use. Shown here are a few basic knives; the paring and utility knives are the most practical and handy for a beginner's kitchen.

steel, plated with stainless chromium, is a costly combination of sharpness and good looks.

Any good knife has a blade that extends 2 or more inches into its handle. Two or more studs (which show as brass circles on either side of the handle) should hold the blade to the handle.

Good blades deserve good care. They should be sharpened briefly on a steel or stone device every few times they are used. Blade edges should not be banged against each other. They also shouldn't be used on counter tops, stove tops, or other hard surfaces. A wooden cutting board preserves the blade and improves the work.

Cutting food like celery or garlic into very fine pieces is a job that can be done skillfully with a French cook's knife. It can also be done with a simple one-blade hand chopper or kitchen shears.

Other Processing Two of the most familiar old utensils in the kitchen are the masher and the grater. The masher's work is pretty much confined to mashing potatoes, turnips, and a few other items. The grater is one-sided or four-sided. Hard cheese or vegetables are rubbed over the sharp holes in it and reduced to the desired bits, shreds, or thin strips. Over the years, the work of both utensils has been taken over by dozens of mechanical and electrical devices. Hand-operated food mills and electric mixers, slicers, and blenders can do the same work. Yet the simple hand tools stay high in popularity and use.

Another special old tool is the pastry blender. It has one job. It mixes shortening (butter or lard) in a special way with flour for use in

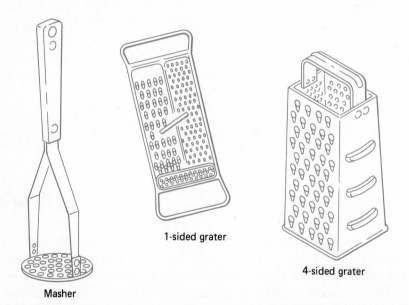

1-sided grater

4-sided grater

Masher

Fig. 13-8 There are various expensive mechanical and electrical devices available that do many tasks, including mash and grate. But the simple hand masher and hand graters shown here are still popular and get the job done.

such foods as cakes or dumplings. Any cook who wants to bake pies or make dumplings or ravioli will also need a rolling pin, a pastry board or cloth, and a flour sifter.

Every cook probably needs a colander. This is a metal or plastic basket filled with holes for draining water from food, from hot spaghetti to cold green salad fixings.

The brewing of coffee might involve any one of a hundred methods and special utensils. Coffee experts say that water should run *once* through the ground coffee. This can be done with a simple drip coffeepot. It can also be done with expensive coffee makers that involve high pressure and filters. Many cooks prefer to defy the experts by using percolators or by simply boiling the ground coffee in a pan of water.

Mixing   The wire whip is another simple old tool that many cooks prefer to mechanical and electrical devices. It is simply a set of shiny wire loops bound together. It can do a great job of beating any egg or other liquid combinations.

Mixing, beating, or whipping food can be a sloppy job. Mixing bowls should be the right size for the job. They should also allow plenty of room. Food moves and splashes. It can also gain air, which increases the space it takes up in the bowl. The cook who tries to beat 30 ounces of batter in a 1-quart bowl is going to have a mess to clean up later.

Good-quality mixing bowls can serve many purposes. If they are made of heat-resistant glass or pottery, and have a handle and a pouring lip, they can be used for many jobs from the refrigerator to the oven.

Cooking on the Stove   Pots, pans, and kettles that have good tight covers permit cooking with less heat and water. This helps preserve food flavors and keeps vitamins from washing away in cooking water. An inexpensive steamer basket can keep vegetables entirely out of water, cooking in steam alone. Pressure cookers carry this method to an extreme. They are tightly sealed. They cook food rapidly under high steam pressure. Instructions need to be followed very carefully, however. They can be dangerous if not watched closely.

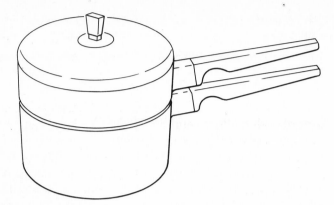

Fig. 13-9 The double boiler is used for delicate mixtures that might burn easily if put over direct heat. Boiling water in the lower pan provides controlled heat. Sauces, melted chocolate, or cheese can be heated in the upper pan.

A Dutch oven is a big, covered pot made of heavy cast iron or cast aluminum. It is excellent for slow cooking of pot roasts, stews, and other dishes good for company. Such dishes require little watching, and more time for guests.

The double boiler is used for delicate mixtures that might burn easily if they were put directly over the heat. Water boils in the bottom pan. The second pan fits tightly into the top of the first. Sauces or syrups put into it will heat well, but won't burn. The buyer will get extra service from a double boiler if both parts can be used separately as saucepans.

Cooking in the Oven   The size of cooking vessels becomes very important when they are used in the oven. Food put into an over-large pan or casserole dish may turn out pale or undercooked. Food piled to the top of the pan or casserole may bubble over. Such oven spills are extra hard to clean up. Thus a variety of utensil sizes is needed to save trouble and get best results. A big casserole for company should be baked with an inch or so to spare at the top of the dish. Small individual portions (of meat loaf or puddings, for example) may even be baked in muffin tins or glass custard cups.

Glass and pottery aren't used for stovetop cooking because they don't carry direct heat well. They are very good, on the other hand, for carrying radiant heat—the waves of heat which fill the oven. (Glass transmits this heat so well that the oven must usually be set about 25° lower than it would be when using a metal utensil.) Because of the greater number of materials available, ovenware comes in a wider variety of designs. Many are so attractive that they can be taken directly from the oven to the table as serving dishes.

Cleaning Up   Good containers for trash and garbage are important in terms of both neatness and health. The garbage can, made of plastic or metal, should have a tight-fitting lid. Food waste should *never* be thrown into open wastebaskets, where it may attract insects and rodents. Waste containers with easy-lift swinging tops aren't much better than the open variety. A tight cover is worth the bit of extra effort it causes.

Food scraps and grease should go into the garbage, not the sink or the dishwater. A rubber scraper helps do this task before dishwashing starts.

Storing Leftovers   The management of leftovers (or "plan-overs") is especially important in a one-person household. There is really no way to make a complete diet of food sold in one-portion amounts. Many foods will have to be used in two or more installments.

Many types of containers for storing food in the refrigerator or freezer section can be purchased. Other containers can be reused after the food bought in them is used up. Plastic and screw-top glass containers should be saved in sizes from a few ounces to a half gallon. Whether bought or reused, these containers should be clear. Leftovers put into an opaque container are often out of sight and out of mind. If opaque containers are used, label them with masking tape labels. (Frozen beef broth looks an awful lot like frozen onion soup.) The tape can be easily taken off and thrown away when no longer needed. Containers should also have wide, flat caps or lids so they can be stacked if necessary. Keep them in the front of the refrigerator so you don't forget them.

Supplies of wax paper, plastic wrap, and aluminum foil should also be kept on hand. They are good for wrapping leftovers. They serve many other purposes, too. Aluminum foil put under a casserole dish, for example, gives extra protection against oven spills.

Appliances   Americans are often called a "gadget-happy" people. Many home kitchens are loaded with expensive appliances that are

Table 13-2 BASIC FOOD STAPLES

Food Group	Item
Cereal (grain) products	All-purpose flour
	Rice
	Cornmeal
	Bread crumbs, plain and seasoned
	Spaghetti
	Macaroni
	Noodles
Aids for baking	Baking powder
	Baking soda
Dairy products	Powdered milk
	Evaporated milk
	Grated cheese
Sugars	Granulated sugar
	Powdered sugar
	Brown sugar
Salts	Plain iodized salt
	Onion salt
	Seasoned salt
	Garlic salt
Peppers	Black pepper
	Paprika
	Cayenne pepper
Spices	Cinnamon
	Cloves
	Chili powder
	Curry powder
	Dry mustard
	Ginger
	Nutmeg
	Allspice
Herbs	Basil
	Bay leaf
	Chives
	Marjoram
	Onion flakes
	Oregano
	Parsley flakes
	Tarragon
	Thyme
Vinegars	White vinegar
	Wine vinegar
Oil and shortening	Vegetable or corn oil
	Solid vegetable shortening
	Olive oil
Flavorings	Vanilla extract
	Lemon extract
	Maple syrup

Table 13-2   BASIC FOOD STAPLES *(Continued)*

Food Group	Item
Flavorings (continued)	Unsweetened chocolate
	Chocolate syrup
Soups and sauces	Tabasco sauce
	Soy sauce
	Chili sauce
	Worcestershire sauce
	Steak sauce
	Gravy flavoring or base
	Bouillon cubes, chicken, beef, and onion
	Ketchup
	Applesauce
	Dry or powdered soup packets
	Canned soup (including tomato, cream of chicken, cream of celery, and cheddar cheese, to use undiluted as sauces)
Spreads and relish	Honey
	Marmalade
	Jam and jelly
	Peanut butter
	Mayonnaise
	Prepared mustard
	Pickle relish
Beverages	Tea
	Cocoa
	Coffee
	Juices (tomato, orange, lemon, pineapple)
Desserts	Gelatin, plain and flavored
	Tapioca
	Puddings (vanilla, chocolate, butterscotch and lemon)
Mixes	Cake mixes
	Pancake flour
	Biscuit mix
	Frosting mix
	Pie crust mix
	Stuffing mix
	Dehydrated mashed potatoes
Quick-meal suggestions (canned)	Tuna fish
	Sardines
	Spiced ham
	Corned beef hash
	Macaroni in sauce
	Baked beans
	Brown bread
	Whole potatoes
	Boned chicken
	Codfish cakes

Table 13-2 BASIC FOOD STAPLES (Continued)

Food Group	Item
	Chicken fricasee
	Chili with beans
	Vienna sausage
Basic fresh foods	Potatoes
	Onions
	Garlic
	Eggs
	Milk
	Sliced cheese
	Butter or margarine
	Salad greens
	Bread
	Crackers
	Celery
	Carrots
	Horseradish

rarely, if ever, used. A first rule in thinking about appliances is considering how often they will be needed and used. Some appliances do tasks that can't be done as well, or can't be done at all, in any other way. The person who loves waffles and wants them every other day will enjoy having a waffle iron. The person who thinks it might be nice to have waffles once in a while will probably find the appliance a waste of time, money, and space.

The electric toaster is one of the most commonly used appliances because it does its work better than any other appliance could. Other appliances are useful *if* the owner is willing to learn special methods and special recipes. Appliances like the blender, the slow cooker, the electric frypan, and the electric griddle require some study about all the things they can do. If the cook doesn't take the trouble to find out these things, the appliance may be of little use.

Among the appliances that seem most useful for the one-person household is the small oven/broiler. This appliance is low in price. It can save a great deal of money for the person whose landlord doesn't pay the utility bills. Cooking one hamburger in a big oven is a waste of energy and money. A smaller unit can get the job done more efficiently. Another fairly new "gadget" is an electric mini-grill, which cooks one hamburger or toasts one sandwich in minutes. This would seem to be most useful and enjoyable for the cook who

Fig. 13-10 A number of electrical appliances can be useful in the one-person kitchen as well as in the family kitchen. A small oven/broiler, for example, is relatively inexpensive and uses less energy than a full-size oven. (General Electric)

lives alone. The microwave oven (for those who can afford it or are lucky enough to have one provided in an apartment) is a modern wonder that changes many of the traditional ways of cooking. It is faster, cooler, and cleaner than standard ovens.

Stocking Up on Food

As the tools are gathered, the cook also needs "building materials." A surprising number of food items are included in the list of *staples*. These are basic elements that appear over and over again in many different dishes. A big investment would be needed to buy them all at once. Yet most of them will have to be bought sooner, rather than later, as the beginning cook tries out different recipes.

Table 13-2 on page 220 covers most of the food items that the live-alone cook will need on hand to put a variety of meals together. Some of the items are suggested for short-notice meals in a hurry.

Most are the important "supporting actors" needed in dishes featuring vegetables, meat, fish, poultry, or cheese. Most of them can be kept on hand for fairly long periods without refrigeration.

Many of the items on the list, of course, can be used straight from the can or package. A more pleasant use of it, however, is combining the elements to make hundreds of interesting dishes, from snacks to whole meals. Consider some simple possibilities. Peanut butter on a cracker is an old standby snack. Put a dab of horseradish on top of it and—strange as that may seem—find a zesty new taste. A cup of grated carrots and a cup of drained crushed pineapple combine with a package of lime gelatin to make a great salad.

Many people addicted to plain food may shudder at the thought of such inventions. As the old saying goes, don't knock them until you've tried them. Good cooking and good eating are adventures.

THINKING IT THROUGH

1. What qualities do good cooking tools have in common with the tools of other crafts and trades, such as woodworking, car repair, electronics, painting, sculpture, office work, gardening, etc.?
2. Chapter 13 points out that Americans are considered "gadget-happy." Is this true or not? Do you think that being gadget-happy is a good or bad quality? Why?
3. Explore the kitchen in your home. How many cooking utensils or appliances are there that are unfamiliar to you? How many are rarely, if ever, used? Make a list of the utensils and appliances that you consider to be essential and those that you feel are optional.

More Basics: Terms and Safety Tips

A few years ago, a New York city grandmother won a contest for cooking the best chicken soup. A New York *Times* reporter tried to get her recipe exactly for his story. Her instructions began with "a glass of water."

"What size glass?" he asked.
"Whatever size you got," she replied.

Grandmothers' recipes—a bit of this and a handful of that—seem very uncertain. They know exactly what they are doing, of course, from long experience. They simply have no clear terms for telling someone else. Recipes written in standard form do much to solve that problem. Two forms are most common. The first lists all ingredients and then tells what to do with them. The second form, often found in newspaper food columns, tells a step-by-step story of what goes into the dish and how it is prepared. Figure 14-1 shows the same recipe in both forms. It also points out some important kinds of information that *ought* to be included in a recipe.

Sometimes recipe writers forget an important point or two. They say that ingredients should be mixed "in a bowl." How large a bowl? Or they say a dish should be "cooked until done." How long a time should that be? Or they say "bake in a moderate oven." What temperature is "moderate"?

Before doing anything else, the cook ought to read the recipe all the way through. Is everything clear? Are all the ingredients on hand? Are all the right utensils on hand? Will the recipe make too much, too little, or just the right amount for the number of people to be fed? All doubts should be settled before anything else happens.

SIZE OF COOKING UTENSIL?

SEVEN-LAYER CASSEROLE

1 C uncooked rice
1 C canned whole kernel corn, drained
1 C tomato sauce
1/2 C water
1/2 C finely chopped onion
1/2 C finely chopped green pepper
3/4 lb uncooked ground beef
4 strips of bacon, cut in half

COOKING TEMPERATURE?

Use a 2-qt casserole with a tight-fitting cover. Place the rice in a layer at the bottom. Add the corn as the next layer. Pour half the tomato sauce and the water over the corn. Mix the chopped onion and pepper in a separate bowl and add it as the next layer. Add the layer of ground beef. Pour the rest of the tomato sauce over the beef. Cover the top with strips of bacon.

COOKING TIME?

Put the cover on the casserole and bake for one hour at 350°F (177°C). Take the cover off and bake about 30 min longer until bacon is crisp. Makes 4 to 6 servings.

HOW MANY SERVINGS?

SEVEN-LAYER CASSEROLE

Place 1 C of uncooked rice in a layer on the bottom of a 2-qt casserole. Add a layer of 1 C drained whole kernel corn. Mix 1/2 C tomato sauce and 1/2 C water and pour over corn layer. Finely chop 1/2 C onion and 1/2 C green pepper. Mix onion and pepper and add as next layer. Add layer of 3/4 lb uncooked ground beef. Pour 1/2 C tomato sauce over beef. Top with 8 half strips of bacon. Cover tightly and bake at 350°F (177°C) for 1 hr. Uncover and bake about 30 min longer until bacon is crisp. Makes 4 to 6 servings.

Fig. 14-1 Recipes are usually written in two standard formats. One format (top) lists all ingredients, then tells what to do with them. The other (bottom) explains in step-by-step form what goes into the dish and how it is prepared. Both formats should provide the cook with basic information.

Temperature

Most published recipes leave some questions unanswered for the beginning cook. They also have many traps for the cook who doesn't read or think ahead carefully. Suppose that the cook put the whole casserole together and then read it was to bake in a "slow" or "moderate" oven. This is a kind of cooking language that is often confusing, especially to the beginning cook. Use the following if you're confused:

Recipe direction	Oven temperature	
	°F	°C
Very slow	250	120
Slow	300 to 325	150 to 165
Moderate	350	175
Medium	375	190
High or hot	400 to 425	205 to 220
Quick or very hot	450 to 475	230 to 245
Broil	500	260

When the recipe says *preheat,* it means just that. The oven should be brought up to the proper temperature *before* the dish is put in. (This takes about 5 or 10 minutes.) Failure to do this is likely to leave the dish undercooked.

Quantities

Abbreviations used in recipes can cause trouble for the careless reader. It is not hard to recognize *lb* for pound, *oz* for ounces, and *C* or *c.* for cup. But many cooks have trouble telling the difference between *t* or *ts.,* or *tsp.* for teaspoon and *T* or *tb.* or *tbsp.* for tablespoon. There may be a great deal of difference between *2t* of garlic powder or baking powder and *2T* of the same things in a recipe.

The words for very small amounts are not very exact. A recipe may call for a *speck (spk).,* a *few grains (f.g.),* or a *pinch* of something. They all mean the same thing—an amount less than ⅛ *t.*

Fig. 14-2 Read recipes closely and measure out spices and other flavorings carefully. A stew will taste very different if you've added two tablespoons instead of two teaspoons of garlic!

Cutting the Recipe   Many cooks are completely scared off by the idea of making a recipe bigger or smaller. The live-alone cook misses many good things unless family-size recipes can be cut down to one or two servings.

How can a six-serving recipe be cut down to one or two? It is not always easy, but it is almost never impossible. It takes careful arithmetic, and sometimes a little judgment and invention. The wisest first step is doing the arithmetic all the way through. Since two servings equal one-third of the recipe, for example, you want to divide all amounts by 3. This should include the size of the cooking container (but *not* the cooking time or temperature). Figure 14-3 shows it done with a familiar recipe. The $\frac{1}{3}$ cup amounts are no trouble at all; that is a standard marking on measuring cups. The quarter pound of ground beef is equal to a big hamburger. What about the $\frac{1}{6}$ cup amounts? Well $\frac{1}{6}$ cup equals $\frac{8}{6}$ ounces or $\frac{4}{3}$ ounces or $1\frac{1}{3}$ ounces or 8 teaspoons. The teaspoon measure would

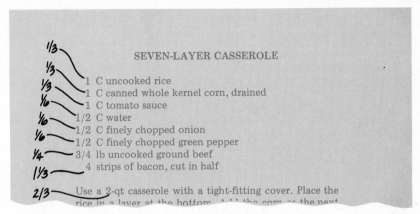

Fig. 14-3 The secret to cutting a recipe is to figure out your arithmetic carefully and to write down all the new measurements *before* you begin cooking.

be used if the cook wanted to be very exact. Close measurement is very important when using some ingredients. These may be things like baking powder or yeast, which cause baked goods to rise. Or things like flour or cornstarch, which thicken the dish. Or strong spices. In the casserole a little onion and pepper more or less probably won't make that much difference. The cook can simply estimate what is halfway to the ⅓ mark on the measuring cup.

The size of the utensil is often important to the way a dish cooks and browns. In this case, it would be hard to find a 21-ounce casserole. Cutting down to the 1-quart size would probably do. Baking a cake, on the other hand, would demand a container that was smaller, but *in proportion* to the one in the original recipe. To bake half a cake recipe, for example, the cook would want a pan about half the length and width but the same depth as the one in the recipe. Otherwise the cake would be likely to come out much differently than it was supposed to.

There are other problems. How do you measure one-third of one-fourth of a teaspoon of salt or spice? That comes out to a *pinch,* and it's pretty much the cook's guess what that is. How do you measure one-third of one egg? If it seems important, the egg might be slightly beaten and actually measured. The leftover can go into scrambled eggs the next morning. It may be enough just to use a small egg rather than a large one. Most cooks take a chance to try a change in recipes just for the sake of discovery.

A few equivalents are important to remember in cutting down recipes:

- 3 teaspoons = 1 tablespoon
- 4 tablespoons = ¼ cup = 2 ounces
- ⅓ cup = 5⅓ tablespoons = 16 teaspoons
- 48 teaspoons = 16 tablespoons = 1 cup = ½ pint = 8 ounces
- 1 quart = 2 pints = 4 cups = 32 ounces

It is also important to remember that most, but not all, measurements given in recipes are by volume—the amount of space an ingredient fills. A half cup of oil and a half cup of flour don't *weigh* the same as each other and neither *weighs* 4 ounces. On the other hand, some things like meat and cheese are listed in recipes by weight. If the recipe is cut down to 5 ounces of ground beef, that means weight and not the space it fills in a measuring cup. If the recipe says to shred 8 ounces of American cheese, that means weight. But beware. If the recipe calls for *half a cup of shredded cheese,* that means volume. Don't go out and buy 8 ounces of cheese for this purpose. Only 4 ounces of cheese (by weight) is needed for 8 ounces (by volume) of shredded cheese.

Puzzles like these may help explain why the United States is turning to the metric system of measurement used in most of the rest of the world.

The Metric System   The metric system sets standards for all measurements. It dates back to the eighteenth century and is used by most foreign countries. The United States is the last major country in the world to make the changeover. In 1975, it became official United States policy to adopt these standards too (Metric Conversion Act of 1975). American industries involved in foreign trade have already had to work with metric measurements for many years. For the rest of America, the changeover is taking place gradually. Soon, however, all Americans will use *meters* (units of length), *liters* (units of volume), and *kilograms* (units of weight) as easily as they now use feet, miles, quarts, gallons, ounces, and pounds. In fact, we will probably use metrics more easily since metric measurements are a far more logical and efficient system than our present system of measurement.

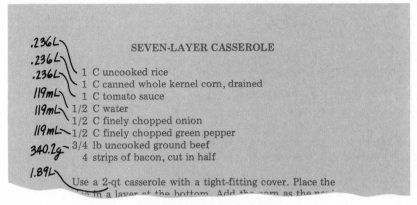

.236L
.236L
.236L
119mL
119mL
119mL
340.2g
1.89L

SEVEN-LAYER CASSEROLE

1 C uncooked rice
1 C canned whole kernel corn, drained
1 C tomato sauce
1/2 C water
1/2 C finely chopped onion
1/2 C finely chopped green pepper
3/4 lb uncooked ground beef
4 strips of bacon, cut in half

Use a 2-qt casserole with a tight-fitting cover. Place the

Fig. 14-4 Translating a recipe with customary measurements into metric measurements results in odd amounts and doesn't make much sense.

The metric system is *decimal*—based on tens, hundreds, and thousands. Units of length, for example, are made in these terms:

10 millimeters (mm) equals 1 centimeter (cm)

100 centimeters equals 1 meter (m)

1,000 meters equals 1 kilometer (km)

Compare that to our present system:

12 inches (in or ") equals 1 foot (ft or ')

3 feet equals 1 yard (yd)

1,760 yards (or 5,280 feet) equals 1 mile (mi)

There are no easy connections between our present system of measurement and the metric system. Translations are awkward. Consider these translations, for example:

1 mile equals 1.609 kilometers

1 kilometer equals .621 miles

Similarly, converting the recipe on page 226 to metric measurements would not make sense. It would end up looking like Figure 14-4.

Presently, food packaging just translates customary measures to metric measures. Metric recipes are not always readily available, although metric measuring equipment is not hard to find. When food packaging is changed (and it will be) to standard metric units, metric measuring equipment will be needed to prepare "metric" meals. But don't throw away your cookbooks or measuring equipment! In the years to come, it is likely that cooks will be using both

Fig. 14-5 Eventually, food will be packaged using metric measurements. An example is this 2-liter bottle of soda. (Pepsico)

types of measurements, one for old favorites and the other for new discoveries.

The metric measurements used in cooking are those for weight, volume, and temperature.

Weight Grams and kilograms will replace ounces and pounds. One ounce of cheese weighs about twenty-eight grams, and so you can see that the gram is a very small measure. (A paper clip weighs about 1 gram.) The kilogram is a larger unit of weight. One thousand grams equals one kilogram.

Fig. 14-6 On the Celsius temperature scale, water freezes at 0°C and boils at 100°C. (Ginger Chih)

Volume   The liter (L) is the most commonly used unit for liquid and dry volume measure. You may have already seen liter bottles of soda (a little more than 1 quart) in your supermarket. (See Figure 14-5.) Units of liters will replace gallon, quart, and pint measures. Smaller units of volume will be replaced by the milliliter (mL). About 15 milliliters equals 1 tablespoon, and 60 milliliters equals ¼ cup.

Temperature   For baking and roasting, metric recipes will include oven temperatures in degrees Celsius. The Celsius scale uses the freezing point of water (32° F) as 0°C and the boiling point of water (212°) as 100°C. Until new control dials are made available for ovens, translation from Fahrenheit to Celsius is necessary. Turn back to page 227 for common oven temperatures in both Fahrenheit and Celsius degrees.

The Verbs of Cooking

The language of cooking includes many special words and many common words used in special ways. Here is a short list of verbs— "doing" words—that are often found in cooking instructions:

Add alternately   To add part of one ingredient to a mixture, then part of another, then part of the first, etc., until both are completely mixed in.

Bake   To cook in dry heat in an oven.

Baste   To spread pan drippings or a sauce over food while it cooks. This keeps the food moist and adds flavor.

Beat   To use a hand utensil with a lifting, stirring motion to mix food smoothly. (This is also done, of course, with a mechanical or electric beater.)

Blanch   To dip food for a short time into boiling water. This is done to loosen skin (as with almonds). It is also done to ready food for freezing and canning.

Blend   To mix two or more ingredients together so that all have the same appearance.

Boil   To cook in a liquid heated to bubbling (such as water at 212°F or 100°C).

Braise To cook slowly in a small amount of liquid in a tightly covered pan on the stove top or in the oven.

Bread To coat the surface of a food with bread crumbs.

Broil To cook by direct heat under the broiler element in an oven or over hot coals.

Chop To cut food into small, uneven pieces with a knife or chopping utensil.

Cream To rub shortening, or shortening and sugar, with a spoon against the sides of a bowl until it is smooth.

Cube To cut a food into box-like pieces about a half inch on each side.

Cut in To mix tiny pieces of butter or shortening evenly into a dry ingredient like flour. This is done with a pastry blender or two knives.

Deep fry To cook food in fat deep enough to cover it.

Dice To cut food into small, even pieces. (*Diced* pieces are about half the size of *cubed* pieces.)

Dot To put small pieces of an ingredient, such as butter or cheese, from place to place on top of a food.

Dredge To coat a food with a dry ingredient, usually flour, by sprinkling the food with it or rolling the food in it. This may be done by shaking the food in a bag with the covering ingredient.

Flake To break a food, like fish, into small pieces with a fork.

Flour To dredge, or cover, with flour.

Fold To mix an airy ingredient, such as beaten egg whites or cream, into another gently. This is done by cutting down into the ingredients with a spoon or spatula, across the bottom of the bowl, then up and over, until mixing is complete.

Garnish To decorate a prepared food with touches of another, such as parsley flakes or paprika.

Glaze To coat a food thinly with a jelly or syrup for flavor or decoration.

Grate To cut a food into fine pieces by rubbing it over a grater.

Julienne To cut a food like string beans or potatoes into long, thin strips.

Knead To mix dough by folding and pressing it with the heels of the hands.

Level off To move the flat edge of a knife or spatula across the top of a measuring container, pushing away excess amounts.

Marinate To set foods for a period of time in a liquid mixture. The food absorbs moisture and flavor from the *marinade*.

Mince To cut into very small, fine pieces with a knife or scissors.

Panbroil To cook meat uncovered in an ungreased pan. Grease is poured away as it drips from meat.

Panfry To cook in a frypan with a small amount of fat.

Parboil To cook briefly in boiling water. Cooking is then completed in another way.

Pare To cut the skin from a fruit or vegetable with a knife or another utensil.

Pit To remove the stone, or pit, from a fruit, such as a peach.

Poach To cook in gently boiling water.

Pound To hit meat with a mallet or the edge of a dish. This breaks up tissue and makes the meat more tender.

Preheat To heat a pan or oven to the correct temperature before starting to cook a food.

Puree To press food through a sieve or strainer until it is smooth and soupy. This can also be done in an electric blender.

Roast To cook uncovered and without added moisture in dry heat. This is most often done in an oven. It may also be done by covering foods such as corn or potatoes with hot ashes or coals.

Sauté To cook very gently in a small amount of fat.

Scald To heat a liquid to a temperature just *below* boiling. Also to pour boiling water over a food.

Score   To make shallow cuts on the surface of a food.

Scrape   To rub off the skin of a vegetable or fruit with the sharp edge of a knife.

Sear   To brown the surface of meat quickly over high heat.

Shred   To chop food into thin uneven strips with a knife or shredder.

Simmer   To cook in a hot liquid kept just below boiling.

Steam   To cook in a covered container in the steam from a small amount of boiling water. The food does not touch the water.

Steep   To soak in a hot, not boiling, liquid. The liquid takes color and flavor from the ingredient, such as tea.

Stew   To cook slowly over low heat in a small amount of liquid.

Stir   To move food around in a container with a circular motion of a spoon or fork. This is done to mix it or to keep it from burning.

Toss   To mix ingredients by lifting them gently and turning them back into the container.

Whip   To beat an ingredient or mixture rapidly and steadily. This is done to get air into it.

Starting Safely

The basics of cookery should also include survival skills. That may sound overserious. Yet the kitchen should always be entered with caution. It is the most dangerous room in the house or apartment, the scene of more recorded accidents than any other. Hazards include electrical shock, burns, falls, cuts, fires, and food-borne illness. The cook's safety may depend on keeping the room uncluttered, well lighted, and clean. Such rules of safety are the first recipe for good health.

Electricity   Any electrical outlet has limits to what it can do. If too much energy is demanded of it, wires may become overheated, blow out, or even catch fire. Heat-making appliances, such as toas-

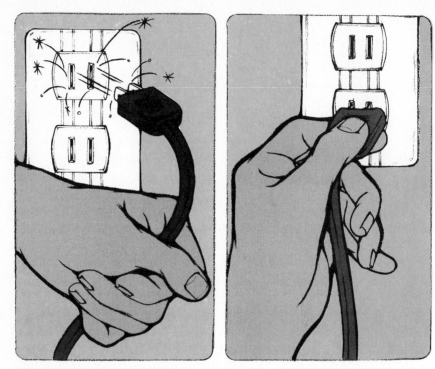

Fig. 14-7 Always grasp the plug and gently pull it out of the outlet to disconnect an appliance. This protects the cord from short circuits and you from electric shocks.

ters and electric frypans, demand a great deal of electricity. Only one at a time should be plugged into an outlet.

Electrical cords that become frayed or cracked should be repaired at once or replaced. Appliances should be removed from the outlet by a firm pull on the plug, never by a yank on the cord.

Electricity and water mix too well. The chance of electrical shock—or worse—increases when the cook has wet hands. Wet spots on the counter or floor increase the chance of shock still more.

Burns The danger of burns is almost everywhere in cooking a meal. Prevention measures begin by making sure that no utensils have loose handles or knobs that might cause them to slip or tip. The cook should not wear loose-fitting sleeves or other loose clothing that can brush against heating elements. Handles of pans should be turned in the same direction, inward on the stove top, where no one can bump into them while walking by.

Hot fat in a pan is very active. Water or other liquids dropped into it can make the fat spatter outward in burning droplets. Food should be dried off before going into fat. It should be *placed,* not dropped, into the fat.

The cook should avoid reaching over hot pans or open burners. Well-padded potholders should be used in handling utensils. The lid of a hot pan or pot should be lifted at the side away from the cook's body. The cover will act as a shield against rising steam.

The lid should be held in place with a potholder when hot liquid is being drained from food. Otherwise the food may slip out of the pan and splash the hot liquid. Hot liquid or foods should always be emptied away from the body.

Falls   Why worry about grown-up people keeping on their feet? Because falls are a main cause of kitchen injuries. The kitchen should be kept as clear of obstacles as possible. Chairs, garbage pails, and other movables should be kept where they belong, out of the cook's hurried path. Slippery spills should be wiped up *at once.* A strong stool or stepladder should be used to reach high shelves or cabinets. Chairs, boxes, or pulled-out drawers just aren't strong enough.

Cuts   The simplest rule for staying cut-free is to keep fingers away from cutting edges. The second rule is to cut down and away whenever possible. Sharp items should never be put loosely into a dishpan or a drawer. Any broken glass should be picked up at once. The tiny fragments may be more dangerous than the big pieces. They should be carefully brushed up or lifted with a few thicknesses of damp paper toweling. A glass that is stuck inside another should not be forced out. The two glasses can be separated by putting the bottom one in warm water and pouring cold water into the top one.

Fire   Fat is the biggest fire hazard in cooking on the stove or under the broiler. Care should be taken at the start. A pan should be deep enough to keep fat from bubbling over or spattering. A thermometer should be used in deep-fat frying to make sure the fat does not

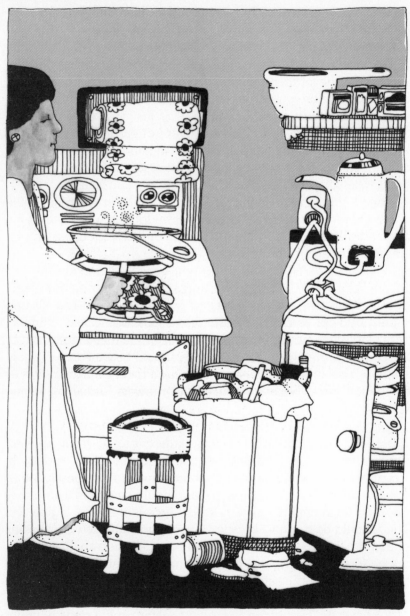

Fig. 14-8 Is your kitchen guilty of any of these safety hazards?

overheat. Extra fat should be trimmed away from meat that is going under the broiler.

Water should *never* be thrown on burning fat. It will simply splatter and spread the fire. The best move is to deprive the fire of air. If fat is burning in a pan atop the stove, turn off the heating element and put a lid on the pan. If the fire is in the broiler, slam the oven door shut and turn off the heat. Then cover any vents through which oven heat escapes.

Very small fat fires may be smothered with salt, or baking soda, *if* there is enough to throw it on by the handful. Don't try to fight a fire with a salt shaker. Call for help instead.

Other materials burn less easily than fat, but may still be dangerous. Don't leave potholders, paper towels, or plastic utensils on top of the stove. Don't leave pans on, either. Sometimes the food will burn or the pans actually melt over the heating element. A whistling teakettle may keep this from happening when the mere boiling of water is involved. But most pots and pans don't have alarms on them.

Food Contamination   Some people have an unreasonable fear of germs. Most of us, however, don't worry enough about bacteria that grow in the kitchen. Many cases of "flu" and "indigestion" are likely to originate in poor handling of food and careless kitchen management.

Places where food is prepared should be kept clear of old food particles. These include counter tops, cutting boards, the sink, and the top of the stove. Also, use clean utensils.

Some foods are more likely to cause illness than others. These include:

- *Poultry.* Always wash poultry thoroughly before cooking, and keep it in the refrigerator until you are ready to cook it. Make sure it's cooked completely before eating.
- *Pork.* All pork or pork products should be completely cooked before eating. Cook until there is no trace of pink in the meat or the juices.
- *Foods made with milk or milk products.* Keep all milk or milk product foods refrigerated. When cooking with milk, keep it refrigerated until ready to cook, cook until thoroughly heated, and

serve food immediately. If it will not be eaten right away (like a custard pie, for example), refrigerate until ready to be eaten.

- *Eggs.* Don't use eggs with cracked shells unless they are to be thoroughly cooked.
- *Canned foods.* Do not buy bent or badly battered cans. Cans that are bulging should never be used—don't even taste the food in them. Home canned foods require careful temperature control in cooking and proper storage.
- *Meats, fish, and shellfish.* Keep all meats, fish, and shellfish refrigerated until ready to cook.

The Food and Drug Administration gives these other tips for keeping food safe:

- Buy perishable foods in small quantities so that you will not keep them too long before using them.
- All cooked foods should be served as soon as possible, and never leave leftovers on the table after a meal. Store them in the refrigerator as soon as possible.
- Defrost frozen foods in the refrigerator.
- Read the labels of frozen foods carefully. Do not try to refreeze food unless the label says it is safe to do so.
- If you suspect that food has been contaminated—it just doesn't look or smell right—don't even taste it.

Once the basic rules of safety are kept in mind, cooking can become an art and a pleasure. The next chapter discusses ways of treating food—and yourself—with respect.

THINKING IT THROUGH

1. What arguments have you heard and read about concerning adoption of the metric system of measurement by the United States? Do you agree or disagree with the argument that the metric system would be helpful to all who might use it? Why?
2. The home is the scene of many serious accidents. Do you think that most people have a clear idea of the danger of accidents in the home? Or do they have a false sense of being safer at home than elsewhere? Explain your opinion.

Meals for One: Surviving in Style

Cooking for yourself is a good way to give food a fair test.

Many people grow up "hating" certain foods. They say they can't stand carrots, spinach, chicken, fish, liver, lamb, or what have you. Sometimes they've never tasted the food more than once, and they won't again.

In some of these cases, people may be truly allergic to certain foods. Milk or onions or eggs or strawberries actually make them sick. The range of food *allergies*—a clash between elements in the food and elements in the person's body—is startling. Some doctors believe most of us are *allergic*, often without knowing it, to one food or another. It may even be a favorite food, too well-liked to connect it to after-dinner discomfort, aches, or rashes. But most of us learn to dislike food that "doesn't like us."

In a far greater number of cases, people get "sick" of the cooking, not the food itself. The food may have high possibilities of good taste and good nutrition—until the cook gets at it. Home cooking or restaurant cooking causes some young people to swear off certain foods for life. The most common major crimes of cooking include:

- Overcooked vegetables, usually boiled until all flavor and texture disappear
- Wilted, badly washed salads, made still more soggy by too much dressing
- Aged and overcooked fish, served dry, leathery-looking and "fishy" tasting

These three top a much longer list of the damages done to good food. Meat seems to get the most attention in cooking. Yet some home and restaurant cooks manage to serve it burned or raw.

Spaghetti and rice *can* be cooked into tasteless, starchy clumps. Even eggs can be made tough and greasy. Many restaurants avoid confusion by coating almost everything with a thick coat of bread crumbs and dropping it into the deep fryer. That leaves clams, chickens, onion rings, and hot dogs all tasting pretty much the same. The customer who can stand one can stand any of them.

Vegetables, Salads, Fish: Handle with Care

Challenge for the person learning to cook alone: Start with some of the things you may "hate" the most. Why? Because you may never have tasted them properly prepared. Foods like vegetables, salads, and fish can demonstrate most clearly the differences that good cooking can make.

Anyone who splurges on an expensive restaurant ought to keep these differences in mind. Vegetables and salads may be the best guides to how much the restaurant really cares about its customers. The surroundings may be beautiful and the main courses delicious. If the vegetables are mushy and the salads limp, the restaurant isn't worth what it costs.

Cooking alone may offer opportunities for enjoyment that most restaurants can't match. The best proof of that is learning how to make good meals at home of the foods that many "fine" chefs seem to ruin. The lone cook can discover how good foods are really supposed to taste. It's a challenge worth a try.

How to Prepare Vegetables   *Any* cooking of vegetables produces some nutritional loss. The greatest benefits come from raw vegetables. Most vegetables need to be cooked, however, to suit taste or the occasion.

Raw   Vegetables are nutritionally best when they are fresh and raw. Try vegetable dippers as a more than ample substitute for chips or crackers. The proof may be found at a party, where they are likely to go as fast as or faster than "empty-calorie" snack foods. They serve equally well as a one-person snack, appetizer, or salad. The vegetable dippers go well with many other kinds of homemade or prepared dips.

Vegetable Dippers

Carrots, cut into pencil-thick strips
Celery, cut into strips
Radishes, whole
Green or red cabbage, cut into small wedges
Cucumber, cut into slices or strips
Cauliflower—the white flowerets
Tomatoes, cut into wedges, or whole cherry tomatoes
Turnips, cut into strips or thin slices

Choose four or more vegetables of different colors—all of them if
you wish. Arrange them on a tray, around a bowl of dip:

½ cup (c) cottage cheese
1 tablespoon (T) lemon juice
1 T mayonnaise
1 teaspoon (t) chopped parsley
1 t minced onion

Mash the cottage cheese with a fork in a small serving bowl until it is
smooth. Add all the other ingredients, and stir until smooth. Serves
four as a snack.

Simmered   Cooking in water is the most common method of preparing vegetables. Unfortunately, it also causes the greatest loss of
nutritional elements and flavor. The best cooks learn to cut these
losses as much as possible. The trick is cooking each vegetable with
the lowest possible heat, in the least possible water, for the shortest
possible time.

The rule applies even to the heating of canned vegetables. They
have already been cooked, of course, and have already lost some
vitamins to the water in the can. To cut further losses, some home
economists say, the water in the can should be drained into the
saucepan first and brought to a boil. Then the vegetables should be
put into the water and left there only until they are thoroughly
heated.

The directions on frozen vegetable packages are a good guide to
most vegetable cooking in water. A small amount of water is
brought to a boil. The frozen vegetables are then put into the water.
As soon as the vegetables thaw and the water returns to a boil, the

heat is turned very low and the pan covered. The vegetable is cooked within the time limits given in the instructions. String beans, for example, may cook 6 to 8 minutes and mixed vegetables 10 to 13 minutes. As a rule, the shorter time is worth trying for crispness and flavor. Some cooks also prefer to take the covered saucepan completely off the burner as soon as the water reaches the second boil. The heat of the water alone is enough to do the cooking.

Fresh vegetables need more preparation, of course. The extra work offers rewards of better texture and flavor. Vegetables should be washed carefully but quickly under running water. A small vegetable brush should be used if needed. Bad spots should be removed. Otherwise vegetables should be peeled as little as possible before cooking. (The only exceptions to the fast-washing rule are vegetables with tightly bunched heads, such as broccoli, artichokes, Brussels sprouts, cabbage, and cauliflower. They need to be soaked in salted water for about half an hour to draw out any hidden dirt or insects.)

The saucepan used to cook vegetables should be the right size to hold the vegetables with only a little room to spare. All-purpose rules for the amount of water to be used and the cooking time are difficult to make. They may depend on how fresh and young the vegetable is and the size of the pieces into which it has been cut. Ideally, the cooking water will have just about boiled away by the time the vegetable is cooked to the perfect tenderness and taste. In other words, cooking vegetables takes personal experience and a number of trials by the cook.

In every case, however, the water should be brought to boiling *before* the vegetables are put in the pan. Green vegetables need a little more water than white, red, and yellow vegetables. This is so because green vegetables must be kept uncovered for at least the first 2 or 3 minutes of cooking time. If kept covered the whole time, they take on a grayish color and lose flavor. The color and flavor of white and red vegetables may be protected by adding a teaspoon of lemon juice or white vinegar to the cooking water.

Steamed   Many cooks believe that steamed vegetables have the best crispness and flavor. A small amount of water covers the bottom of the pan. The vegetables are kept completely out of the water in a basket or tray. Steaming devices can be purchased which have sides that fold in to fit most pans. If special tools are lacking, the vegetables may simply be put on a dish about 2 inches smaller in diameter than the cooking pan. The dish can be put on a stand made out of a small can, such as a tuna fish can, with the ends removed.

The steaming tray is put into place and the pan covered tightly. The water is brought to a boil and kept there with the lowest heat needed to produce the steam. Steaming usually takes 5 to 10 minutes longer than boiling. It tends to leave vegetables fresher-tasting and less soggy.

Steamed String Beans

Buy ½ pound (lb) fresh string beans. Cut off the ends, and wash carefully and quickly.

Lay the beans on the steamer. This may be a specially purchased utensil. It may also be a dish that can be placed onto a tin-can pedestal. The dish should leave plenty of room to spare so that steam can circulate and so that it can be easily removed from the pan.

Put about ½-inch (in) water at the bottom of the pan. Put in the steaming tray. Cover the pan. Bring the water to a boil. Keep the heat high enough so that steam keeps circulating. Add more water if necessary.

Sample the beans for flavor and texture after 20 minutes (min). They should be ready in 30 min at the most. Serves two.

Fried Some vegetables can be nicely cooked by deep frying. French fried potatoes are a big favorite, of course. Other vegetables like onion and eggplant can be coated with an egg–bread crumb mixture or a batter and cooked in deep, very hot fat (375° F, 190°C). This method quickly seals in minerals and vitamins. It is a good way as long as the oil is fresh and clear.

Some vegetables, like mushrooms, can be completely cooked by sautéing. They are cooked gently in a small amount of butter or fat. Sautéing is usually used to soften vegetables like onions and celery before they are combined with other ingredients cooked by other methods.

The Chinese method of stir frying is one of the most useful all-purpose skills for the lone cook. Vegetables, or mixtures of different vegetables, are cut into fairly small, even-sized pieces. They are tossed and moved very rapidly so that all surfaces of the vegetables come into contact with the oiled pan.

Chinese cooks use a special pan called a *wok*. It has a narrow bottom and high, sloping sides. A regular skillet with rounded sides may be substituted, however. It is probably better, in fact, for use on an electric stove. Stir-fried vegetables have a special crispness and flavor and a thin, mellow sauce that is part of the method. Almost all fresh vegetables can be stir fried. Frozen spinach and peas can also be used in stir-fry dishes if they are completely thawed and free of loose water.

Stir-Fried String Beans

½ lb young string beans
1½ T peanut, vegetable, or corn oil
2 T water
¼ t honey
2 t soy sauce
½ t salt

Wash the string beans, cut off the ends, and slice into 1½-in pieces. Combine the water, honey, and soy sauce. Heat the oil in a 7-in skillet with sloping sides. When the oil is very hot, put in the string beans. Stir fry them for 2 min, using a spatula or pancake lifter to scoop and toss them very rapidly. Add salt and stir a little more. Pour in the water-honey-soy mixture, and heat to boiling. Reduce heat, and let simmer 5 min. The beans should be tender but crunchy. Serves two.

Baked   Some vegetables may be baked in their own skins. The list includes potatoes, of course, and sweet potatoes, squash, carrots, onions, and mushrooms. The vegetable is simply washed and laid in a baking pan. A potato will bake thoroughly in about an hour at 425°F, while squash will cook in about an hour at 325°F. Dry baking is by far the best method of preserving the minerals and vitamins in a vegetable.

Many other vegetables are stuffed, scalloped, or prepared *au gratin* for baking in the oven. Tomatoes and peppers may be baked with a variety of fillings. Scalloping involves the use of layers of cream sauce or milk and seasonings with the vegetable. Butter, bread crumbs, and cheese as the top layer are used in the *au gratin*

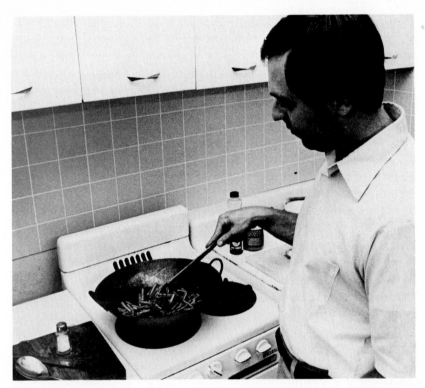

Fig. 15-1 It's easy to prepare vegetables using the Chinese method of stir-frying. First, the wok is oiled and heated. Then the vegetables are cut into fairly small pieces, dropped into the pan, and stirred rapidly. (Susan Berkowitz)

method. Often, however, the vegetables used in these methods must first be boiled or parboiled.

Scalloped Potatoes

Peel 2 medium-sized potatoes. Cut into ⅛-in slices. Grease a 1-q casserole dish that has a cover. Put a layer of sliced potatoes on the bottom. Season with a little salt and pepper. Do it with 2 t butter. Sprinkle 2 t flour over the layer. Repeat until the layers almost fill the dish. Pour ½ C milk over the top layer. Bake at 325°F for 30 min covered and for another 20 min uncovered, until the potatoes are tender and have a light-brown crust. Serves two.

How to Make a Green Salad   A salad is any cold dish served with a dressing. The salad may include mixtures of greens, vegetables, fruits, meat, chicken, seafood, and sometimes gelatin. Salads may be served as appetizers, accompaniments to the main course, main dishes in themselves, and even as a preliminary to dessert or a substitute for it.

A green salad is the simplest type of all. It offers rich amounts of vitamins, minerals, and fiber in an easy way. Yet it is often difficult to find it made well in many homes and restaurants.

A good salad starts with the purchase of the greens in the store. Iceburg lettuce is all too familiar to most people. It is easier to store for longer periods than other types. Thus it is widely used. On the other hand, it also offers less flavor and nutritional value than other types. A better salad is made by mixing in one or two or more other types of greens that are deeper-colored and more flavorful. Among these types are romaine, escarole, curly endive (also called chicory), Belgian endive, raw spinach, Chinese cabbage, red cabbage, watercress, Bibb lettuce, Boston lettuce, parsley, and mint.

The live-alone cook clearly can't keep a supply of all these types on hand. They don't keep well for long periods. The best answer is to buy those greens that can be found in small amounts, rather than a large amount of one type.

Greens should be crisp and colorful when purchased. Skip any that have limp or discolored leaves. They need to be kept fresh, too. Once they are brought home, the greens should be washed in clear running water. Wilted leaves should be removed. The core or stub of iceberg lettuce should be banged hard against the counter and pulled loose. When the greens are shaken dry, they should be put in an airtight bag or container. They should be put into the crisper drawer of the refrigerator or on the lowest shelf. (Special containers called lettuce keepers are available in many stores. They have very tight lids and help keep greens fresh for several extra days.)

When it is time to make the salad, the greens should be torn—not cut—into bite-size pieces. These pieces are put into a colander or strainer and washed again in cold running water. The water should be removed from the greens by shaking the colander occasionally. Better yet, the greens can be shaken in a clean, dry towel to remove the water. (A "spin-dry" device for doing this task can also be purchased.)

The salad greens should be served as quickly as possible. They should be covered with just enough dressing to coat the leaves. The salad may be tossed before serving in a large bowl by adding the dressing and turning the greens with a fork from the bottom up.

Many fine cooks consider a simple mixture of greens and vinaigrette dressing as the "true" basic salad. Although most restaurants present the salad first, it is also refreshing served with the main course or between the main course and dessert.

French (vinaigrette) dressing

3 T olive oil or vegetable oil
1 T wine or malt vinegar (lemon juice can be used instead)
½ t salt
¼ t pepper
¼ t paprika

Combine all the ingredients, and shake well. Try adding small amounts of these for a new taste:

dry mustard
basil
tarragon
curry powder
cayenne or tabasco
Worcestershire sauce
garlic (clove, salt, or powder)
grated onion
oregano
grated Parmesan cheese
crumbs of Roquefort or blue cheese

The basic salad can be varied in hundreds of ways by adding or substituting ingredients. The tossed salad makes a good framework for bits of leftover vegetables, meat, or cheese. A hearty chef's salad can be served as a main course. A typical chef's salad might include three kinds of greens; strips of one or more types of cheese, meat, and poultry; wedges of tomato and hard-cooked egg; and olives. The ingredients are really limited only by the cook's taste and imagination.

A Basic Salad

Add to the basic greens one or more of the following:

Other Vegetables

tomato wedges
carrot slices
onion slices or rings
celery chunks
radishes
mushrooms
cauliflower slices
green pepper strips
marinated artichoke
cucumber slices
leftover cooked beans,
    beets, potatoes, peas

Fruits

black or green olives
avocado wedges
mandarin orange segments
apple slices

Cheese

julienne strips of American or
    Swiss cheese
crumbled blue or feta cheese

Meats and Poultry

julienne strips of roast beef,
    ham, turkey, or chicken
crumbled bacon

Fish

anchovies
flakes of tuna, salmon, or other
    cooked fish
shrimp

Eggs

hard-cooked egg, slices or
    wedges

How to Cook Fish   Fish, whether bought frozen or fresh, is an excellent source of protein and is simple and quick to cook. In fact, the most important thing to remember is that fish does get done quickly, and so be careful of overcooking it. Fish is tender before it's cooked, and cooking brings out the flavor. Overcooking spoils the flavor and texture. When the flesh is milky white and moist and it *flakes* (comes up in layers) with the tip of a fork, it's done.

Most fish can be cooked in the same ways—if you know how to cook one, you can cook them all. Just remember two general rules:

1. Lean fish (also called white fish) are best cooked with moist heat—poached, steamed, or baked in a sauce. These include

flounder, haddock, cod, smelt, yellow perch, pike, and sea bass among others.

2. Fat fish are cooked nicely by dry heat—broiling, baking, or panfrying. Fat fish include salmon, swordfish, shad, mackerel, bluefish, and butterfish.

Poached   One of the most efficient meals for the live-alone cook is a poached fish fillet. (A *fillet* is a piece cut along the side of the fish. It's ready for cooking, and usually the bones have been removed. The skin may also have been removed.) Poaching is simply a matter of simmering (not boiling) the fish for a short time (5 to 10 minutes) in a seasoned liquid. Liquids you can use include lightly salted water, a mixture of water and white wine, milk, tomato sauce, or water seasoned with some or all of the following: carrots, celery, salt, pepper, parsley, onion, bay leaf, and cloves.

Poached fish can be eaten hot or cold and is usually served with a sauce. Try mayonnaise for when eaten cold. When eaten hot, the easiest sauce of all is canned soup—cream of mushroom, tomato, cheddar cheese, or cream of shrimp—taken right from the can and heated without adding any water or milk.

Fish Poached in Tomato Sauce

⅔ C canned tomatoes
1 bay leaf
1 t minced onion
pinch of salt
pinch of pepper
2 fillets lean fish, about 6 oz each
1 t butter or margarine

Grease a 7-in skillet. Cook the tomatoes and seasonings about 15 min, until the mixture begins to boil down and thicken. Add the fish fillets, and simmer 5 min. Turn very carefully, and simmer another 5 min. Remove the fish to serving plates. Strain the tomato sauce, and add the butter. Pour the sauce over the fish. Serves two. (A half cup of prepared tomato sauce may be used in place of the tomatoes and seasonings.)

Steamed   A lightly greased steamer tray or basket and a pan with a tight-fitting cover are all you need to steam fish. Add a pinch of salt and lemon juice to the water in the bottom of the pan. Set the steam tray over the boiling water (the fish should not be touching the water), and cover the pan. Cook about 5 to 10 minutes until done.

Baked   Bake whole fish or fillets in a preheated 350°F oven until just tender. To prevent drying, brush the fish with oil or butter. There's no need to turn it while baking. Cooking time takes 10–30 minutes, depending on the thickness of the fish.

Fillet of Sole au gratin

2 fillets of sole (or flounder), about 6 oz each
1 t butter or margarine
1 t flour
1 t chopped onion
1 bay leaf
⅓ C chicken bouillon
1 t lemon juice
¼ C bread crumbs

Place the fillets in a small, greased baking pan. Dissolve a chicken bouillon cube in hot water. Heat the butter to melting in a small skillet, add the flour and onion, and blend well. Add the bay leaf and chicken bouillon, and simmer about 15 min. Stir until thickened. Remove the bay leaf, and add the lemon juice. Pour sauce over the fish, and sprinkle crumbs over the top. Bake at 425°F for 20 min. Serves two.

Broiled   Brush the fish with oil or butter, and put it under the broiler. Cooking takes about 5 to 15 minutes. Thick fillets or whole fish may be turned once and oil or butter brushed on again during the cooking time.

Panfried   Bread fillets, steaks, or whole fish by dipping them in a little milk (or a mixture of beaten egg and milk) and then in dry bread crumbs, flour, or cornmeal. Let the coating dry a few minutes before cooking. Fry fish in a little melted butter or oil, and turn the fish once during frying. It will begin flaking in about 8 to 10 minutes.

Panfrying is often a smoky, smelly process. The same results without the same discomfort may be had by the method of ovenfrying.

Ovenfried   Breaded fish is baked in a well-greased pan at high heat, 500°F. The breading keeps the juices from escaping during cooking time (about 10 minutes).

How to Cook Shellfish   Shellfish include shrimp, lobster, scallops, oysters, clams, and mussels among others. These also cook up quickly and can be bought fresh, frozen, or canned.

Shrimp   Fresh shrimp can be bought in the shell or with the shell already removed. It's expensive—even more so when bought already shelled—for a family meal. For a special treat, however, it's within the range of the lone cook. Fresh shrimp cocktail can be afforded far more easily at home than in a restaurant. The shrimp should be simmered in water that has been seasoned with a bay leaf, peppercorns (about 3), some celery leaves, and a sliced carrot. Cook until the shrimp turn pink—about 5 minutes for small shrimp, longer for large or jumbo shrimp. Then shell and clean the shrimp. Peel off the shell with a paring knife. With the knife, cut a thin opening along the top to reveal the black, sandy vein (shown in Figure 15-2). Rinse under cold water to remove the vein. Chill the shrimp, and serve on some lettuce with cocktail sauce. A good sauce for a single portion is made by mixing 2 tablespoons of ketchup, 1 tablespoon of horseradish, 1 teaspoon of lemon juice, and a dash each of tabasco sauce and Worcestershire sauce. The amounts can be changed to suit your taste.

Lobster   You can buy lobsters frozen, canned, or fresh. If bought fresh, they should be alive. Keep live lobsters in the refrigerator until ready to cook. Then drop them into a large pan of boiling salted water. Cover, and boil for about 20 minutes. Serve with melted butter and lemon. Lobsters, the aristocracy of shellfish, have become scarce and gone beyond the means of most people.

Scallops   Scallops are bought already shelled, and two types are available—bay scallops (the smaller, sweeter kind) and sea scallops (a larger variety). You can bake, broil, panfry, or ovenfry scallops. When done, they'll be opaque and tender.

Oysters, Clams, Mussels If bought in the shell, you'll need to scrub them well under cold running water to remove the sand. If time permits, they should be left to stand in a pot of fresh water to which a little cornmeal has been added. The cornmeal helps to get rid of more sand and to give them added flavor. They can be steamed in the shell, or the meat can be removed (pry open the shells with a knife and loosen the meat) and then breaded and panfried. Oysters, clams, and mussels can also be eaten raw, but unless you know that the waters they come from are safe from pollution, there is the danger of getting *hepatitis* (disease of the liver). There is no danger if they're cooked.

Steamed Mussels or Clams

water
1 doz mussels or clams in the shell
2 T butter
lemon

A very small amount of water is put in a pot just big enough to hold all the mussels or clams. Add the mussels or clams, cover the pot, and bring to a boil over high heat. They are done as soon as the shells open, about 15 min. Any that do not open should not be eaten. While the mussels or clams are steaming, melt the butter in a small saucepan and squeeze in a little lemon juice. The shellfish are served with a small dish of the butter/lemon sauce and a small dish of the broth from the bottom of the pot. They are dipped in the broth and then in melted butter and eaten with the fingers. It's a messy but enjoyable process.

The Lone Cook's Repertoire

A *repertoire* is a supply of skills. An actor's repertoire is the number of roles that he or she has learned and can perform well. The repertoire of an orchestra is the number of musical pieces it has in its command. The cook's repertoire, by the same definition, is the number of dishes the cook can prepare well and with ease.

The workable repertoire of the live-alone cook is limited by time and storage facilities. The biggest problem is shopping for the right amounts of food. Most one-person apartments do not have much

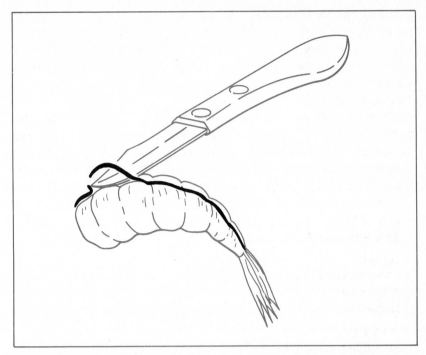

Fig. 15-2 With a knife, cut a thin opening along the top of the shelled shrimp to reveal the black, sandy vein. Rinse under cold water to remove the vein.

refrigerator-freezer space. That means most perishable foods must be used up in a fairly short period of time. The live-alone cook can't normally shop for things like turkeys, roasts of beef, or large fruits and vegetables (for example, a whole watermelon, a big eggplant, or a large head of lettuce). Such items have to be reserved for company meals. Otherwise, even if they are served several days in a row, they are likely to linger beyond safe storage time.

To add to the problem, supermarkets insist on putting small items into large batches. Such items as mushrooms, chicken legs, tomatoes, potatoes, beef livers, and artichokes are bunched into family-size packages. Sometimes the customer can get less by special request. More often, supermarket managers make small orders difficult or impossible.

Most other packages, finally, are designed for more than one person. The list of convenience foods for one begins with TV dinners and soup-for-one and doesn't go much further. A standard can of peas or pears is too much for the usual one-person meal. Even the regular loaf of bread may be too much for one person to keep fresh until it's used up. Quantity is a real challenge for the person who wants something better than a routine of TV dinners and take-out foods.

A Different Pattern   Shopping for one may require far different patterns than shopping for a family. The lone cook may have to go to market more often. Long-range planning is good for the family cook. It may not be as good an idea for the person living alone. For one thing, live-alones are more subject to last-minute invitations or changes in plans. Such freedom of action can mean waste if there are large amounts of perishable food in the apartment.

This problem can be partly solved by purchasing canned foods in the smallest sizes. Many fruits and vegetables are available in 4- to 6-ounce cans, which are just about right for one ample serving. The offering of such items is limited in most stores, however. Besides that, the unit price of these cans is usually much higher than that of the same foods in larger cans.

A somewhat better solution is the wise use of frozen foods. The needed amount of frozen peas or mixed vegetables can simply be poured from the package into the pan, for instance. If the food is frozen solid, it can actually be cut in half with a frozen-food knife or saw. The remaining frozen food should of course be quickly put in a plastic bag, tightly resealed, and returned to the freezer compartment. The same principles may be followed with cooked foods. Some live-alone cooks deliberately make twice as much as they need of dishes such as a meat loaf, a casserole, or even pancakes or waffles. These "plan-overs" should be tightly wrapped or put into a container without much extra airspace. They should be put into the freezer space at once, while they're still warm.

Without much freezer space, however, the live-alone cook is likely to depend more on fresh foods—meat, fish, fruit, and vegetables—than the average family cook. These foods can be bought in smaller quantities than packaged foods. If the supermarket will not offer small quantities, the cook may have better luck at smaller neighborhood stores. It is worth searching for stores where the customer can still buy one chop, one fish fillet, one apple, or one handful of string beans. Unit prices may be higher, but even this is

Fig. 15-3 Don't try out new dishes for the first time when you're cooking for company. You'll feel far more confident with a dish you've learned in daily home cooking. (Susan Berkowitz)

not automatically true. Small markets sometimes offer prices that are surprisingly *lower* than supermarkets for such items as fresh meat and vegetables. Any extra cost in time and money may be offset by the possibilities of greater variety, better nutrition, and less waste.

The Supply of Skills   The lone cook's repertoire needs dishes that are good, practical, and interesting *every day*. Cooking skills can't be well developed if they are used only for large gatherings. Thus the live-alone cook should try to find recipes that serve one person well, but may be expanded to serve two or four or even ten guests. One clear benefit of such recipes is the chance to practice them alone. It's not usually a good idea to try out new dishes for the first time on company. The cook is likely to feel far more confident with a dish that's been learned in daily home cooking.

The lone cook ought to know a number of dishes that are good for absorbing leftovers. For the reasons noted above, leftovers are more prominent in cooking for one than in cooking for a family.

Besides that, they're a good dieting idea. The person eating alone shouldn't feel obliged to clean the plate at every meal. That can be fattening. Food can be left over comfortably when the cook knows there is a place for it in tomorrow's salad or soup or fried rice dish.

Finally, the lone cook ought to have enough know-how for a system of "plan-overs." Even a small head of cabbage is too much, for example, if the cook can prepare it only as coleslaw. It won't become boring, on the other hand, if part of the head can be used as a salad, part of it boiled plain for the next day, and the rest scalloped with cheese a few days later. The three dishes are quite different in flavor and texture. In the same way, half a can of cream soup can be served as soup and the other half "planned over" as a sauce for fish or vegetables. The best basis for plan-overs is usually one of the cook's favorite foods. Starting from there, the cook keeps an eye on cookbooks and periodicals for new ways to prepare that food. The possibilities for many foods, such as potatoes or chicken, seem almost endless. The cook's plan-over skills may permit breaking the rule against buying larger quantities. Some foods can be prepared in so many ways that they can be served day after day without seeming monotonous.

Recipes for One

The skills of cooking vegetables and fish and making salads have already been described at the start of this chapter. They make up an important part of the repertoire of any good cook. The recipes and skills described on the following pages are suggested especially for the live-alone cook. Most are quick. Many can be changed to suit the cook's inventions and the leftover or plan-over situation.

Soups and Sauces Soups and sauces used to be the heart of home cooking. When kitchen stoves were fueled with wood or coal, many family cooks kept a big pot of soup stock simmering day in and day out. Scraps of meat and vegetables were constantly added, with water and herbs, to make the rich base for many kinds of soup. Other types of stock were made from poultry or fish. Sauces were made with great care for all sorts of special dishes.

Most soups and sauces used today come, in hundreds of varieties, from cans and packets. Most cooks have neither the time nor the patience to watch a meat stock simmering for several hours. They can simply add water to the contents of a can or a packet of dried ingredients. In many cases, as mentioned earlier, they use condensed soup directly as a sauce. Many other sauces are available in instant powder form.

Besides their many basic varieties, soup producers offer suggestions for all kinds of combinations and additions of leftovers or flavorings. Here are just a few examples:

- Sprinkle grated cheese over tomato, vegetable, or onion soup. Or drop shreds of cheddar cheese into hot tomato soup.
- Add leftover rice or spaghetti to a can of consommé.
- Add leftover flakes of tuna fish to a can of cream of mushroom soup.
- Combine leftover whole-kernel corn, a dash of Worcestershire sauce, and a dash of chili powder with canned cream of chicken soup.

The possibilities for such inventions are almost limitless. For all that, the lone cook can sometimes find both satisfaction and practical benefits in making soups and sauces from scratch. It might be done just for old time's sake. It might be done to get the just-right amount for one, or to avoid the additives in canned and powdered products. Or it might be done for the special flavor added by the cook's own efforts.

None of these motives may be enough to get the live-alone cook to make a basic meat stock. That takes 4 or 5 hours of simmering, with occasional skimming and straining and other special attention. Chicken stock, on the other hand, is a natural by-product whenever chicken is cooked in water. The broth formed by the cooking should be put in a closed container in the refrigerator. There the fat will rise to the top and harden. This layer of fat should be carefully removed and discarded just before the soup making begins.

The broth can be heated, seasoned, and served clear. Leftover pieces of chicken can be added. The soup can be "built up" still more by adding sliced onion, celery, carrots, and parsley. Shredded cabbage is another interesting addition. So is leftover ham, and perhaps a little milk.

The recipe is pretty informal, of course. One of the good things about soup is the chance to invent a dish that goes with the cook's taste and the ingredients that happen to be on hand.

Soup possibilities become much greater when the cook learns to make cream sauce (also called white sauce). This is the basic material for many different kinds of soup which can be used as appetizers or main-course dishes. It is also the base for many sauces used with meat, fish, poultry, and vegetables.

Here is a traditional recipe for a small portion of white sauce.

White Sauce

1 t butter or margarine
1 t flour
⅓ C milk
pinch of salt
few grains of pepper

Melt the butter in a skillet or saucepan. Add the flour, stirring continuously for about 5 min until the mixture is very smooth. Add the milk gradually, continuing to stir until the sauce just reaches the boiling point. Add the seasonings, and keep over low heat for 3 min.

The recipe is for a *thin* white sauce of the type used to make soup. The amount of flour and fat is *doubled* for a medium sauce and *tripled* for a thick sauce. The result is a basic ingredient that can be used in many dozens of dishes and that is fresher and more economical than store bought. Figure 15-4 includes just a handful of some uses for white sauce.

Eggs Eggs are a highly nutritious food and easy to digest. You'll find them as an ingredient in many recipes. Eggs are used in meat loaf to hold all the ingredients together. In fried foods, they hold on the flour or bread crumb coating. Eggs act as thickeners in custards, puddings and pies. They're used for decoration in salads and sandwiches. Beaten egg whites add air and lightness to soufflés and angel cakes. In mayonnaise, they keep the oil from separating and rising to the top. Shell color depends on the breed of hen and does not change the grade, nutritional value, flavor, or cooking of the

CREAM SOUPS

1/3 C thin white sauce
plus
3 oz cooked, mashed
carrots
cauliflower
asparagus
peas
mushrooms
celery
potatoes
onions
tomatoes
lima beans
spinach
fish
lobster
shrimp
. . . and more. Take your
choice, mix and match.

CREAMED VEGETABLES

1/3 C medium white sauce
1/2 C cooked celery, (or use
small onions, peas, diced
potatoes, radishes or spinach)

Drain vegetable, mix into sauce,
and heat. Salt and pepper to taste.

SAUCES

1/3 C medium white sauce
plus
1/3 C grated cheese and a pinch
of dry mustard
or
1 chopped, hard-cooked egg
or
3 oz chopped, cooked shrimp
or
1 slightly beaten egg yolk, 1 T
butter, 1 T lemon juice.
(This is called *mock
hollandaise* sauce.)
or
3 oz drained canned
mushrooms

SCALLOPED VEGETABLES

1/3 C boiled cabbage
(or cauliflower)
1/2 C grated cheese
1/3 C medium white sauce
1 C bread crumbs

Grease a small casserole dish. Put
down a layer of vegetable, then a
layer of white sauce, then a layer
of cheese until dish is filled. Top
with crumbs. Bake at 350°F
(177°C) about 20 min, until
crumbs are browned.

**Fig. 15-4 White sauce is used as the base for a wide variety of soups, sauces,
and vegetable dishes.**

egg. Remember to keep eggs refrigerated until you're ready to use them.

Overcooking is a common problem in the preparation of egg dishes. High temperatures and overcooking toughen eggs.

Eggs should not be "hard-boiled" or "soft-boiled." Instead they should be started in cold water that is heated just until the water starts to boil. For soft-cooked eggs, the pot should be removed from the burner and the egg left in the hot water for about 4 minutes. For hard-cooked eggs, heat should be reduced and the eggs simmered for about 15 minutes. Then place them under cold water. This makes them much easier to peel.

Scrambled eggs also benefit from slow cooking. They can be made livelier with the addition of grated or cream cheese, chopped ham or dried beef, mushrooms, chopped parsley, or chives. Once the eggs start to "set," they'll cook quickly, so keep your eye on them.

The omelet is regarded as an example of fine cooking. It's easily and quickly prepared for one person, or if all the ingredients are laid out in advance, a number of guests can be served. It can be served for breakfast, lunch, or dinner—as a main course or sometimes even a dessert. Most omelets are simply an egg "pancake" with filling inside. Ingredients can be bought specially for the filling, but the omelet is just as good using leftovers and "plan-overs." A partial list of the many fillings that can be used alone or in combination includes:

- Mushrooms
- Grated or sliced cheese
- Diced fresh tomatoes
- Minced cooked ham
- Mashed leftover vegetables
- Cooked fish, chopped fine and moistened with a little cream
- Diced cooked chicken, moistened with white sauce
- Small whole shrimp
- Artichoke hearts
- Any jelly or jam and powdered sugar

Sometimes, ingredients are added directly to the beaten eggs. This is done with a French favorite called *omelet aux fines herbes*

Fig. 15-5 Follow these steps to cook an omelet.

Step 1: Prepare filling and have it ready on a saucer. Break two eggs (three if your skillet is bigger than 9 inches in diameter) into a small mixing bowl. Beat the eggs briskly with a fork for a few seconds. Have a small spatula ready.

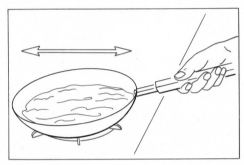

Step 2: Put 1 tablespoon of butter or margarine into the skillet. Turn heat to high or medium high. When the butter in the skillet is bubbling and "popping," empty the eggs into it. Immediately lift the skillet about an inch above the burner and shake it gently back and forth. This keeps the omelet from sticking to the skillet. Move and tip the skillet over the heat so that most of the egg runs to the sides.

Step 3: When the top surface of the omelet is still a little runny, spread the filling across the midsection of the omelet. Do this quickly, with the skillet back on the burner.

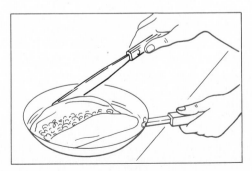

Step 4: Use the spatula to flop both sides of the omelet over the filling. Slide the omelet from the skillet to the serving plate. The whole process should take little more than three minutes.

(omelet with herbs). It's made with ½ teaspoon each of parsley, thyme, and sweet marjoram. Another version calls for 1 tablespoon of chopped onion and 1 teaspoon of chopped parsley.

Special omelet pans are sold, but it's as easily done with a plain skillet. Just make sure that the sides of the skillet are rounded, not straight up and down. Figure 15-5 shows step-by-step instructions for a basic omelet.

Meat Supermarket packaging often makes meat choices for the live-alone cook seem quite limited. The best-known beef steaks, for example, are too large for all but oversized appetites. Filet mignon, the most tender and most expensive of all steaks, is just the right size—if just one can be bought. If the lone cook wants both the right quantity and low price, beef choices often seem to come down to hamburgers and cube steaks (minute steaks).

A broader view may come from a market where the customer can still talk to the butcher. Such a friend behind the counter can provide items like a blade steak (or front of the blade) or a cut of eye of the round. These are less tender than sirloin or porterhouse steaks, but they are usually just right in size, flavor, and price for a one-serving meal. Like the more tender cuts, they are best broiled about 3 inches under the heat. Cooking time of 5 to 6 minutes on one side and 3 minutes on the other side should produce medium-rare meat. (Tender meat should never be seasoned or washed in water before broiling. Tougher cuts usually need treatment with meat tenderizer or long cooking in moist heat.)

Here is a partial checklist of meats that should be available in the right amounts for one person. Those that can be broiled (as long as they are cut ¾ inch thick or more) are marked with a star (*). Those that can be expected to provide some leftovers for one person are marked with a plus sign (+).

- *Beef.* Hamburger*; stew meat, club steak (rib steak)*+, cube steak (minute steak), rib eye steak (Delmonico steak)*, blade steak (front of the blade)*, filet mignon (tenderloin)*, beef liver.
- *Pork.* Bacon*, Canadian bacon*, loin chops*, rib chops*, ham slice*, boiled ham, sausages (such as German knackwurst and Polish kielbasa)*, pork steak+, pork tenderloin.

- *Lamb.* Ground lamb patties*, rib chops*, loin chops*, shoulder chops*, shank, kidney.
- *Veal.* Loin chops, rib chops, cutlet, calve's liver, kidney.

The following suggestions cover several types of meat and some plain and fancy skills for cooking them. Some of these dishes are old standards, while others are worth the adventure in cooking and eating.

Meat Loaf An old standby, meat loaf offers a switch from plain hamburgers. It is also a bit less expensive and provides plan-overs. The following recipe provides two servings. The second can be wrapped in aluminum foil and put in the refrigerator for sandwiches, or put in the freezer for a future meal.

The same general principles apply to dishes like veal loaf (add a tablespoon of oil or top with a strip of bacon to provide fat) or salmon loaf (skip the milk and add a tablespoon of oil and a couple of dashes of lemon juice).

Meat Loaf

1 small egg
¼ C milk
½ C dried bread crumbs
½ lb ground beef
1 T finely chopped onion
¼ t salt
pinch each of pepper, dry mustard, and garlic salt
½ t Worcestershire sauce

Mix all the ingredients thoroughly. Put into a small loaf pan (about 7½ × 3½ × 2¼ in), and bake at 350°F for about 45 min. Small individual loaves may also be baked in a muffin tin. Fill each cup about two-thirds full. Baking time in this case should be 5 to 10 min less. Serves two.

Pork and Ham Pork must always be well cooked to prevent the possibility of a pork-carried disease called *trichinosis*. This does not mean that it must be tough, however.

Simple Pork Chops

1 rib pork chop
pinch each of salt and pepper
¼ C hot water (or apple juice, pineapple juice, or red wine)
dash of Worcestershire sauce

Brown both sides of the chop in an ungreased skillet over high heat. Salt and pepper to taste. Reduce the heat, and add the liquid and Worcestershire sauce. Cover, and simmer about 30 min until tender. Serves four. (Veal chops may be cooked exactly the same way.)

Chinese cooking includes varied and delicious uses of pork. One interesting method involves putting a piece of boneless pork in the freezer. When it becomes firm (not frozen solid), it can be taken out and cut in very thin slices. The slices can then be cooked very rapidly by stirfrying, and combined with stir-fried vegetables. This helps to make a small amount of meat go a long way.

A ham steak can be expensive. Yet it is a no-waste purchase that can be bought or cut into just the right portions for one-person meals and plan-overs. Here are several suggestions for cooking a half-inch ham steak weighing 4 to 8 ounces:

1. Brown both sides under the broiler until fatty parts just start to brown. Then spread both sides with orange marmalade and broil each side 5 minutes more.
2. Bake at 325°F for about 25 minutes in a pan with a cup of milk and ½ teaspoon each of ground cloves, nutmeg, and cinnamon.
3. Sprinkle with 2 tablespoons of brown sugar, and cover with ½ cup of pineapple juice, grape juice, or any other kind of breakfast fruit juice. Again bake at 325°F about 25 minutes.

Poultry   Fresh young chicken is available all year long in many different cuts and quantities. The chance to buy just one chicken leg, one breast, or half a small broiler is a real benefit for the live-alone cook. Here is an example of a one-person recipe:

Spicy Broiled Chicken

2 chicken legs or 1 breast, cut in half
2 T melted butter, margarine, or vegetable oil
1 T white vinegar
1 t chili powder
½ t salt

In this and all other recipes, chicken parts should be washed and dried with paper toweling before cooking. Mix the fat, vinegar, chili powder, and salt. Put the chicken on the rack in the broiler pan, and set the pan 9 in below the heat. Brush the chicken with the liquid mixture. Broil 3 min, basting from time to time. Turn the chicken over, and broil about 20 min more until tender. Baste from time to time with the rest of the liquid. Serves one.

Most good meals begin long before the cook goes to work in the kitchen. Chapter 16 moves back a step to discuss some important preliminaries: budgeting, planning, and wise food-buying habits.

THINKING IT THROUGH

1. Chapter 15 notes that many restaurants—even those regarded as "fine"—serve soggy salads, overcooked fish, and badly cooked vegetables. What should a customer do about badly cooked food? Among the possibilities are (a) keep quiet and eat, (b) leave the food uneaten but tell the waitress or manager that the cooking was unsatisfactory, or (c) complain to the waitress or manager about the cooking and ask for new servings, properly cooked. Which of these do you think are correct? Why?

2. What should a customer do in a store that packages such things as fruit, vegetables, and meats in quantities larger than the customer wants or needs? Among the possibilities are (a) take what is available and try to make use of it by changing menus for the week, (b) break open the packages and take out the needed quantities, or (c) ask store personnel to make up a special, smaller package of the desired food. Which one of these approaches do you think is correct? Why?

Food Foresight: Budgeting and Shopping

Most live-alone cooks can recall being caught, at one time or another, in a funny/sad odd-lot situation. Picture this: It's payday eve. You're broke. You're hungry. Your whole food supply consists of a jar of dill pickles, a half cup of mustard, a can of peanuts, and a slab of chocolate cream pie. What now?

You might test the strength of your stomach by making do with what you've got. You might beg a dinner invitation from a friend. You might scrape a meal together by some sharp trading with a neighbor. Half of the pie, peanuts, and pickles, for example, might be a trade for some soup, bread, and cheese.

The best answer, hindsight tells you, would have been better planning a week earlier. You had plenty of cash for food then. You spent it freely at the supermarket. This led to some fine meals for a few days, and some strange combinations for the next few. Now you're munching on a main course of pickles and wondering where you went wrong.

Such a last-resort meal is a timely occasion for thinking about six ways to see it doesn't happen again:

1. Keep good records of your experiences with food and cooking.
2. Set up a food budget figure that suits you and your life-style.
3. Plan menus and food shopping to cover the longest practical period of time and the fewest possible trips to the supermarket.
4. Develop a simple system for keeping track of your food supplies and needs.
5. Shop sensibly and carefully, using all the available information you can to save time and money.
6. Learn to prevent waste by proper buying, storage, preparation, and cooking of food.

Most lists of rules sound forbidding and time-consuming. This one takes a lot less time than it saves in other ways. It can also produce a large net profit in cash and good nutrition.

Keeping Records

Good meals are often described as "unforgettable." Yet most cooks, as time goes by, have trouble recalling their hits and errors. Many good dishes, for example, are seasonal. It is entirely possible to forget them completely or to "lose" them in a collection of cookbooks during the off-season.

The obvious memory aid in this and other such cases is the traditional recipe box, stocked with 3 × 5-in cards. The recipe box is worth the effort just to store copied and clipped recipes in one compact place. But the advantages can be far greater than that. The recipe card can remind you of the extra touches and impressions that make the dish your own. If you have cut the recipe down and recorded the amounts, you won't have to do the math again. If you've made a slight mistake in preparing the dish, you can remind yourself not to do it again. If you have added or subtracted or substituted an ingredient, you can record how well (or badly) your experiment worked. You can also note what other foods went well (or badly) with the recipe. The recipe box can also include sections on such subjects as complete menus (by season, or occasion, or number of people, etc.) and recipes you want to try one day for a change of pace.

Budgeting

How much should one person spend for food? The question sounds sensible, but it may be one you can answer only for yourself. Statisticians can indeed tell you what the *average* person spends for food and what the *average* family spends. You may learn, for instance, that the average person spends about 20 percent of income for food. Yet the average lumps together a lot of people who aren't you. It may include some who spend $5 a week for food and some who spend $200 a week.

How much should *you* spend for food? That depends on your own income, tastes, and values, and the difference between what you're doing about food and what you want to do. Your budget should begin with a careful accounting of all you spend now. This expense record should cover *every* penny you spend for meals at home, meals in restaurants, and between-meal snacks for at least two weeks. Only then are you ready to ask if you've gotten your money's worth in food. You may decide you're spending far too much for what you get. You may decide you should be getting far more quality for the amount you spend. Either way, you set a target figure that suits your values and satisfactions. Make it realistic, though. A budget figure set too low may cause you to be unhappy about undereating, or overspending, or both. It is better to fine-tune your budget gradually, as you learn more about food and about yourself.

Planning

The basics of food planning are the things you know about your own tastes and life-style. What combinations of dishes are tried and true? They should form the backbone of your menus from week to week. What new dishes do you want to try? They should be reserved for days when you are sure you will have enough time to give them a fair test. Is your diet nutritious? The basic four should be a first consideration in the meals you plan. The frills—fancy desserts, appetizers, or soft drinks, for example—should be added to your menus only if you've planned for basic nutritional needs and then found you have enough money left over for extras.

How often should you shop for food? Family cooks often learn to plan menus and food shopping for a week or even two weeks at a time. This can rarely be done by live-alone cooks. For one thing, small apartments don't often have enough freezer space and other storage space to handle a long-term food supply. For another, people who live alone often appreciate their freedom to accept spur-of-the-moment invitations or simply to change their minds about eating at home. It would be a pity, however, to let fresh meat and greens go bad at home while accepting last-minute hospitality elsewhere. Thus the live-alone might learn to plan for the unexpected. This may mean food shopping two or three times a week—but it shouldn't mean shopping two or three times a day.

Fig. 16-1 Poor planning results in making several trips to the supermarket for just a few items. The wise shopper tries to plan a week's menus, make a list of all the necessary canned and packaged groceries, and do most of the shopping in one major trip. (Susan Berkowitz)

The live-alone cook should recognize a pattern of events and know how many home-cooked meals may be scheduled each week.

Taking Stock

The live-alone may go to market more often than the family homemaker. Yet the greatest part of food shopping can still be done in one major trip. Menus can be planned for seven days or more, even if they won't necessarily be served one day after another.

Then the largest amount of the food needed can be purchased in one trip to the store. All canned and packaged foods on the menus can be bought then. They won't go to waste if the menu has to be postponed for a day or two. Only perishable foods need to be purchased in other, briefer trips to the market, when the cook is sure that they will be used within a day or two.

The supply of staple foods (like those listed in Chapter 13) should be checked every week or two. They are easy to forget—but very hard to do without when in the middle of a recipe. One good practice is *writing* a note whenever a staple item starts to run low. Remember to put it in easy reach for use in doing the shopping list.

Wise Buying

Some people think of food shopping as a dull routine, hardly worth attention. That attitude may cost them dearly. Perhaps shopping is best seen as a game in which considerable amounts of cash may be lost or won each week. Consumers can "win" a great deal by learning selling strategies—especially by knowing when a "bargain" is real or not.

Good shopping tactics should begin long before the customer gets to the store. These tactics grow both from common sense and from close attention to advertising and other plentiful information about food prices and quality. One commonsense trick of menu planning is the inclusion of fresh vegetables and fruits when they are in season locally. A New England shopper, for example, will have to pay heavily for fresh strawberries and tomatoes in March. The budget will be better served by postponing these pleasures a few months. Fresh, frozen, and packaged foods may all bear different prices at different times of the year. One good guide is food store advertising. When *several* stores in your area advertise low prices on items like blueberries, corn, and potatoes, you can tell those items are in good supply.

Another type of food price special is the result of competition among food producers and stores. A favorite competitive weapon of brand-name producers is the price-cut coupon. A week's worth of newspapers and magazines may yield dozens of such coupons for various food items. They may offer cents off the purchase price listed in the store, or two items for the price of one, or return of part

Fig. 16-2 Loss leaders are items advertised by a supermarket at a price well below normal. Price-cut coupons, published in newspapers and magazines by food producers, offer items at a few cents off the regular price.

or all of the money you spend for an item. Careful attention to coupon offers can bring real savings to the shopper.

The most prominent weapon of price competition among food stores and supermarkets is called the "loss leader." This is an item advertised at a price well below normal, sometimes less than half what it usually costs. Loss leaders are not caused by oversupply of the food item, but instead by the desire of the store to bring you in and keep you as a customer for all your needs. Thus, loss leaders may offer impressive savings on items that are known to be in short supply and high-priced.

Choosing a Store   The choice of a store for regular shopping may be a matter of very personal values. Some shoppers may pick a supermarket because it is colorfully decorated, because it has piped-in music, because it has a great variety of food brands, or because it offers a range of special delivery services. Many shoppers may convince themselves, whether it's true or not, that this type of store also offers the best price values for food. If price and basic food quality are the main standards, however, it is best for the shopper to compare stores from time to time. This can usually be done *only* by actual visits to different stores for actual shopping or, if you have time, research using a typical shopping list of your own. Advertised loss leaders are a poor means of comparing stores. The shopper should look for the store that gives greatest value for the *whole* shopping list. Stores that advertise the most sensational price cuts for certain items may in fact charge a good deal more for the week's food needs as a whole.

Shopping Strategy Food shopping wisdom is generally gained through experience. A whole shelf of books might not summarize all you need to know to meet your own needs with the smallest spending of time and money. Most wise shoppers agree, however, on a starting set of rules:

1. Watch your timing. Never, never shop when you are very hungry. If necessary, have a snack before you go. Learn from experience when your store is likely to be very crowded or cluttered. Try to avoid shopping at times when the store aisles are clogged with people or with cartons of goods waiting to be stocked on the shelves.
2. Plan your route. After a few visits, you should learn where things are in the store. Make up your shopping list so that you can move through the store on a straight-ahead route without backtracking or crisscrossing the store.
3. Stick strictly to your shopping list. This rule should be bent only when you discover an item that is a true value and that you really need. A bargain is no bargain at all if it will go to waste or go unused after you get home. However little it may cost, it merely puts you over your budget.

Altogether, these three rules will help protect you from the strategies stores use to stimulate "impulse buying." The target of all these strategies is the shopper who wanders through the store without a list, trying to make food decisions on the spot. Stores use tempting signs and displays to earn extra dollars from this type of shopper. The most costly items may be put on shelves at eye level or in colorful bin displays in the store aisles. Gaudy placards may suggest that the displayed item is a "Good Buy" or a "Star Value" or simply ask you to "Look at What 25 Cents Will Buy." Think about signs like these. None of them says that the price is lower than usual. Such displays are best ignored unless they tell the shopper both the sale price and the regular price of the item.

Shopping wisdom grows with study. It's a good idea, for example, to compare the prices of the same food in different forms. Will you find the best combination of price and quality by buying fresh oranges, bottled or canned orange juice, or frozen orange juice concentrate? Are fresh, canned, or frozen string beans your best buy? Answers to such questions can be helpful and money-saving. On the other hand, the search for answers may increase your travel time in the store and expose you to more possibilities of impulse buying. It's best, perhaps, to study such questions separately before you start throwing items in your shopping cart.

Many valuable comparisons can be made without departing from your shopping list. What box of cereal is the best buy for you? You'll have to think about price, quantity, and quality of different brands and sizes. Some are far different in quality or nutritional value. The nutritional label will give you this information. If it's not on the label, you may simply have to buy and try different products to find out which you like best. The "house brand" of cereal (bearing the store's own label) may be far lower in price but also lower in grade than the nationally advertised brand. Yet the house brand may taste as good or even better to you. You can only find that out by trying some.

If there's no nutritional labeling, or if you can't tell the difference in quality, rely on price to guide your purchase. But higher prices don't always mean higher quality. And prices can be hard to compare because the size of the package is different. Some containers that look the same may actually hold different amounts too. Prices for different-sized packages can be compared by figuring out the cost per unit, for example the cost per ounce, per pound, or any other standard measure. More and more supermarkets are displaying unit prices because it's required by law or because of store policy (often under the pressure of consumer groups). If unit prices are

```
 D M PEAS
   SIZE    17 OZ.

 UNIT PRICE          YOU PAY
   42.4¢ 16 OZ.       $.45¢
```

```
 KEY PEAS LARGE
   SIZE   16 OZ.

 UNIT PRICE          YOU PAY
   39.0¢ 16 OZ.       $.39¢
```

Fig. 16-3 Containers that look the same may actually hold different amounts. Read the label to find out the volume of the package. Some stores display unit price information. If your store doesn't, you can figure it out easily. Simply divide the price by the quantity for each item you're comparing. (Susan Berkowitz)

displayed, as in Figure 16-3, use them to compare the cost per unit of different sizes and different brands.

If unit prices are not displayed, you'll need to figure out the unit price yourself. A little arithmetic know-how is all you need. It's simply a matter of dividing price by quantity for each item you are comparing. If you were always bad at arithmetic, remember that estimating can sometimes give you the information you need. Before starting, remember some basic equivalents: 16 ounces = 1 pound; 16 fluid ounces = 1 pint; 32 liquid ounces = 1 quart.

Some decisions need common sense only. If lettuce is being sold at 39 cents a head, for example, you may want to buy the biggest, heaviest head on the counter. If it is priced at 39 cents *a pound,* however, you may find it budget-wise to buy a smaller head.

Read. Think. Then hundreds of skills like these can become part of your shopping adventures. Once you've started to master the arts of both shopping and cooking, you may want to demonstrate your accomplishments to friends.

THINKING IT THROUGH

1. Guess what hot dogs cost this week. Guess what a sirloin steak costs. Guess what _____ costs. Perhaps you can try calling out your estimates of prices on specific food items in a sort of auction style. How wide a range do the estimates cover? How many in the class have a relatively good idea of what food costs? How many estimates are far off?
2. How many styles of selling food can be found in your community? Which style do you find preferable? Why?
3. Practice comparison shopping. Choose a couple of your favorite packaged foods that are sold in more than one size. Compare the price, quantities, and unit prices of the various sizes and decide which is the best buy.

PART FOUR

All About Clothes

Find Your Own Look

When fashion writers look back on the 1970s, they will surely call that period the "Dungaree Decade." But this term would not tell the whole story. It's true that the denim craze swept the nation. More importantly, though, it led to a "Clothing Revolution."

At first, people didn't want to spend money on what might have been just another fad (a short-lived fashion). But denims grew from a fad into a standard of dress for students everywhere, and they were soon being worn by many fashion-conscious adults. The result was something that rarely happens in the fashion industry: people were wearing the same style of clothing for nearly 10 years! But even more important than this development was the change in attitudes toward clothes that went along with it.

The denim fad was started by the students of the 1970s. It soon led the way to a freedom of choice in clothing for everyone. Rules and regulations about how to dress became more relaxed. People started dressing to please themselves instead of others. Today, wherever you look, on a college campus or in a supermarket, you see people dressed in all sorts of outfits. Everyone is doing their own thing. But while society no longer tells you what to wear, certain standards still apply to how you look.

What Is Your Appearance Quotient?

How many times have you judged someone just on how they look? How many times have you yourself been judged that way? Suppose you're at a party and two men walk up to you. One is dressed in a three-piece suit and the other is wearing jeans and a shirt. The man in the suit needs a shave, his tie is stained, and his white shirt is a dirty gray. The man wearing jeans, however, has on a freshly ironed shirt, his boots are shined, and his beard is neatly trimmed. Which man gives the better impression? Of course, it's the one who is neat and well groomed. His *appearance quotient* is high, and your first impression of him will be a good one.

What does "looking neat" mean? People generally agree that it includes the following standards:

- Clothes that are clean and pressed
- Shoes that are shined and in good repair
- Clean hands and fingernails
- Clean, well-trimmed hair
- Weight that's in the "normal" range
- A clothing style that fits the occasion

The last item on this list is the one that causes the most problems. It's often hard to figure out what to wear. If you're going skiing, you know you'll need warm sweaters and pants, boots, gloves, and a hat. But if you're going on a job interview, you may not know how formally or informally to dress. Standards for on-the-job clothing have become more relaxed over the past few years as a result of the clothing revolution. But this sometimes causes more problems than it solves. Some bosses allow you to wear jeans to work. Others insist that you dress more formally or conservatively. The best way to find out what you should wear is to visit the firm before the interview and see how the employees are dressed. However, this isn't always practical. You can ask about clothing regulations during the interview, but by then it may be too late. That all-important first impression has already been made. If you can't get to see what the other employees wear ahead of time, the next best choice is to dress up a bit more than usual. This doesn't mean that you should wear a dinner jacket or a sequined dress. A plain, knee-length dress for women and a suit or jacket and tie for men are fine.

Dressing conservatively may not get you the job, of course. Other things, such as talent, background, and experience, are important considerations. But looking neat certainly won't count against you. Moreover, it's a well-known fact that when two people of equal ability apply for the same job, appearance can be the deciding factor.

What to wear to a party can be just as puzzling a question as what to wear to a job interview. If you're getting together with a bunch of friends, you usually don't have to worry about this. But a dance or dinner party often presents a problem. Must you wear a dress or will

Fig. 17-1 You don't have to be Sherlock Holmes to discover how to dress for an interview at a particular firm. Visit the firm beforehand if possible, to see how employees dress. If you can't do this, then just dress conservatively and you can't go wrong.

a pantsuit be all right? Should you wear a suit rather than a turtleneck and sports jacket? The easiest solution is to call your host or hostess and ask what the other guests are wearing. But what if you don't know the person who's giving the party? Again, your best bet is to dress up a little more.

If you're going to a restaurant and don't know what to wear, there's one rule of thumb you can follow: the more expensive the restaurant, the more formally you have to dress. Most restaurants now allow women to wear pants, but many still insist on jackets and ties for men. A call to the restaurant can usually settle the question.

The Principle of Building on Basics

Unless you're very wealthy, it's almost impossible to have a different outfit for every occasion. But you've surely known or seen people who never seem to wear the same thing twice. Since they all can't be rich, how do they manage to have such large wardrobes? The answer is that they follow the principle of *building on basics* (BOB).

The BOB principle means choosing a basic color and classic lines as the basis for your wardrobe. *Basic colors* are those that can be worn with many other colors. For example, black, gray, white, beige, brown, and medium to dark blue are basic colors. Your personal taste, skin tone, and hair shade should guide your choice of a basic color that's most flattering to you. Finding your best basic color will be easier after reading Chapter 18.

The other part of the BOB principle—*classic lines*—refers to styles that have passed the fad status and become steady favorites in the fashion world. Trench coats, blazers, A-line dresses, and single- and double-breasted coats and suits are all examples of classic styles. (You'll learn more about these styles in Chapter 18.) Figures 17-2 and 17-3 show how different outfits can be made using the same basic suit. The trick is to mix and match different blouses, shirts, and other accessories with the classics. Such *coordinates* don't have to be expensive. A piece of costume jewelry, a belt, or a scarf can change the dress you wore to school into the dress you'll wear to dinner. Take off your tie, slip a crewneck sweater over your shirt, and put on a pair of loafers, and you're set to go from the office to a party. By using the BOB principle, you can easily have a wardrobe that fits your needs and your life-style.

Anything Goes?

By now, it must sound like all we're giving you are rules and regulations about what to wear and when to wear it. What happened to all

Fig. 17-2 By using different types and other accessories with the same classic style suit, you can put together two totally different outfits.

that freedom of choice you read about at the beginning of the chapter? Why can't you wear what you want when you want to? Why have any guidelines at all?

Fig. 17-3 Here again, by changing the shirt and other accessories, you give a classic suit two completely different looks.

Well of course you can wear anything you want to. There's no law that says you can't wear brown socks with a blue suit. If you feel comfortable going to a formal dance in blue jeans and a torn T-shirt, do so. But most people wouldn't feel at ease dressed like that. The suggestions in this book are not unbreakable rules that must be blindly followed. They are meant as guides to help you feel comfortable in any situation. But this doesn't mean that you can't wear the clothes you like. The trick is in knowing *when* to wear them!

The following chapters offer some helpful tips on how to get and maintain the look you want. The topics include finding the correct size and color clothing; cleaning and storing clothes; taking care of stain removal; and sewing and mending.

THINKING IT THROUGH

1. Employers often have written rules about the dress and appearance of their employees. Sometimes the rules may seem overly strict or arbitrary. If you were the owner of a new department store which was about to open in a small shopping mall, what rules, if any, would you make about the personal appearance and clothing of sales employees? If you were the owner of a new French restaurant, what *grooming* regulations would you make for waiters and waitresses?

2. It sometimes seems as if fashion and styles change so fast that a person would have to spend a small fortune just to keep up with the fads. However, it is not always clear how fads or style changes come about. Who do you think is responsible for these changes, the public or the fashion and clothing industry? Does one lead and the other follow? Give examples.

3. What are the prevalent social attitudes and expectations about dress in your school? In your community? Among your friends? Are there major differences among these groups or are the attitudes and expectations generally the same?

Analyze Your Clothing Needs

18

Suppose a friend asks you to go shopping with her for a new dress. She is going to a fancy party and isn't sure what kind of dress to buy. Also, she's a little overweight, so she sometimes has trouble getting a good fit. After looking at a few dresses, your friend chooses a long, cotton "granny" dress in a large, flowered print. The dress is pretty, its colors look good on her, and it's a perfect fit. Still, you advise your friend not to buy the dress. Why?

Your first reason is that it's not dressy enough. Even though the dress is long, it's too informal and casual for a fancy party. Secondly, the type of print is wrong for your friend's figure. She is already overweight, and the large flowers make her look even heavier. Finally, this type of dress is out of style. Granny dresses are an example of the fads you read about in Chapter 1. While many people were wearing them a few years ago, they are no longer considered fashionable.

Unless you know what to look for, it's often hard to tell whether something looks good on you or not. This chapter will help you in choosing the clothes that best fit both your needs and your figure or build.

There are three things you should consider when buying clothes:

- Function: Does it fit your needs? Does it look right for when you're going to wear it?
- Flattery: Does it fit well? Do the colors and lines look good on you?
- Fashion: Is it in style?

Function

Some people always seem to know just what to wear for any occasion. If you aren't one of those people, don't give up hope. No one

289

Fig. 18-1 When you buy a suit or any other clothing, consider the three F's—function (does it fit your needs?); flattery (does it fit well?); and fashion (is it in style?).

is born with this ability. It's a skill you get by watching how others dress in different situations. Not that you want to look like a carbon copy of everyone else. But you probably don't want to stand out like a neon sign either!

Chapter 1 gave you some suggestions on how to dress when you're not sure what other people will be wearing. As you become more and more familiar with different situations, you will find that choosing the right clothes becomes less of a problem. After you've been to four or five dinner parties, you will know what to wear to the next one. After watching the way your boss and co-workers dress, you will no longer be in doubt about what to wear to work. If an invitation says "formal," you know that women should wear a long gown and men should wear a tuxedo or a very dressy suit.

The toughest decision is usually choosing what to wear when you're going to a place for the first time. As we discussed in Chapter 1, in situations like this it's best to wear something that's in-between—not too dressy and not too casual. For women, this means basic dresses and suits. For men, it means basic suits or jackets and slacks. The building on basics principle explained in Chapter 1 applies here. A basic outfit is one that has simple, unclut-tered lines, is in a basic color, and can be dressed up or down with different shirts, sweaters, and other accessories.

At this point, you're probably wondering if you have to give up your personal style in order to dress "properly." The answer is "No!" Once you know the type of clothes to wear, you can add your own personal touches. One way of doing this is to wear accessories that you like and feel comfortable with. Another way is to choose clothes in a style that flatters you. The next section, on flattery, will show you how to choose the clothes that look best on you.

Flattery

There are three things to look for when choosing clothes that will flatter you: fit, color, and line. All are equally important.

Fit   In order to get the right fit, you must know your own figure type. The easiest way to learn this is to take a complete set of body measurements (best done in your underwear), as shown in Table 18-1.

Table 18-1   TAKING BODY MEASUREMENTS

Body part/how to measure	Diagram
	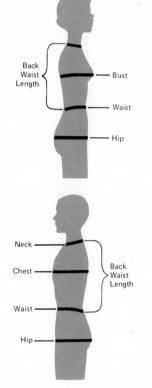

Neck (men): Pull tape measure loosely in to base of neck.

Bust or chest: Measure loosely over fullest part. Tape should slant slightly down in the back.

Waist: Pull tape snugly around the same spot you'd wear a belt.

Hip: Pull tape snugly over the fullest part.

Back waist length: Measure the distance between the bone at the back of the neck and the back of the waist.

Inseam: Measure from the center of the crotch, down the inside of the leg to whatever length (for example, shoe top) you wear your slacks.

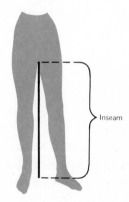

Table 18-1   TAKING BODY MEASUREMENTS

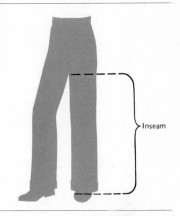

Inseam

Arm (sleeve length): Measure in stages. Start at the bone at the back of the neck and measure out to the center of the shoulder bone. Hold the tape in place with a finger and measure from there down to a slightly bent elbow. Hold the tape in place at the elbow, then measure down to the wrist bone.

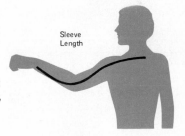

Sleeve Length

Bust (for bra size): *Chest:* Measure under armpits, above any bust fullness. Pull tape snugly. *Over bust:* Measure over fullest part. Slant tape down slightly in the back. Keep tape loose. *Band:* Measure directly under the bust in the front and down slightly in back. Pull tape snugly.

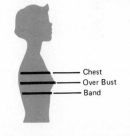

Chest
Over Bust
Band

Before you can convert body measurements into sizes, you must also know how tall you are. But height is not as important as two other measurements: the length of your *trunk* (the distance between your shoulders and your legs) and the length of your *inseam* (the inside length of your leg). For example, suppose you and your friend are both 5 feet (ft) 10 inches (in) [178 centimeters (cm)] tall.

Fig. 18-2 These two people are the same height but should dress differently because they have different builds. The woman on the left should wear solid, dark colors and vertical stripes. The woman on the right should wear light colors and horizontal stripes. (Ginger Chih)

You have a short trunk and long legs. Your friend has a long trunk and short legs. Though you're both the same height, you would each have to take a different size jacket. Since it's hard to do it alone, ask someone to measure your height and your trunk length.

Adults have a wide range of body builds. The clothing industry uses different names to describe different size categories. But some of these names sound more like age groupings. Be careful not to get confused. "Junior" and "Young Men" do not mean that the clothing is for young people only. They mean that the clothes are made to fit the measurements of that size category.

Women's Sizes   Table 18-2 is a sizing chart for women. It will help you to figure out what size to look for when you shop. The measurements are not exact: they can be a couple of inches larger or smaller and still fit.

Women's separates are sold both by body measurements and by sizes. If you have a 36-in [91.5-cm] bust, you should buy a size 36 blouse or sweater. If you have a 26-in [66-cm] waist, you would buy a size 26 pair of slacks or skirt. However, if your hips are more than 12 in [30.5 cm] larger than your waist, choose the size that fits your hips and alter the waist.

Women's underwear and sleepwear are often marked Small (S), Medium (M), Large (L), Extra Large (XL), and Extra, Extra Large (XXL). As a rule, Small fits sizes 6–8; Medium, sizes 10–12; Large, sizes 14–16; Extra Large, 18–20 and 38; and Extra, Extra Large, sizes 40–42. Panties go from size 5 (the smallest) upward. The conversion chart from hip measurement to size is usually on the package. If you're in doubt, ask the salesperson.

Wearing the right size bra is important for your posture and comfort as well as for looking good. A bra should cover the bosom completely in front. It should also be small enough around so that the band rests well down on the back. After taking your bust measurements, look at Table 18-3 to see if you're wearing the right size.

Your measurements might be a little different from those given in the table. If they are, the following rules can be used. Chest measurements measure the "around" size of a bra. Band measurements are generally 4 to 5 in [10-12.5 cm] less. Cup sizes depend on the difference between the chest and over-bust measurements. For example, 1 in [2.5 cm] equals an A cup, 2 in [5 cm] equal a B cup,

Table 18-2 SIZING CHART FOR WOMEN

Size Categories	Characteristic body builds			
	Height	Back and shoulders	Back waist length	Bust and hip to waist ratio
Misses: Even numbers, sizes 6–20; size 6 = 33 in–23 in–33 in [84 cm–58.5 cm–84 cm] (Add 1 in [2.5 cm] for each larger size.)	5 ft 6 in [167.5 cm]	Broad	15½–17¼ in [39.5–44 cm]	*Bust:* 10 in [25.5 cm] larger than waist; *Hips:* 10–12 in [25.5–30.5 cm] larger than waist
Tall Girls: Same as Misses	5 ft 7 in [170 cm] and over	Broad	17–19 in [43–48.5 cm]	Same as Misses
Misses' Petite: Even numbers, sizes 6–16; measurements same as Misses	5 ft 3 in [160 cm]	Broad	14½–15¾ in [37–40 cm]	Same as Misses
Junior: Odd numbers, sizes 5–15; size 5 = 32 in–23 in–33 in [81.5 cm–58.5 cm–84 cm] (Add 1 in [2.5 cm] for each larger size.)	5 ft 4 in [162.5 cm]	Narrow	15–16¼ in [38–41.5 cm]	*Bust:* 9–10 in [23–25.5 cm] larger than waist; *Hips:* 10–12 in [25.5–30.5 cm] larger than waist
Junior Petite: Odd numbers, sizes 3–13; measurements same as Juniors	5 ft [152.5 cm]	Narrow	14–15¼ in [35.5–38.5 cm]	Same as Juniors
Young Junior/Teen: Sizes 5/6–15/16; size 5/6 = 30 in–22 in–30 in [76 cm–56 cm–76 cm] (Add 1 in [2.5 cm] for each larger size.)	5 ft 2 in [157.5 cm]	Narrow	13½–15¾ in [34.5–40 cm]	Bust and hips 8 in [20.5 cm] larger than waist
Women's: Even numbers, sizes 38–50; size 38 = 44 in–35 in–44 in [112 cm–89 cm–112 cm] (Add 2 in [5 cm] for each larger size.)	5 ft 6 in [167.5 cm] and over	Broad	17¼–18 in [44–45 cm]	Bust and hips 9 in [23 cm] larger than waist
Half sizes: Even numbers, sizes 10½–24½; size 10½ = 35 in–27 in–35 in [89 cm–68.5 cm–89 cm] (Add 2 in [5 cm] for each larger size.)	5 ft 2 in [157.5 cm]	Narrow	15–16¼ in [38–41 cm]	Bust and hips 8 in [20.5 cm] larger than waist

Table 18-3 DETERMINING BRA SIZES

Bra size	Body part	A cup in	A cup cm	B cup in	B cup cm	C cup in	C cup cm	D cup in	D cup cm
32	Chest	32	81.5	32	81.5	32	81.5	32	81.5
	Over bust	33	84	34	86.5	35	89	36	91.5
	Band	27–28	68.5–71	27–28	68.5—71	27–28	68.5–71	27–28	68.5–71
34	Chest	34	86.5	34	86.5	34	86.5	34	86.5
	Over bust	35	89	36	91.5	37	94	38	96.5
	Band	29–30	73.5–76	29–30	73.5–76	29–30	73.5–76	29–30	73.5–76
36	Chest	36	91.5	36	91.5	36	91.5	36	91.5
	Over bust	37	94	38	96.5	39	99	40	101.5
	Band	31–32	78.5–81.5	31–32	78.5–81.5	31–32	78.5–81.5	31–32	78.5–81.5
38	Chest	38	96.5	38	96.5	38	96.5	38	96.5
	Over bust	39	99	40	101.5	41	104	42	106.5
	Band	33–34	84–86.5	33–34	84–86.5	33–34	84–86.5	33–34	84–86.5
40	Chest	40	101.5	40	101.5	40	101.5	40	101.5
	Over bust	41	104	42	106.5	43	109	44	112
	Band	35–36	89–91.5	35–36	89–91.5	35–36	89–91.5	35–36	89–91.5

and so forth. If your measurements are 32-in [81.5-cm] chest, 33-in [84-cm] over bust, and 27- to 28-in [68.5-71-cm] band, you would wear a size 32A bra. For a bust this small, a bra is not absolutely necessary. But if you are more than an A cup, you should wear a bra for support. Without one, breasts will tend to sag over a period of time.

Men's Sizes   There are two basic size categories in men's clothing: Young Men's (Cadet or Collegiate) and Men's. If you are less than 5 ft 9 in [175.5 cm] tall, you will probably find a better fit in the Young Men's department. Table 18-4 will help you choose the best size for you.

As mentioned earlier in the chapter, your trunk length is as important as your overall height in figuring out what length jacket or suit to buy. Most jackets should end where the leg begins. The best coat length for most men is one that touches the knee. If you have a very long trunk and short legs or are taller than average, coats that come just above the knee will be most flattering.

A Short suit allows for 28- to 30-in [71- 76-cm] pants; a Regular allows for 30- to 32-in [76- 81.5-cm] pants; and a Long has 32- to 34-in [81.5- 86.5-cm] pants. To avoid expensive alterations, trousers are usually sold unfinished at the bottom. Cuffs and hems are then made to fit.

Slacks come in nearly every size and shape. For example, they are sized according to crotch depth ("high rise" for men who are short- or high-waisted and "low rise," or hip-huggers, for men who are long-waisted); hip and leg size (Slims, Regulars and Huskies); and inseam lengths.

If you are taller than 6 ft 2 in [188 cm] or larger than a size 48, you will probably have to buy your clothes at a specialty store. To find such a store near you, look in your local yellow pages under "clothing."

Men's dress shirts come in neckband–sleeve-length measurements: 14-33, 15-34½, 16½-35, and so forth. The first figure is the neck size. Shirts should be bought ½ in [1.3 cm] larger than what your neck actually measures. The second figure is the sleeve length. The sleeve length should match your arm length exactly.

The neckline of a dress shirt is designed to be worn with a tie or some other type of neckwear. Dress shirts are made with many

Table 18-4 SIZING CHART FOR MEN

SIZES

CATEGORIES

Young men's

	14 in	14 cm	16 in	16 cm	18 in	18 cm	20 in	20 cm
Neck	13	33	13½	34.3	14	35.5	14½	36.8
Chest	32	81.5	33½	85.3	35	89	36½	92.8
Waist	27	68.5	28	71	29	73.5	30	76
Hip	32½	82.8	34	86.5	35½	90.3	37	94
Height	5 ft 1 in	155	5 ft 4 in	163	5 ft 6 in	168	5 ft 8 in	173
Sleeve	29	73.5	30	76	31	78.5	32	81.5
Backwaist	14	35.5	14¾	37.5	15½	39.3	16¼	41

Men's

	34 in	34 cm	36 in	36 cm	38 in	38 cm	40 in	40 cm	42 in	42 cm	44 in	44 cm*	46 in	46 cm	48 in	48 cm
Neck	13½	34.3	14	35.5	14½	36.8	15	38	15½	39.3	16	40.5	16½	41.8	17	43
Chest	34	86.5	36	91.5	38	96.5	40	102	42	107	44	112	46	117	48	122
Waist	28	71	30	76	32	81.5	34	86.5	36	91.5	38	96.5	40	102	42	107
Hip	35	89	37	94	39	99	41	104	43	109	45	115	47	120	49	124.5
Height	5ft 10in	178	5ft 10in	178	5ft 10in	178	5ft 10in	178	5ft 10in	178	5ft 10in	178	5ft 10in	178	5ft 10in	178
Backwaist	17½	44.3	17¾	45	18	46	18¼	46.5	18½	47.3	18¾	48	19	48.5	19½	49

different collar styles. You will learn more about choosing a flattering collar style in the section on line.

Some stores sell shirts, suits, and jackets that are *tapered* (cut in) to fit a waist that is smaller than the standard waist, which is 6 in [15 cm] smaller than the chest. This tapered cut, called the "Continental" or "European" style, has a waist that is 7 in [18 cm] smaller than the chest. This style is good for broad-shouldered, slender-waisted men who usually have to have the waists altered on pants and jackets.

Men's sleepwear and underwear are usually marked Small (S), Medium (M), Large (L), and Extra Large (XL). Chest and waist measurements are also given. T-shirts made of 100 percent cotton tend to shrink in length when laundered, so buy them longer than needed. Sports shirts and sweaters are also marked S, M, L, and XL. Generally, Small fits sizes 32–34; Medium, sizes 36–38; Large, sizes 40–42; and Extra Large, sizes 44–46.

Fitting Pointers   Many clothing manufacturers realize that standard body measurements, as given in Tables 18-2 and 18-4, are not always exact. So it's a good idea to find brand names or manufacturers that cut their clothes closest to your figure type. Even then, minor alterations may be needed. If you don't want to be bothered with altering clothing, you can buy separates or have your clothes *custom made;* that is, you select the material and a tailor makes your clothes to your actual measurements.

Figures 18-3 and 18-4 show some fitting pointers to check when trying on a shirt, slacks, or a suit. After studying these illustrations, you should be ready to go out and buy perfectly fitting clothes. But a perfect fit is only one part of looking your best. Choosing the right colors is equally important.

Color   Color is the second part of "flattery" to consider when choosing clothes. It is often the reason why you receive so many compliments when you wear a certain outfit. But be careful not to fall into the "favorite color" trap. What looks good on you and your favorite may not be the same color. Finding the colors that flatter you the most depends on three things: skin color, hair color, and general body build.

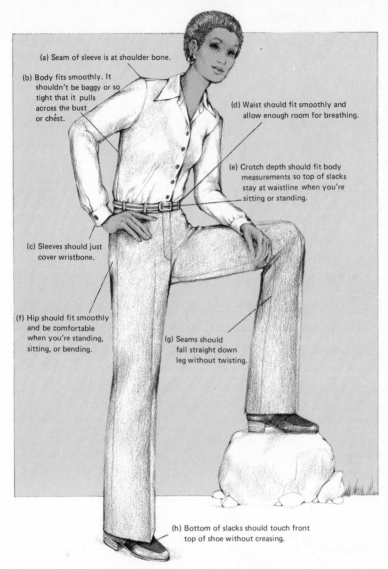

(a) Seam of sleeve is at shoulder bone.

(b) Body fits smoothly. It shouldn't be baggy or so tight that it pulls across the bust or chest.

(d) Waist should fit smoothly and allow enough room for breathing.

(e) Crotch depth should fit body measurements so top of slacks stay at waistline when you're sitting or standing.

(c) Sleeves should just cover wristbone.

(f) Hip should fit smoothly and be comfortable when you're standing, sitting, or bending.

(g) Seams should fall straight down leg without twisting.

(h) Bottom of slacks should touch front top of shoe without creasing.

Fig. 18-3 Here are some fitting pointers to look for when trying on shirts and slacks.

But before considering these three factors, you should understand some of the words used in the language of color.

- *Color, hue,* and *tone* all mean the same thing. They refer to the many combinations of the three *primary colors* (yellow, blue, and

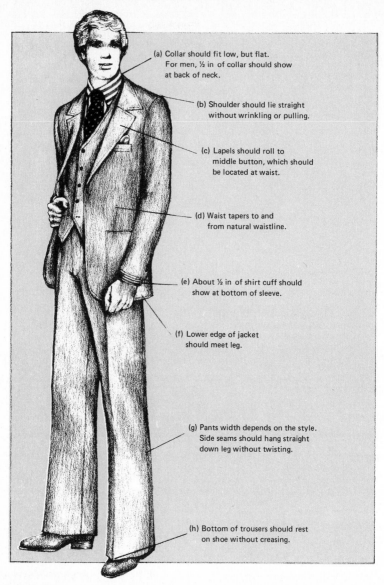

(a) Collar should fit low, but flat. For men, ½ in of collar should show at back of neck.

(b) Shoulder should lie straight without wrinkling or pulling.

(c) Lapels should roll to middle button, which should be located at waist.

(d) Waist tapers to and from natural waistline.

(e) About ½ in of shirt cuff should show at bottom of sleeve.

(f) Lower edge of jacket should meet leg.

(g) Pants width depends on the style. Side seams should hang straight down leg without twisting.

(h) Bottom of trousers should rest on shoe without creasing.

Fig. 18-4 Here are some fitting pointers to look for when trying on suits.

red) from which all other colors are made. They also refer to the values of those colors. The same words are also used for the two noncolors: white (the absence of all colors) and black (the combination of all colors).

- *Tint* is any color that is made lighter by adding white.

- *Shade* is any color that is made darker by adding black.
- *Value* is the amount of light (tint) and dark (shade) in a color.
- *Pure colors* are bright, clear hues of full intensity.
- *Intensity* is the strength or weakness of a color.
- *Neutral colors* are white, black, and gray.
- *Basic colors* are those that can be combined with many other colors. They include the neutral colors plus beige, luggage (both tints of brown), and dark blue.
- *Warm colors* have a lot of yellow or red in them. They seem to come toward you.
- *Cool colors* have a lot of blue (colors of the sky, the ocean, trees) in them. They seem to move away from you.

Skin Tone and Color   *Skin color* is based on a scale from white to black and can be divided into these categories: fair, medium, dark, and black. *Skin tone* refers to the amount of pink in your skin, and the groupings are: neutral, pink, and sallow. Take a few minutes to read the following generalizations about skin color and tone. Which categories best describe your own complexion?

- Fair skin is very light and tends to freckle or burn when exposed to the sun.
- Medium skin is a shade darker, seldom freckles, and usually tans easily.
- Dark skin stays dark all year and tans to a very dark brown.
- Black skin does not show a tan and stays the same color when exposed to the sun.
- Neutral skin tones have very little pink or yellow in them. Some pink will show up during exercise or extreme cold.
- Pink skin tones are often called "ruddy." People with pink skin tones blush easily and turn very pink with active exercise or during cold weather.
- Sallow tones give a yellowish hue to any skin color. Sallow skin rarely shows any pink during exercise or cold. A sunburn will turn a sallow complexion pink, but this soon turns to freckles or a tan.

Choosing a color that flatters your skin tones is not as hard as it sounds. The best way to choose a color is, of course, to try on various colors and simply note which looks best. However, here are a few guidelines for choosing colors: People with warm skin coloring (lots of pink) generally should not wear reds or oranges. People with sallow complexions should avoid yellow-orange, yellow, and yellow-green. Shades look better on light skins and tints look better on dark skins. Refer to Table 18-5 for further help in choosing colors that flatter you.

Table 18-5   SKIN TONE COLOR CHART

| Skin color | Skin tone | Colors | | | Best values |
		Best	Avoid	Basic	
Fair	Neutral	Reds Blues Greens	Yellows White	Black, beige, gray, luggage, dark blue	Shades Intense
	Pink	Yellows Blues Greens	Reds Browns	Black, gray, dark blue	Shades Intense
	Sallow	Reds Blues Blue-greens	Yellows White Navy	Black, gray, beige, luggage, medium blues	Shades Intense
Medium	Neutral	Reds Blues Greens	Yellows	White, black, gray, beige, luggage, dark blue	Shades Intense Tints
	Pink	Yellows Blues Greens	Reds Browns	White, gray, black, dark blue	Shades Intense Tints
	Sallow	Reds Blues Blue-greens	Yellows White Navy	Gray, beige, luggage, medium blue	Shades Intense
Dark or black	Neutral	Reds Blues Greens	Yellows	White, gray, beige, dark blue, luggage	Tints Intense
	Pink	Yellows Blues Greens	Reds Browns	White, gray, black, dark blue	Tints Intense
	Sallow	Reds Blues Greens	Yellows White Navy	Gray, beige, luggage, medium blue	Tints Intense

Hair Color   While hair color is not as important as skin tone in choosing your most flattering colors, it should be considered. For example, some people with light or medium brown hair do not look good in black, and some redheads should avoid wearing reds.

Body Build   Different colors can make you look slimmer or heavier. If your body build is heavy, wear cool colors of full intensity shades of those colors, or black. Light colors (tints) and white make a person appear larger. Shades slim you down. Wearing a light-color shirt with dark-color slacks will make you appear larger on top and smaller from the waist down. You will learn more about how your body build affects your choice of clothing in the next section.

Men's Fashion Association of America

McCall Pattern Company

Fig. 18-5a To look slimmer, you should wear dark colors (left) and vertical lines which continue from shoulder to hem with little break at the waistline (right).

Men's Fashion Association of America/Hoechst Fibers

Men's Fashion Association of America/Pendleton

Simplicity Patterns

18-5b To look broader and heavier, you should wear horizontal stripes (top left), multiple layers (bottom left), and plaids (right).

Line Line is one of the most confusing parts of clothing selection. What is line? *Line* refers to the shape of the garment and the print or design of its fabric. It can be flowing or fitted, cut diagonally or straight, sewn vertically or horizontally, woven in a bold stripe or fine pin stripe, etc. Try to remember the two basic principles of line:

1. *Vertical,* or up-and-down lines, give the appearance of height.
2. *Horizontal,* or crosswise lines, give the appearance of width.

The trick is to use these principles to make the most of your physical characteristics. If you want to look slimmer, you should wear clothes that have vertical lines. If your arms are too thin, you will avoid certain types of sleeves. To make the best use of line, you should be aware of both your good and bad points.

Starting at the top, study the shape of your face and neck. Your face shape and the length of your neck are important things to consider when choosing collars and necklines. For example, if you have a short, wide neck, you should not wear turtle or high-cowl necklines. Table 18-6 will help you choose lines that flatter your facial structure. Figure 18-6 illustrates various neckline and collar styles. Of course, other physical characteristics should also be considered.

Besides the shape of your face, you should be aware of whether you have broad or narrow shoulders, a long or short *torso* (the area between your neck and your legs), heavy legs, thin arms, and so forth. To disguise figure problems and emphasize your good points, you must know what they are.

Shoulder and sleeve lines are important clothes features. Sleeve styles come in many different lengths: short, above the elbow, below the elbow, and long. Figure 18-6 shows some of the many types of necklines and collars and sleeve and shoulder lines that are available. Once you know the styles that look best on you, choosing clothes will be a lot easier.

If you have narrow or sloping shoulders, the set-in, saddle, kimono, or *split raglan* (set-in sleeve in front; raglan in the back) shoulder will look best on you. If you have broad or square shoulders, the dolman, extended, and raglan shoulders will be most flattering and give you extra fullness across the back and shoulders.

People with slight or short builds should avoid dolman and raglan shoulders because their fullness will make them look top heavy. Don't wear full or flowing sleeves if you're shorter than average. Such lines should be kept simple so you are not overpowered.

To learn how to appear taller and slimmer, look at the clothes in Figure 18-7. Note that they have vertical lines with very little break at the waistline. Dark and solid, matching colors work together with the vertical lines to give a slender look.

Table 18-6 COLLARS AND NECKLINES FOR DIFFERENT FACE SHAPES

Face shape	Description	Necklines	Collars
Oval (a)	Forehead and chin the same width. Not too long. Evenly balanced	*Wear:* Any style	*Wear:* Any style
Round (b)	Widest at cheek-bones. Round at forehead and chin.	*Wear:* Slit; V-neck; scoop; bateau; *Avoid:* Turtle; mock turtle; jewel; crew	*Wear:* Wide spread; long-point; deep notch; high roll; shawl *Avoid:* Medium spread; buttoned-sports; mandarin; bow tie
Heart (c)	Wider at forehead than at chin. Pointed chin.	*Wear:* Turtle; mock turtle; crew; jewel; bateau *Avoid:* Slit; V-neck; scoop	*Wear:* Medium spread; mandarin, bow tie *Avoid:* Wide spread; long point; deep notch; high roll; shawl
Diamond (d)	Narrow at forehead and chin. Wide, high cheekbones.	*Wear:* Turtle; mock turtle; crew; jewel; bateau *Avoid:* Slit; V-neck; scoop	*Wear:* Medium spread; bow tie; mandarin *Avoid:* Wide spread; long point; deep notch; high roll; shawl
Oblong (e)	Square at forehead and chin. High forehead, long chin	*Wear:* Turtle; mock turtle; bateau; jewel; crew *Avoid:* Slit; V-neck; scoop	*Wear:* Medium spread; buttoned sports; mandarin; bow tie *Avoid:* Long point; deep notch; high roll; shawl
Triangle (f)	Narrow at forehead with wide, square chin.	*Wear:* Slit; bateau; V-neck; scoop; *Avoid:* Turtle mock turtle; crew	*Wear:* Wide spread; long point; deep notch; high roll; shawl *Avoid:* Medium spread; mandarin; bow tie

Face shape	Description	Necklines	Collars
Square (g)	Same width at forehead and chin. Wide cheekbones.	*Wear:* Slit; bateau; V-neck; scoop;	*Wear:* Wide spread; long point; deep notch; high roll; shawl
		Avoid: Turtle; mock turtle; crew	*Avoid:* Medium spread; mandarin; bow tie

a

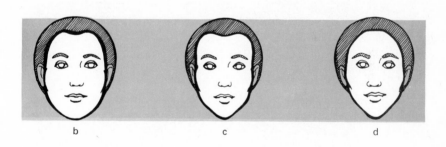

b   c   d

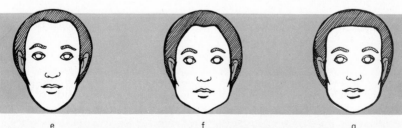

e   f   g

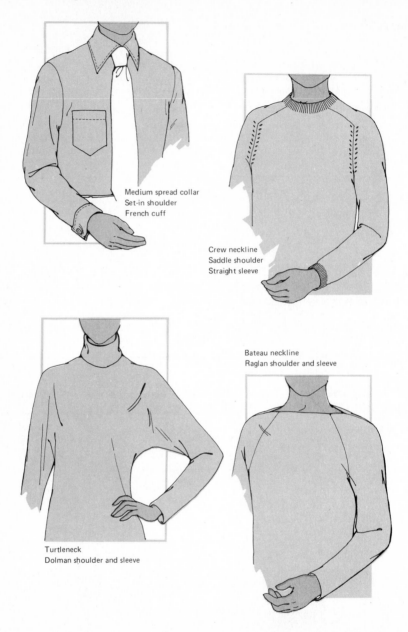

Medium spread collar
Set-in shoulder
French cuff

Crew neckline
Saddle shoulder
Straight sleeve

Bateau neckline
Raglan shoulder and sleeve

Turtleneck
Dolman shoulder and sleeve

Fig. 18-6 Study the shape of your face, the length of your neck, the breadth of your shoulders, and the length of your torso. When you buy a shirt or blouse, choose one with a shoulder, collar, or sleeve that flatters your features and your build.

Slit neckline
Drop shoulder and sleeve

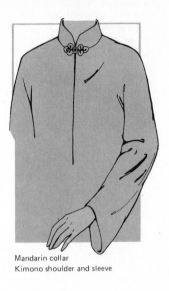

Mandarin collar
Kimono shoulder and sleeve

High roll collar
Gathered sleeve

Jewel neck
Cap sleeve

Fig. 18-6 (*continued*)

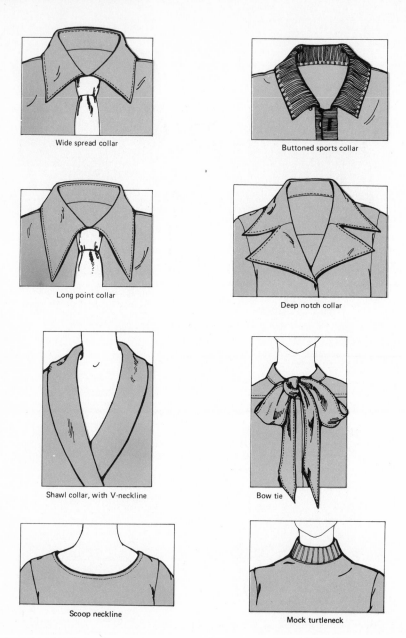

Wide spread collar

Buttoned sports collar

Long point collar

Deep notch collar

Shawl collar, with V-neckline

Bow tie

Scoop neckline

Mock turtleneck

Fig. 18-6 (*Continued*)

Fig. 18-7 Here again are some clothing ideas to help you appear slender. The top and slacks (a) in a matching color give a taller, continuous line. Solid dark colors, as in the trousers (c) have a slimming effect. The striped shirt gives a vertical line. Skirts without a waistband, like the A-line style in (b), deemphasize the waist.

These are just some of the ways that you can make line work for you. But line is just part of the picture. Color and texture must be used together with line to create the look you want. You will learn more about *texture* (how something feels) and fabrics in Chapter 19.

Flattery Dos and Don'ts   If you are tall and slender:

- Do wear bulky fabrics, loose-fitting clothes, contrasting colors, horizontal stripes, any line that cuts you in the middle.
- Don't wear slinky, clinging fabrics or tight-fitting clothes.

If you are heavy:

- Do wear medium-weight fabrics; loose-fitting clothes; solid, darker colors, lines as in Figure 18-7. (Clothes should flow smoothly from the shoulder or bustline to the hem.)
- Don't wear contrasting colored tops and bottoms, contrasting belts, wide waistbands.

If you are short and slender:

- Do wear light- to medium-weight fabrics, small prints or stripes, solid colors, slightly full tops and bottoms.
- Don't wear wide waistbands or bulky fabrics.

If you are a mixture (heavy on top and small on bottom or the other way around):

- Do use the basic rules of line in the areas that need them. Bulkiness in clothes adds width; light- and medium-weight fabrics make you look slimmer. Medium to dark colors slim you; large or bold prints, stripes, and bright colors add weight.

Fashion

Fashion is the third F of clothing selection. Most people like to dress in fashion. A line, an item of clothing, or an overall look that is accepted and worn by thousands of people is considered fashion.

But don't confuse fashion with fad. Fads are short-lived styles that come and go very quickly. If a certain fad or new style appeals to you, buy one or two items in that style. Don't spend your entire clothing budget on it or you may soon find yourself with a closet full of clothes that are out of style. If the fad becomes widely accepted, you can always add to your wardrobe. If not, you haven't wasted a lot of money.

Classics   Lines, looks, and types of clothing that have been around for a long time are called classics. Some of these classics are shown in Figure 18-8. Build your wardrobe around the styles that flatter you. Then you can add to it each year without worrying about being out of style. A good selection of shirts, blouses, and sweaters will provide many changes of wardrobe at less cost than a collection of one-piece outfits.

If you don't want to keep putting up and taking down hems, wear your dresses and skirts at or just below the knee. This length is always in fashion and it also looks best on most figures.

Because coats are so expensive, buy one in a classic style that will last for several years. Coats should also be worn at knee length. But there are exceptions. Short people look better in longer coats and tall people look better in coats that come just above the knee.

All of the fashion classics shown here offer good value for your money. In fact, the reason they are called classics is that they combine the three F's of clothing selection: function, flattery, and fashion.

Taking a Clothing Inventory

Before you can decide what your clothing needs are, you should know what clothes you already have. What you need will depend on your life-style: your job, the type of social life you lead, the activities you're involved in, the climate where you live, and so forth. The sample clothing inventory shown in the workbook that goes with this text includes seasons, condition of clothes, and colors. It also gives suggestions about how many blouses, sweaters, suits, etc., you should have. This list can be expanded to cover sleepwear, sportswear, and any other types of clothing you may have or need.

Queen Casuals, Inc.

Men's Fashion Association of America/Big Smith, Inc.

Simplicity Patterns

Men's Fashion Association of America/Ratner Corporation

Fig. 18-8 A good addition to your wardrobe would be a fashion classic; it would never go out of style. Here are some classics: casual pantsuit, dungarees, wrap skirt, crewneck sweater and leisure shirt.

Simplicity Patterns

Men's Fashion Association of America/The Aries Group Ltd.

McCall Pattern Company

Men's Fashion Association of America/The Aries Group Ltd.

Fig. 18-8 (*continued*) **Some fashion classics: vested pantsuit, reefer style trench coat, shirtwaist dress, fly-front coat.**

Fig. 18-8 (*continued*) Some fashion classics: blazer and turtleneck sweater, 3-piece dress suit, jewel-neck dress, V-neck sweater.

When you've completed the clothing inventory, it will be very easy to see what you have and what you need. Anything that's in fair condition will probably have to be replaced in a year or two. If you know you're going to have to buy a winter coat next year, you can start saving for it now. Hosiery and underwear need to be replaced more often than most other types of clothing. A good idea is to buy a few items every month and stock up if they're on sale. In fact, a lot of money can be saved if you buy your clothes on sale. Sales generally follow peak selling seasons, occurring after Labor Day, after Christmas, and during summer and winter clearances. But don't buy something just because it's on sale. Make sure you need the item first.

If you practice the three F's of clothing selection, your clothing budget will stretch further. But even more important, you will build up a wardrobe that's functional, flattering, and fashionable. Nothing gives people more confidence than to know they look their absolute best.

THINKING IT THROUGH

1. Good decisions about function, flattery, and fit require an objective knowledge of our own life-style and physical characteristics. But being objective may not be easy, considering the many ways in which clothing is advertised and displayed. In what ways can clothing ads or displays influence our judgment? Can they lead us into buying something that isn't really right for us? If so, how?

2. Do our attitudes about clothing and appearance reflect our attitudes about the places where we live? What similarities are there between wardrobe planning and other household planning (for shopping, decorating, etc.)?

3. What is your attitude toward fashion fads? Do the members of your class think that keeping up with the "latest" styles is important? What influences your decision to purchase or not to purchase fad items?

Treat Your Clothes to TLC

19

In Chapter 18, you learned how to choose the clothes that are right for you. Now it's time to learn how to keep them clean. This may sound pretty easy. But keeping your clothes looking fresh can be a problem if you don't use the right method. Just washing everything you own in soap and hot water can often lead to disaster. How many of us have closets full of ruined clothing because we didn't follow the right cleaning methods? Clothes, like people, need TLC (tender, loving care).

Fig. 19-1 Learn how to clean clothes the right way before disasters happen.

Fibers and Fabrics

In order to clean your clothes properly, you should know what they are made of. Different fabrics need different cleaning methods.

Cloth that is made by weaving or knitting fibers is called *fabric*. *Fibers* are long, thin threads. There are two kinds of fibers: natural and manmade. *Natural fibers* are those produced by an animal or plant; these include cotton, silk, and wool. *Manmade fibers* are those produced artificially from chemicals (called *synthetics*) or by combining natural fibers and chemicals (called *cellulosics*). Fibers must be twisted or spun into *yarn* before they are woven or knit into a fabric. Yarn that is made of a combination of two or more fibers is called a *blend*. A fabric woven from two or more yarns of different fibers is called a *mixture*. It is the yarn and the method of weaving or knitting that gives a fabric its *texture* (the way it feels) and *finish* (the way it looks). Figure 19-2 shows some common types of yarn and fabrics and how they are made.

To Dry Clean or to Launder—A Matter of Values

Doing your laundry can take a lot of time if you follow all the care instructions. Unless you have a machine with automatic dispensers, first you put in soap or detergent, then you wait; then you put in your clothes—and wait; then you put in the bleach—and wait; then you put in the fabric softener—and wait; and so on and on. If your time is limited, it might be a good idea to dry-clean many of your clothes. Dry cleaning can be expensive, but the time you save may make it worthwhile. The term "dry cleaning" means that clothes are washed in a chemical solution that cleans them and dries very quickly.

Almost all fabrics can be dry-cleaned. If your budget is as limited as your time, you might want to use a bulk dry-cleaning machine. You can dry-clean from 3 to 5 pounds (lb) [1.5-2.5 kilograms (kg)] of clothes for a single price. These machines are great for cleaning woolen sweaters, slacks, and skirts economically and with very little bother. With heavier items, such as suits and coats, professional dry cleaning is better since it's not based on weight and also includes steam pressing.

A word of caution: Clothing that is to be dry-cleaned in a machine should be carefully sorted. A mohair sweater should not be

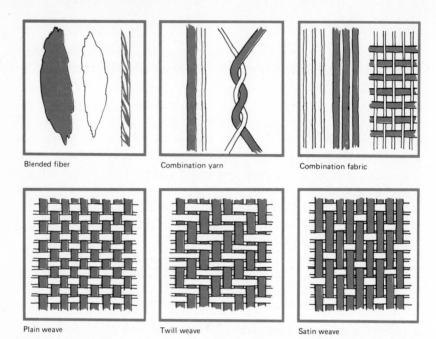

Blended fiber   Combination yarn   Combination fabric

Plain weave   Twill weave   Satin weave

Fig. 19-2 A blended yarn is made by spinning two fibers together into one. A combination yarn is made by twisting together two yarns of different fibers. A combination fabric is woven with two yarns of different fibers. The crosswise (woof) threads in the weaves shown here are white. The lengthwise (warp) threads are green. The way in which they cross over and under each other gives them their *finish*. Plain weaves have a smooth surface. Twill weaves have a diagonally ribbed surface. Satin weaves have a shiny, smooth surface.

cleaned with black wool slacks—unless you like looking as though you've slept with your dog! Light and dark colors should also be dry-cleaned separately since the cleaning solution often causes colors to *bleed* (run into each other).

Laundry Products

Tide, Gain, Bold, Cheer, Fab—the list could go on forever. There are so many laundry products on the market, each one claiming to get your clothes cleaner, whiter, brighter, and fresher than the next one. They promise that your spouse will love you more, your children will appreciate you more, and your friends will envy you more. Though most of the laundry products on the market do get your clothes clean, it's important to know how they differ. Some perform a particular job. Others combine two or more jobs, such as cleaning and bleaching. Read the labels on the containers so you won't buy two products when one would do just as well.

Cleaning Products   Cleaning products include soaps, detergents, and wool cleansers.

Soaps   You should add soap to the machine while it's filling and then dissolve the soap by swishing it around *before* you put in the clothes. Soap flakes are sometimes combined with a water softener. *Advantages:* They clean better than detergents. They are completely *biodegradable* (able to be broken down so they don't harm the environment). *Disadvantages:* Soap can't be used to wash animal fibers (such as silk and wool). It must be used in warm or hot soft water.
     Water can be either *soft* or *hard,* depending on the chemicals that are found in it. Hard water causes soap and mineral deposits to build up that may leave a film or stain on clothes. Figure 19-3 shows you some ways to find out if you have hard water.

Detergents   Unlike soaps, detergents can be added to the machine after it is loaded—either through a dispenser or on top of the clothes. Detergents come in powder or liquid form. *Advantages:* They can be used in either soft or hard water. They clean well in all water temperatures and can be used for all washable fabrics. *Disadvantages:* Detergents are not as biodegradable as soaps. They are less effective in removing grease and grass stains. They can also wash out certain finishes, such as flame resistance.

Wool Cleansers   Wool cleansers come in liquid or powdered form and are usually used in cold water. Wool cleansers are suggested for colors that bleed as well as for woolens and other fabrics that might shrink in hot water.

Bleaches and Stain Removers   Bleaches and stain removers include chlorine bleach, fine-fabric bleach, prewashes, and presoaks.

Chlorine Bleach   Chlorine is a bleach that is generally recommended for cleaning 100 percent cotton or linen fabrics that are

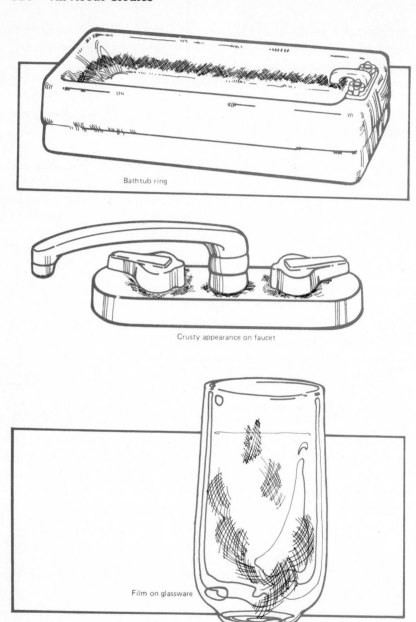

Bathtub ring

Crusty appearance on faucet

Film on glassware

Fig. 19-3 Does your water usually leave deposits or film like these shown? Then you have hard water.

white or light-colored. Check the cleaning instructions on the garment before using chlorine bleach with blends and mixtures or with trims and elastic that could be damaged by chlorine.

Fine-Fabric Bleach Any powdered, nonchlorine bleach is safe for all washables unless the care tag on the garment states otherwise.

Prewashes and Presoaks Available in spray, liquid, and powder form, prewashes and presoaks are used before regular washing to remove stubborn spots and stains.

Water Conditioners   Cleaning products work best in soft water. If your area doesn't have soft water, a water softener should be added to your wash water.

Finishes   Finishes include bluing, starch, fabric softeners, and waterproofing products.

Bluing You can use bluing to give the look of whiteness to white fabrics. Bluing comes in powders or liquids; some laundry products come with bluing already added.

Starch Available in liquid, powder, and spray form, starch adds crispness and smoothness to fabrics and also increases soil resistance. The liquid or powder should be added to the final rinse water. The spray can be used while ironing.

Fabric Softeners When liquid fabric softeners are added to the final rinse water, they help remove any soap or detergent from your clothes. Softeners also come in a fiber form that can be put into the dryer. Fabric softeners help to remove static electricity that causes synthetics to cling to the body and to other clothes. Fabrics feel fluffier and are less wrinkled when a fabric softener is used.

Waterproofing Products Since washing and dry cleaning remove waterproofing finishes, you should respray your clothing with a waterproofing product after each cleaning.

Sorting the Laundry

Since we all have to do laundry sometime, we might as well make it as painless as possible. One way of avoiding problems is to carefully sort your clothes before washing them. Some other tips for preparing the laundry are shown in Figure 19-4.

Separate whites and pastels from bright and dark colors. From these two bundles, sort out any heavily soiled clothes. These must be prewashed to remove some of the dirt. Prewash the clothes either by hand or in a machine that has a prewash cycle. Then soak them in a bleach solution, rinse, and add them to your regular wash. Or, instead of soaking them, you can wash them with a load of clothes to which bleach has been added. Stains and spots should be sprayed with a prewash laundry product.

When laundering bright colors for the first time, wash them by hand to see if they bleed. If they don't, they can be machine-washed along with the dark colors.

Lingerie, hosiery, and other clothing made from delicate fabrics can be washed with the regular wash if warm water is used. Place such clothes in a nylon mesh bag so they won't be torn by zippers, hooks, or other sharp objects.

Manmade and natural fibers and blends or mixtures of both can be washed together if:

- Warm water is used
- A fabric softener is added to the final rinse
- The manmade fabrics and blends are removed before the spin-dry cycle is over

Doing your laundry may not be much fun. But, by following these suggestions, you can at least have the satisfaction of knowing you're doing it right.

Choosing the Right Cleaning Method

A federal law states that a tag showing cleaning instructions must be attached to all clothes. But what happens if:

- The tag gets lost?
- The tag becomes unreadable after a few washings?

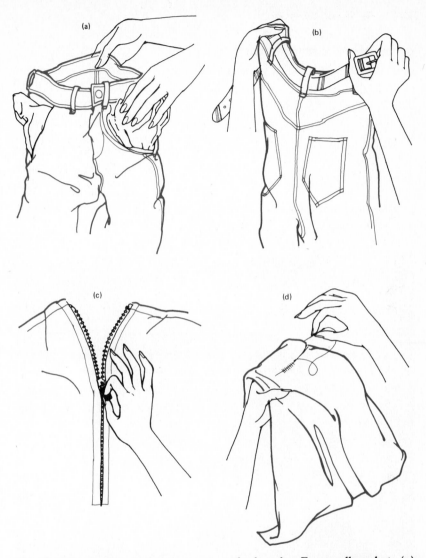

Fig. 19-4 Check your clothes as you sort the laundry. Empty all pockets (a); remove belts (b); close zippers (c); and make any necessary repairs (d). These few precautions will ensure that your clothes wear longer and remain in better condition.

- There wasn't one attached to begin with?
- You've made your own clothes?

The answer is to know what the clothes are made of. For example, are they 100 percent cotton, all-wool, or a blend of cotton and polyester? All clothing today is supposed to have a fabric label sewn in giving the fiber content and recommended care. If there is no care label or tag, the salesperson may know what kind of material the item is made from. If not, you can write to the clothing manufacturer for the information. Most clothes have tags hanging somewhere on them that give the name of the manufacturer and extra cleaning instructions.

Tables 19-1 and 19-2 are clothing care charts that will help you choose the right cleaning method for each fabric. Much time and money can be saved by knowing how to care for all types of clothing.

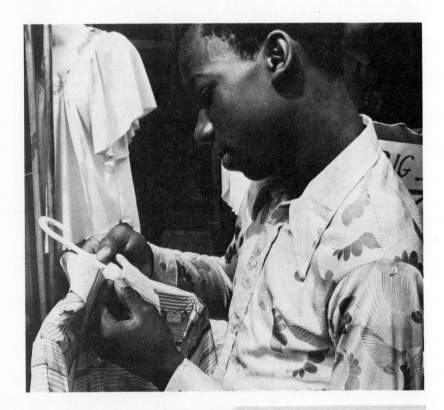

Fig. 19-5 When you buy a shirt or other clothing, check for the manufacturer's labels stating fiber content and cleaning instructions. (Susan Berkowitz)

Special Laundering Problems

According to some TV commercials, the worst thing that can happen to a person is to have "ring around the collar," "tattletale gray," or "dirty yellow tinge." Of course, soap manufacturers make such laundry problems seem much worse than they are. But these problems often do need special attention.

If your clothes look a bit gray after you've washed them, it usually means that the water wasn't hot enough, too little soap or detergent was used, or the washing machine was overloaded. Repeated washings in hotter water, more soap or detergent per load, and a loosely packed machine will remove "tattletale gray."

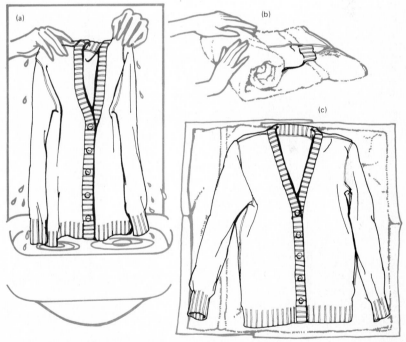

(a)

(b)

(c)

Fig. 19-6 Follow these instructions to wash and block a sweater. (a) Lift the sweater out of the sink. Don't wring or twist because this would stretch the yarn and ruin the shape of the sweater. (b) To remove excess water, place sweater in a dry towel, fold the towel over, and roll both up tightly. (c) Spread sweater out on a dry towel laid upon a flat surface, like the floor or a table. Place a layer of newspapers under the towel to absorb any extra moisture.

Table 19-1 CLOTHING CARE FOR FABRICS MADE OF NATURAL FIBERS

Fiber/fabric	To wash or clean	To dry	To press
Wool and hair			
Woven	Dry-clean only. If combined with a synthetic in a blend or mixture, it can be washed.	Blends: Hang to dry or use warm setting on dryer.	Press with damp pressing cloth at "cotton" setting or with steam at "wool" setting.
Knits	Dry-clean or wash. Hand-wash in lukewarm to cold water, using a detergent or laundry product made for woolens. Squeeze (don't wring) water out and roll in a towel to remove excess water. Blends can also be washed this way.	Block and let air dry (see Figure 19-6).	Same as above, if necessary.
Silk			
Woven	Dry-clean unless instructed otherwise. If it can be washed, follow directions for wool.	Hang to dry or use lowest setting on dryer.	Steam on wrong side at "wool" setting.
Knits	Same as above.	Lay on flat surface to dry.	Same as above.
Cotton			
100 percent cotton (Woven and knits)	Machine- or hand-wash in warm to hot water, unless otherwise instructed because of trim, lining, finish, etc. Use soap or detergent. Use chlorine bleach for heavily soiled, light-colored, and white clothes; use fine-fabric bleach for soiled colored clothes.	Machine-dry at medium to high settings or hang to dry.	Sprinkle, then dry-iron, or steam-iron at "cotton" setting. Fold knits with or without ironing.

Fiber/fabric	To wash or clean	To dry	To press
Blends or mixtures (Woven and knits)	Machine- or hand-wash in warm water. Use fine-fabric bleach if necessary. Turn clothes inside out to prevent the formation of *pills*, or little round fiber balls. (If pills do form, they can be shaved off with a safety razor.) Remove from washer before spin-dry cycle is completed.	Machine-dry at "low" to "medium" setting. Remove from dryer and hang immediately; hang to dry.	Touch-up ironing may be necessary. If so, use "wool" setting on steam iron.
Linen	Follow instructions for 100% cotton.		Dampen and dry or steam-iron. Set between "cotton" and "linen."

Table 19-2 CLOTHING CARE FOR FABRICS MADE OF MANMADE FIBERS

Fiber/fabric	To wash or clean	To dry	To press
Cellulosics			
Acetate	Dry-clean. If label says it can be washed, do so by hand, using lukewarm water and soap or detergent. Don't wring or twist.	Wrap in terry cloth towel.	While still wet, dry-iron on wrong side at lowest setting.
Rayon	Unless dry cleaning is indicated on label, wash, either by hand or machine, in warm water, using soap or detergent. Use fine-fabric bleach if necessary. Don't wring or twist. Remove from washer before spin-dry cycle is completed.	While still wet, hang to dry or place in dryer at "warm" setting.	Steam-iron at "wool" setting on wrong side.
Triacetate	Same as above, but hand-wash pleated garments.	Same as above.	Same as above.
Synthetics			
(Nylon, acrylics, modacrylics, polyester, spandex, etc.)			
Woven	Dry-clean deep piles ("fake-fur" fabrics). Wash others according to the following directions. Turn inside out to prevent pilling. Machine- or hand-wash in warm water. Use detergent or soap. Add fabric softener to final rinse water. Remove from washer before spin-dry cycle is completed.	Hang to dry or dry at warm setting. Hang immediately after removal from dryer.	If touch-up is needed, set iron at lowest steam setting.
Knits	Same as above.	Machine-dry at "warm" setting. Fold or hang as soon as dry.	Same as above.

A piece of clothing that develops a yellowish tinge after a few washings may have been specially treated to give it a smooth, crisp finish. Such finishes, often put on cottons and rayons, turn yellow and smell like chlorine when they are washed with a chlorine bleach. Use a commercial color remover (made by the same firms that make dyes) to get rid of this type of yellowing. Then wash the clothing with a nonchlorine or fine-fabric bleach if extra whitening is needed.

Yellowing or yellow spots can also be caused by minerals that are in your water, especially if you live in a hard-water area. This kind of yellowing can usually be prevented by adding a water softener to every wash load. But if you already have yellow spots on your clothes, the best way to get rid of them is to dissolve about ½ cup [0.12 liter (l)] of a silicate-type cleanser (found in water softeners) in the wash water and then run the clothing through a regular wash cycle.

Stain Removal

Special stains that can't be removed by using regular washing products need extra treatment. Nonwashables should be taken to a professional dry cleaner as soon as possible. If you know what caused the stain, tell the dry cleaner so it can be properly treated.

The following list gives some tips on getting rid of stubborn stains:

1. Discoloration from deodorants and antiperspirants: These stains can be removed by soaking, then scrubbing, the areas in white vinegar. If this doesn't remove the stain, try denatured alcohol instead of vinegar. Denatured alcohol is very flammable, so be careful when using it. The garment should be washed by hand before placing it in the washing machine.

2. Yellowish spots caused by body oils and other oils: Oil and grease stains can be easily removed from fabrics that can be washed in very hot water (e.g., cotton, polyester, and blends of each). Such stains can be treated by dissolving twice the usual amount of soap or detergent and 1 cup [0.25 l] of chlorine bleach in a washer full of very hot water. Run the machine for a few minutes, then turn it off and let the clothes soak for about 20 minutes before completing the wash cycle.

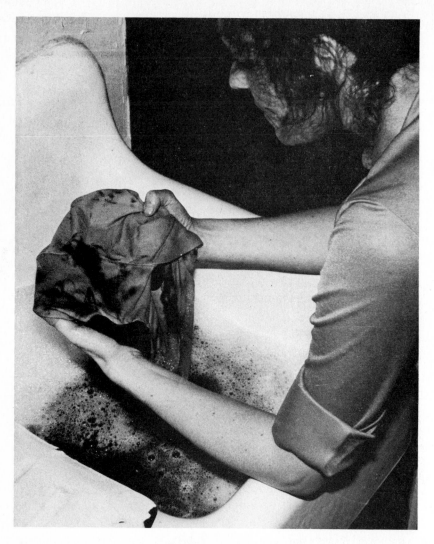

Fig. 19-7 You don't have to throw away a blouse or shirt just because you've stained it. Instead, try some of the simple stain-removal tips given in this chapter. But hurry! The sooner you treat stains, the more likely it is they'll come out. (Susan Berkowitz)

3. Blood, egg, milk, and other food stains: These should first be sponged (for nonwashables) or soaked in cool, salted water or club soda (for washables). Then sponge the nonwashables with dry-cleaning fluid. The washables can be laundered as usual.

4. Heavy grease stains: Rub in petroleum jelly, wiping off any excess with a paper towel. Sponge nonwashables with dry-

cleaning fluid. Spot-treat washables with a strong solution of detergent or with *petroleum solvent* (a chemical solution that dissolves oil and grease). Then wash the garment in hot, soapy water.

5. Fresh oil-based paint: Sponge with turpentine or paint thinner. Then dry-clean or wash in hot, soapy water. Paint stains that have dried are just about impossible to remove from nonwashable fabrics.

6. Nail polish: Sponge with nail-polish remover any fabric *except* acetates, acrylics, and modacrylics. To remove nail polish from these fabrics, sponge with a solution of one teaspoon [5 milliliters (ml)] of sodium perborate in 1 pint [0.5 l] of hydrogen peroxide. (Both of these products are sold in drugstores.) This solution can also be used to remove scorch marks caused by a too-hot iron.

7. Rust stains: Rub in a solution of lemon juice and salt. Place in the sunlight for a few hours. Rinse, then wash or dry-clean. Or try one of the products now on the market that are made to remove rust spots.

8. Chewing gum: Rub an ice cube over the stain. Then scrape off the gum and sponge with dry-cleaning fluid.

9. Ink stains: Sponge with rubbing alcohol. Then wash or dry-clean.

If you get a food or beverage stain on your clothes while you're away from home, remember this tip: Sponge such stains with seltzer water or club soda. As a rule, the longer a stain sets, the harder it is to remove. So this is a safe, temporary step to take until the garment can be treated more completely.

Besides the laundry products listed earlier, your first-aid kit for home care of clothing should contain rubbing alcohol, nail-polish remover, a container of cleaning fluid, seltzer, and a stain removal chart. This chart can be obtained from your County Extension office.

Drying Your Clothes

By now, you should have a pretty good idea of how to wash your clothes properly. But if you think you've got your laundry problem licked, you're wrong. Some of the worst mistakes happen not in the washing machine but in the dryer. By the time all the sorting and prewashing and bleaching are done, most of us are pretty tired of the whole process. So we throw everything into the dryer at once and set it to the hottest temperature in order to get it done as fast as possible. But care in drying your clothes is just as important as care in washing them.

Light and dark colors can be dried together. But manmade fabrics and blends should be separated from cottons and linens because they need a much lower drying temperature. The biggest mistake that's made with manmade fabrics is drying them at too high a temperature for too long.

Ironing and Pressing

The next step in keeping your clothes looking fresh is ironing. The difference between ironing and pressing is the way that the iron is used. In pressing, the iron is lifted up and placed down on the area to be pressed. In ironing, the iron is moved along the fabric in a gliding motion. Most clothes need both pressing and ironing.

To do a good ironing job, you will need the following equipment, shown in Figure 19-8.

1. A well-padded ironing board with a clean cover and, to get into the small areas, a mini-sized ironing board, called a *sleeve board*.
2. A steam iron. It's a good idea to get one that sprays as well. You can also dry-iron with a steam iron.
3. A sprinkling bottle. You can make one by putting a sprinkling top (sold at hardware stores) on any small bottle. If you have a "plant mister" handy, that could be used instead.
4. A pressing cloth or a piece of medium-thick 100 percent cotton.
5. A velvet board or strip of heavy fabric covered with "nails" on which to steam pile fabrics like velvet and corduroy.

Steps in Ironing   The first, most important step in ironing is to read the instruction booklet that comes with the iron when you buy it. Then, read the additional steps listed below; these will make your ironing easier.

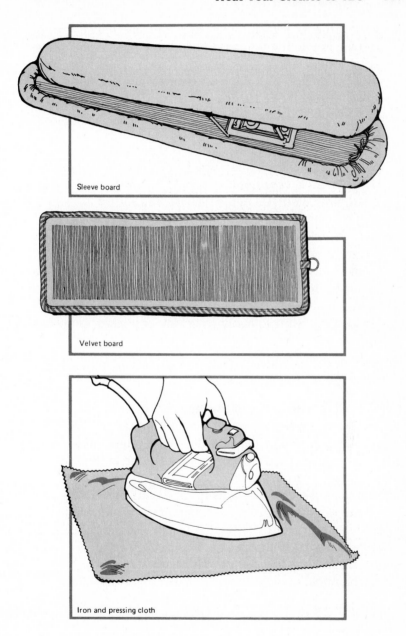

Sleeve board

Velvet board

Iron and pressing cloth

Fig. 19-8 Here is some equipment you will need to do a good ironing job.

1. Follow the directions on the iron for filling it with water.
2. Set the iron to the temperature indicated on the dial. Most irons have four settings:

   a. "Synthetics" is the lowest temperature setting; it should be used for manmade fabrics.

   b. "Wool," the next setting, should be used for wool, blends or mixtures of cottons and synthetics, and for silk.

   c. "Cotton" should be used for 100 percent cotton; this setting is also used when ironing any fabric with a pressing cloth.

   d. "Linen" is very hot and should be used only for predampened, untreated 100 percent linen. Since most linen clothing is treated with a finish, it's safer to iron it between the "cotton" and "linen" settings or at the "cotton" setting.
3. Find the grain line of woven clothing (see Figure 19-9). The *grain line* usually runs along the center front and back on a shirt, blouse, skirt, or slacks and along the fold opposite the sleeve seam on a shirt or blouse. When ironing, follow the lengthwise grain of the fabric to avoid stretching or puckering the garment.

Figure 19-10 shows the steps to follow when ironing a shirt or blouse. These are:

- Press all seams open (unless they're meant to go in one direction). Press *facings* (the lining at the edges of a garment that sometimes show on the outside: collar, cuffs, lapels, etc.); the inside of pocket flaps and cuffs; areas around buttons *(a)*; and any trim, bows, or ruffles first.
- Press the collar *(b)* and cuffs *(c)* of a shirt or blouse next. Then iron the sleeves *(d)*. When ironing a tailored shirt, fold the *yoke* (the fitted piece of material that lies across the shoulders) upon the back and iron it from sleeve to sleeve *(e)*.
- Iron or press the body of the garment last *(f)*. Then hang it up to dry and cool.

Figure 19-11 shows the steps to follow when pressing and ironing slacks or trousers. These are:

- Press the inside of the waistband, zipper facing, and pockets first. Then, put the top of the slacks over the end of the ironing board

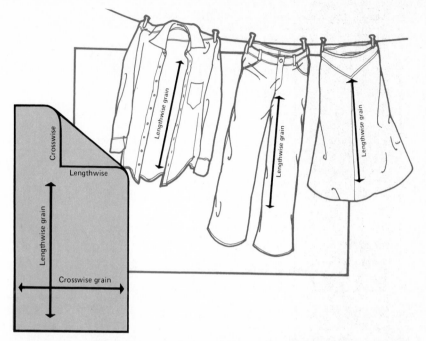

Fig. 19-9 Woven fabrics are made by running crosswise yarns under and over lengthwise yarns. The grain of each of these yarns is the direction they take in relation to the finished edges, or selvage, on each side of the fabric. If the crosswise grain forms a perfect right angle to the lengthwise grain, clothes that are made properly will follow the lengthwise grain of the fabric and hang straight, without twisting on the body. When you are ironing your clothes, follow the lengthwise grain.

and press the outside from the top of the waistband to the bottom of the crotch seam.

- Place the slacks lengthwise on the ironing board so that the seam down the inside of the leg rests on top of the seam down the outside of the leg. Steam-iron the inner side of this leg from the waist to the hem.
- Turn the slacks over and steam-iron the *inside* of the other leg.
- With both legs together, steam-iron the outside of each from the waist to the hem.
- Then hang the garment up to dry and cool.

Tips to Remember   Now that you know the basics of ironing your clothes correctly, here are a few tips to keep in mind:

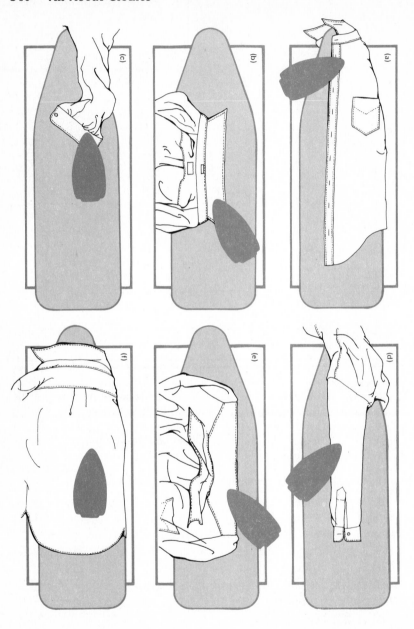

Fig. 19-10 Follow these steps in ironing a shirt. (a) Press the areas around the buttons. (b) Next press the collar and (c) the cuffs. (d) Fold and iron the sleeves. (e) Next iron the yoke, and finally (f) iron the body of the shirt.

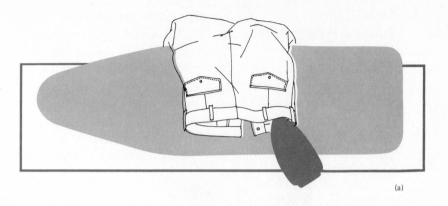

(a)

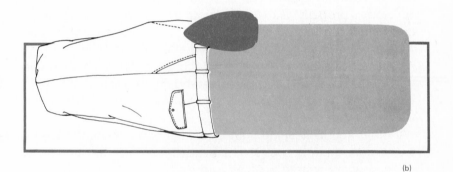

(b)

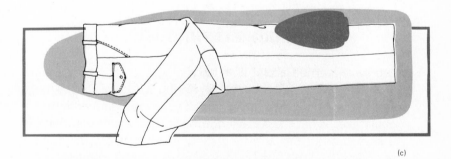

(c)

Fig. 19-11 Follow these steps in ironing slacks or trousers. (a) Press the inside of the waistband, zipper facing, and pockets first. (b) Press the outside from the top of the waistband to the bottom of the crotch seam. (c) With the inside seams directly over one another, iron the inner side of one leg, then the other.

1.   Steam cottons, linens, rayons, silks, woolens, and *pile* fabrics (fake fur, velvet, corduroy, etc.) on the inside.
2.   Dampen any clothing that comes out of the dryer very wrinkled. After sprinkling or spraying the garments with water, put them in a plastic bag to keep them damp. Iron without steam. If you've sprinkled something and can't iron it the same day, store it in your freezer to prevent mildew.
3.   Wire hangers are not good for your clothes. Buy some wooden, plastic (for drip-drying), and padded hangers to keep that "just pressed" look in your clothes.

Wash Often and Wash Right

If you've read this chapter carefully, you should know how to wash your clothes properly. But washing your clothes often enough is just as important as washing them correctly. You may not wish to *iron* your jeans, but they should be washed after two or three wearings. Any item of clothing that's worn next to the body, such as under-wear, stockings, socks, and pajamas, should be washed after each wearing. This will make your laundry task easier, and your clothes will keep that fresh look longer.

Another key to keeping your clothes in good shape is knowing how to store them properly. The next chapter will give you some tips on how and where to store your clothes.

THINKING IT THROUGH

1.   You have learned about time budgeting and caring for a place of your own in earlier chapters. Caring for your clothes is an activity that could be a larger part of your time budget than you would like. What ways have you observed or can you think of to save time in this activity without sacrificing proper clothing care? Are "no-iron" or "drip-dry" fabrics a total solution? Why or why not?
2.   Clothing care has changed dramatically over the years. Can you describe some of the clothing care practices of 1900? 1930? 1950? What changes could the future bring to this activity?

A Stitch in Time

Do you feel helpless when it comes to replacing a zipper or sewing on a button? Does the thought of hemming a skirt or altering a jacket send you running to the tailor? Haven't you ever wished that you could jazz up your jeans by adding a few well-placed patches? Well, don't give up hope. All you need are a few basic sewing skills and some inexpensive supplies, and you, too, can repair, alter, and decorate your clothes like an expert.

But, you may ask, why bother learning how to sew when a tailor or dressmaker can do it for me? Well, for one thing, it's hard to find a tailor at 7 p.m. when you're getting dressed for a big date and your best dress splits a seam or a button falls off your favorite jacket. Of course, you can always change your dress or wear another jacket. But why should you have to when repairing them would take just a few minutes? And why spend money on a tailor when you could be spending it on new clothes? Suppose you buy three pairs of slacks and they all need to be shortened. If you take them to a tailor, it could cost you around $12. If you hemmed them yourself, you could take that money and buy another pair of slacks!

This chapter will introduce you to some of the basic sewing skills needed to do repairs and minor alterations. But you don't have to stop there. Once you've learned the basic techniques, you can decorate your clothes, make your own ties and scarves, sew curtains, and do any number of other creative projects.

Equipment and Supplies

Besides the pressing and ironing equipment you learned about in Chapter 19, you'll need a few more tools and supplies to repair and alter your clothes. Most of the items discussed in this section can be found in variety stores and all of them, of course, in stores that sell sewing equipment. And each item, except perhaps the cutting tools, is inexpensive. Cutting tools are sold in all price ranges, but quality really counts here. A good pair of scissors, for example, will cut right up to the tip of the blade and is a worthwhile investment.

Measuring Equipment   From the following list of measuring equipment, choose the tools you think you will need to repair or alter your clothes. (Your choices, of course, will depend on what types of clothes you wear.)

1. *Tape Measure.* To take body measurements, you will need a tape measure. Most tape measures are 60 in [152.5 cm] long. Those made out of plastic-coated fabric are best because they last longer and don't stretch.
2. *Yardstick.* You'll find you have many uses for a yardstick, from measuring lines on fabric or paper to marking for hems. Metal yardsticks are more expensive than wooden ones, but they last longer and won't bend out of shape.
3. *Skirt Marker.* If you plan to do a lot of hemming on skirts or dresses, a skirt marker is a worthwhile investment, since it is more accurate than a yardstick. There are two types of skirt markers available: *(a)* the pin marker, which has a metal clamp to grip the hemline and hold it in place so a friend can mark it with straight pins; and *(b)* a chalk marker, which allows you to mark the hem yourself by turning around as you squeeze the marker's rubber handle, causing chalk marks to be placed at the desired hem level. Both types of skirt markers are shown in Figure 20-1.
4. *Sewing Gauge.* In addition to a skirt marker, it's a good idea to buy a sewing gauge, which is a short ruler with a sliding marker attached to it. The sliding marker can be moved to show the measurement you want. For example, suppose you're shortening a skirt or a pair of trousers by 4 in [10 cm]. Since this would be too large a hem to work with (2-in [5-cm] hems are best), you would use the sewing gauge to mark off 2 in on the turned-up fabric. This will give you an accurate measurement of hem width. Figure 20-1 also shows you what a sewing gauge looks like.

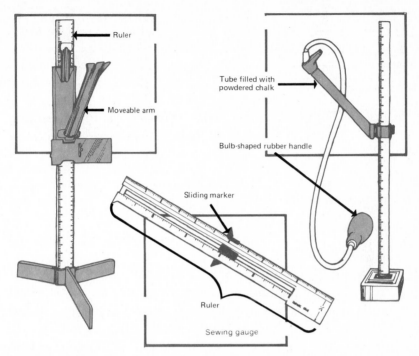

Fig. 20-1 To do accurate alterations, you may need some of the measuring equipment shown here.

5. *Mirror.* If you don't already own one, you will have to buy a full-length mirror. You can't decide where you want your hem if you can't see it!

Cutting Equipment   To do adequate repairs and alterations, you'll need some of the following cutting equipment.

1. *Shears.* You'll find that shears (which are longer than scissors) come in various designs, including right- and left-handed versions. The type with a bent handle is best because one blade rests flat on the cutting surface for a smooth cut. This type of shears is shown in Figure 20-2. When buying shears, take some fabric scraps (light and heavy) with you to the store. Using the full length of the blade, make several long cuts in the scraps. Is the cut smooth? Is the blade smooth or are there nicks in the metal? Test the tips of the blade by making some short clips in

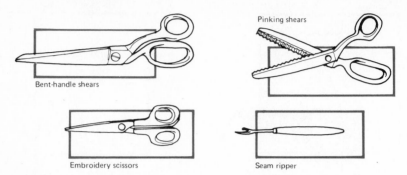

Fig. 20-2 Each pair of scissors here has a special usage: The bent-handle is helpful when cutting material on a flat surface; pinking shears cut a zigzag line that prevents fabrics (like a seam) from fraying; the embroidery scissors and seam ripper are good for removing stitches.

the fabric. It's important to keep your shears sharp, so keep one pair aside just for sewing. Blunt scissors do not cut well and can also damage your garment.

2. *Embroidery Scissors.* You'll also need 3½-in [9-cm] embroidery scissors; these are used for cutting threads and for removing stitches. A pair is shown in Figure 20-2. A seam ripper (Figure 20-2) can also be used for removing stitches.

3. *Pinking Shears.* Seams and hemlines can be finished easily with pinking shears (Figure 20-2). They make a zigzag cutting line that keeps fabric from fraying.

Marking Equipment   You'll need marking equipment for taking up hems or altering a dress or jacket. Here are some tools to choose from:

1. *Tailor's Chalk.* Used for marking hems or seams, tailor's chalk is a hard-finish chalk that comes in flat squares. You hold the flat part between your thumb and fingers; the edge of the chalk marks the fabric. Tailor's chalk also comes in pencil form for thin line markings. Both types are shown in Figure 20-3. Tailor's chalk comes in white, pink, and blue. Use the white or dark fabrics and the pink or blue for light-colored fabrics.

2. *Tracing Paper.* You can use tracing paper and a tracing wheel to trace seam lines and alteration lines. The tracing paper works like carbon paper in a typewriter and comes in many colors. Use the color that shows up best on the fabric. But don't use the

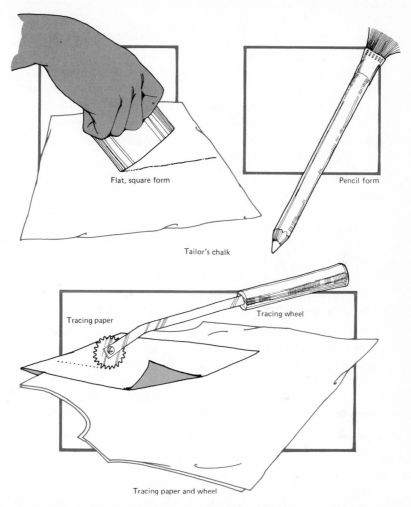

Flat, square form

Pencil form

Tailor's chalk

Tracing paper

Tracing wheel

Tracing paper and wheel

Fig. 20-3 Here is some equipment for marking alterations and hemlines. Tailor's chalk comes in flat squares or pencil form. A tracing wheel is used with tracing paper to draw seams and alteration lines onto fabric.

dark blue and red sheets to mark light colors because their markings are difficult to remove. A tracing wheel and tracing paper are shown in Figure 20-3.

Sewing Equipment You should put together a sewing kit containing all of the following equipment. Then you will always be prepared for any emergency or repair.

1. *Needles.* The most important sewing tool, needles come in different lengths and thicknesses, with differing eye shapes and sizes. (The *eye* is the hole in the needle through which you put the thread.) Longer needles are best for long stitches and shorter needles should be used for short stitches. The proper thickness of the needle depends on the thickness of the fabric. For example, if a thick needle is used on thin fabric, it may leave too large a hole in the fabric. You don't have to buy or learn about all the needles that are available since many of them are used for special work. For general sewing and repairing, buy a package of assorted *sharps* (all-purpose needles) and crewel needles. The crewel needles with large, long eyes are easier to thread. If you want to repair knits, you will also need a darning or yarn needle.

2. *Thread.* You should have an assortment of thread in all the neutral colors (white, black, dark blue, beige, and brown) so you'll be prepared for any last-minute repairs on almost anything you own. Of course, if you don't want the seams to show at all, you can find thread to match any color fabric. When buying a particular color thread, take a piece of the fabric along with you. It'll help when you're faced with 30 shades of green! To blend in with the fabric, the thread should be a shade darker. For prints and plaids, match the thread to the main color in the fabric. Cotton-covered polyester and plain polyester are good all-purpose threads. For areas that need extra reinforcement, such as seams and buttons, you may need heavy-duty or *buttonhole-twist* (strong silk) thread.

3. *Pins.* You will need a supply of straight pins for pinning hems, seams, and alteration lines. While you can save the pins that come with the shirts you buy, thin, rustproof brass pins are best, and they are very inexpensive. Many of them come with colored heads, which are easier to see and handle.

4. *Beeswax.* To keep your thread from knotting or twisting as you sew, you can use beeswax to strengthen and wax it. Beeswax can be bought in a container with grooves in it for pulling the thread through.

5. *Pin Cushion.* You can either keep your needles and pins in a box or store them in a pin cushion. Some pin cushions are

shaped like a tomato, with a "strawberry" attached. The "strawberry" is filled with emery and is used for sharpening and cleaning your pins and needles.

6. *Needle Threader.* This inexpensive little device will save you many annoying moments. See Figure 20-4 for directions on how to use a needle threader.

7. *Thimbles.* While thimbles are not a necessity, they will protect your finger, especially when you're sewing a thick fabric. Thimbles fit on your middle, or needle-pushing, finger. They come in different sizes, so be sure to try one on before buying it.

8. *Seam Binding.* Thin strips of fabric or lace—called *seam binding*—are used to prevent seams and hems from unraveling. Seam binding is sewn on the top of a seam or hem to finish it.

9. *Fasteners.* At some time, you will need a safety pin, some hooks and eyes, snaps, or an extra button for emergency repairs. Keep a supply of these items in a box so you'll know where to find them when you need them. Later in the chapter you will learn how to sew on buttons and other fasteners.

Basic Sewing Skills

The first two skills you need to learn for hand sewing are how to thread a needle and how to knot the thread. Simple, you say? Yes, it *is* simple, but you should learn the right way to do it. Figure 20-4 shows you, step by step, how to thread a needle by hand, as well as with a needle threader. Figure 20-5 explains the steps in knotting.

Hand sewing is done with either single or double thread, depending on the stitch and the amount of reinforcement that's necessary. Double thread is stronger, but it tends to knot and twist. You can untwist it by dropping the needle and running your thumbnail between the two strands.

When instructions call for a single thread, pull the thread through the needle (or use a needle threader), knot that end, and leave a shorter "tail" on the other end. When double thread is used, the two ends can be knotted either separately or together. After the thread is knotted, wax it with beeswax before you start to sew.

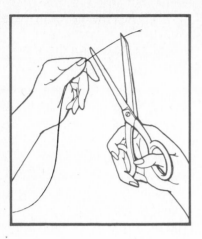

Fig. 20-4 Follow these steps to thread a needle by hand.

Step 1: Cut polyester thread straight across. Cut cotton and silk thread at an angle.

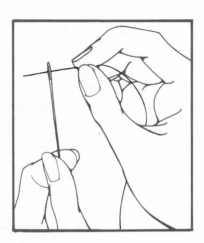

Step 2: Wet the tip of the thread and push it through the eye of the needle.

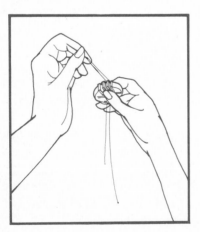

Step 3: Pull the thread, starting at the eye end of the needle through the beeswax.

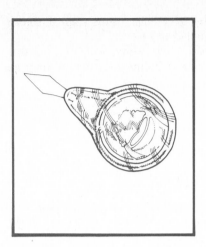

Fig. 20-4a Follow these steps to use a needle threader.
Step 1: This is what a needle threader looks like.

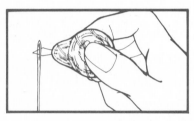

Step 2: Put the loop of the threader through the eye of the needle.

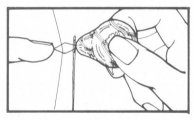

Step 3: Push the point of the loop to expand it and slip the thread through.

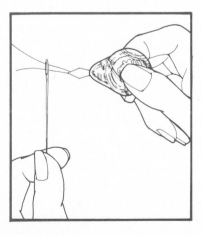

Step 4: Pull the threader out of the needle and the thread will come with it.

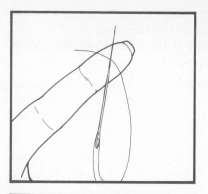

Fig. 20-5 Follow these instructions to knot a thread.
Step 1: Place tail of thread and the needle at right angles, across finger.

Step 2: Hold in place with thumb.

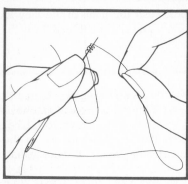

Step 3: Wrap loop of thread around needle three or four times.

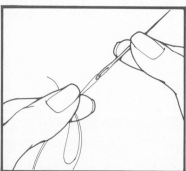

Step 4: Pull needle through thread loops, as you hold them between finger and thumb.

Many different types of hand stitches are employed in sewing, each one having a particular use. Sewing machines offer even more types of stitches. If you find that you enjoy sewing or if you want to make your own clothes from patterns, you might want to invest in a sewing machine. But for general repairs and alterations, all you really need to know are a few basic hand stitches.

Basting Stitch   Basting—a temporary stitch—is used instead of straight pins to hold the fabric together before you permanently stitch the pieces. Don't worry if your stitches aren't perfect, because you will be removing them later on.

Use a long needle and single white or pastel thread. Working from right to left, take long, even stitches that are about ¼-in [6 millimeters (mm)] long and ¼-in apart, as shown below. The reason for using a long needle is that it lets you weave the needle in and out of the fabric, making several stitches at a time, before pulling the thread through.

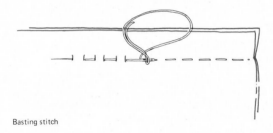

Basting stitch

Running Stitch   The most basic hand stitch, the running stitch, can be used either for basting or as a permanent stitch. A single row of stitches is sewn for mending, seaming, and quilting; a double row is sewn for gathering in fullness.

Use a long needle and single thread. Working from right to left, weave the point of the needle in and out of the fabric until several stitches are on it before pulling the thread through. This procedure is shown below. When used as a permanent stitch, the stitches and spaces between them should be even and very short (about $\frac{1}{16}$ in [1.5 mm]).

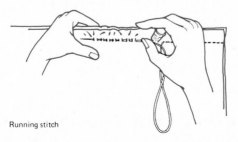

Running stitch

Back Stitch   Because the back stitch is a series of overlapping stitches, it is the strongest of all hand stitches. The back stitch is used for sewing and mending seams and other areas that need to be reinforced.

Use a short needle and double thread. Working from right to left, place the needle in the fabric and take a ⅛-in [3-mm] stitch on the underside. Pull the thread through to the surface. For the next stitch, insert the needle about ⅛ in *behind* the first stitch, push it underneath your work, and bring it up ⅛ in ahead of the first stitch, as shown below. Follow this procedure for the rest of the stitches. The pattern of the back stitch is a continuous line of overlapping ¼-in [6-mm] stitches on the underside and one nearly continuous line of ⅛-in [3-mm] stitches on the surface. To get an idea of what this looks like, take a scrap of fabric and work the stitches yourself. Use thread that contrasts in color with the fabric so you can clearly see the pattern.

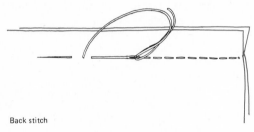

Back stitch

Zipper, or Pick, Stitch   Used to sew in zippers, the zipper, or pick, stitch is a type of back stitch, except that the stitches are smaller. The zipper stitch is also used as a decorative stitch around the neck, collar, or sleeves of a garment.

Use a double thread for zippers and a single thread for decorative stitching. The stitch that goes backward should be about $^1/_{16}$ in [1.5 mm] long, and the underneath forward stitch should be about ¼ in [6 mm] long. This stitch is shown below.

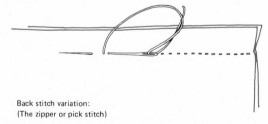

Back stitch variation:
(The zipper or pick stitch)

Combination Stitch   Called a combination stitch because it combines the running and back stitches, this stitch is used for permanent seams and for mending. Although it's stronger than the running stitch and faster to sew, it's not as strong as the back stitch.

Use a short needle and either single or double thread, depending on how strong the stitch has to be. Take three or four running stitches about ⅛ in [3 mm] long; then take a back stitch about ⅛ in long, as shown below. The underneath stitches before and after the back stitch should be ¼ in [6 mm] long. Again, it would be helpful if you tried this stitch on some scrap fabric to see the pattern.

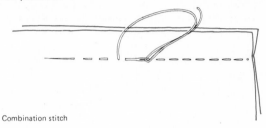

Combination stitch

Overcasting   You can use the overcasting stitch to sew on patches, *appliqués* (a cutout decoration applied to a fabric), and fasteners. Overcasting is also used to finish raw edges on seams and hems.

Use a medium-length needle and single thread. Working from right to left over the edge of the seam (see below), take one stitch at a time on bulky fabrics or several stitches at a time on thinner fabrics. Stitches should be ⅛ to ¼ in [3-6 mm] apart and $1/16$ to ⅛ in [1.5-3 mm] deep.

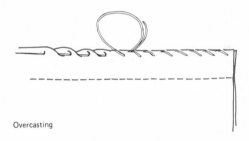

Overcasting

Hem, or Blind, Stitch   Use the hem, or blind, stitch when you don't want the stitches to show on the surface of the fabric. The hem stitch can be used on any type of fabric and with any hem finish except a *pinked* (saw-toothed) edge.

Use a medium-length needle and single thread. Working from right to left, start the first stitch under the hem, $1/16$ in [1.5 mm] from the edge. Pull the needle through and insert it, at an angle, into the fabric, ⅜ in [9 mm] from the last stitch, just under the edge of the hem. This procedure is illustrated below. Only pick up a thread or two of the fabric—less than $1/16$ in [1.5 mm]. Tilt the needle up and out through the underside of the hem, $1/16$ in [1.5 mm] from the edge. After sewing four stitches like this, lock the thread by sewing two stitches in place over the edge of the hem.

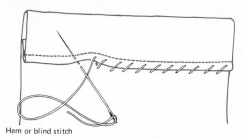

Hem or blind stitch

Whipped Stitch When a fine, narrow edge is needed, such as on scarves and handkerchiefs, use a whipped stitch.

You'll need a medium-length needle and single thread. Working from right to left, roll a very narrow edge between your thumb and index finger and take slanting stitches into the fold as you roll. The needle goes over and under the roll, not through it. The illustration below shows you what this stitch looks like. The stitches should be about ⅛ in [3 mm] apart.

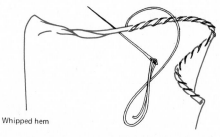

Whipped hem

Catch Stitch A You could use catch stitch A instead of the blind stitch to finish hems. Catch stitch A stretches, so it's good for hemming necklines, sleeves, and other areas that will stretch in a knit garment.

Use a short needle and single thread. Working from left to right, insert the needle (¼ in [6 mm] deep) under the edge of the hem, then bring it up and over ¼ in to the right. Make a right-to-left, $1/16$-in [1.5-mm] stitch into the body of the garment. Pull the thread through, up, and over ¼ in [6 mm] on the hem and make a right-to-left, ⅛-in [3-mm] stitch. (The stitch on the hem can be larger because it doesn't show through on the outside.) This stitch is shown below.

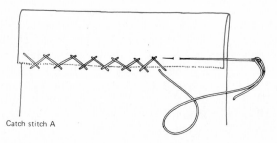

Catch stitch A

Catch Stitch B   Since catch stitch B doesn't stretch as much as catch stitch A, use it just for hemming knits and bulky fabrics where an over-the-edge hem would leave a ridge showing on the outside.

Fold the garment back so that the raw edge of the hem shows ⅛ in [3 mm] above the fold. Use a short needle and single thread. Working from left to right, take a right-to-left stitch (¹/₁₆ in [1.5 mm] long) into the hem at the point where it meets the fold. Bring the thread over ¼ in [6 mm] to the right and take a right-to-left stitch (also ¹/₁₆ in [1.5 mm] long) on the edge of the fold. The illustration below shows you what this stitch should look like. Continue this pattern. When you're finished, the stitches should be almost invisible on both the hem and the garment.

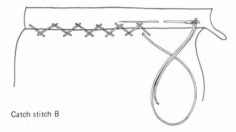

Catch stitch B

Slip Stitch A   When you don't want the stitches to show, use slip stitch A. However, since it isn't very strong, use slip stitch A only for areas that do not stretch or need reinforcement. For example, slip stitch A is good for hemming and sewing on patches or for attaching any folded edge to a piece of fabric (a lining to a jacket, for example).

When using this stitch for hemming, fold your work as you did in catch stitch B. Baste the hem into position. Use a short needle and single thread. Working from right to left, take a ¹/₁₆-in [1.5-mm] stitch into the garment at the point where it meets the fold of the hem. From the point where the needle comes out, cross directly over to the fold. Insert the needle into the fold and run it ¼ in [6 mm] inside the folded edge. Then bring the needle out and directly across for another ¹/₁₆-in [1.5-mm] stitch in the garment (see below).

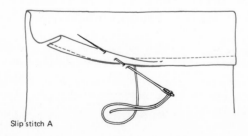

Slip stitch A

Slip Stitch B   You can use slip stitch B to join together two folded edges, such as a split seam that can't be reached from the inside to be repaired.

Pin the folded edges together. Use a short needle and single thread. Work from right to left. Insert the needle underneath the fabric and into the fold of one side. Bring it through and into a point directly across from it in the fold of the other side. Run a short (⅛-in [3-mm] stitch) along the inside of the fold. Bring the needle out and repeat the procedure. (In the illustration below, a broken line is used to represent the placement of the stitches. This is because the needle and thread would normally be hidden from your view.)

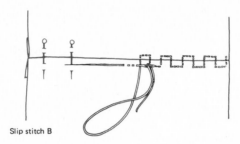

Slip stitch B

Blanket Stitch   Usually used for embroidery, the blanket stitch is also used for outlining appliqués and patches.

Use a short crewel needle and single, heavy-duty thread or two to three strands of embroidery thread. Working from left to right, bring the needle from underneath through your work about ¼ in [6 mm] from the edge. Make the first stitch by going over the edge, into the fabric to which the patch is being attached, and out again through the same hole. This procedure is shown below. The stitches (about ¼ in apart) are made by holding the thread coming from the previous stitch with your other hand as you insert the needle ¼ in from the edge, pick up the underneath layer, and bring the needle up at the edge of the patch. Hold the strands of the thread loop under the needle as you pull the thread through to form an outline along the edge.

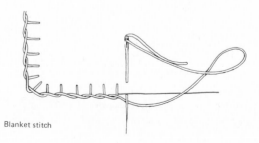

Blanket stitch

Buttonhole Stitch   Use the buttonhole stitch to make or repair buttonholes.

You'll need a crewel or embroidery needle and single, heavy-duty or buttonhole thread. Start in the corner of the buttonhole that's farthest from the front. Working from right to left, overcast the edge with stitches about ⅛ in [3 mm] deep and ⅛ in apart. Starting in the same corner, do a blanket stitch around the hole, ⅛ in deep and ¹/₁₆ in [1.5 mm] apart. This procedure is shown below. Finish the back of the buttonhole with a bar, made by sewing blanket stitches over the last two stitches on each side of the back end of the buttonhole.

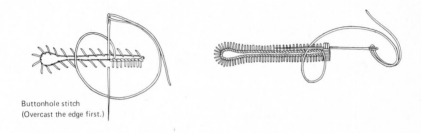

Buttonhole stitch
(Overcast the edge first.)

Sewing Patches and Appliqués

Patches and appliqués have many different uses. They can be used to cover tears and holes in a garment. You can also use them to decorate jeans, T-shirts, bags, tablecloths, and just about anything that you want to give new life to.

If the garment you're patching is to be laundered, use a washable fabric for the patch or appliqué and finish the edge with one of the stitches you've learned (for example, the overcast stitch, slip stitch A, or the blanket stitch). Edges should be finished even on iron-on patches because, after several washings, the edges can start to lift up.

Patches and appliqués can be made in several ways:

1. Buy an iron-on patch or appliqué from a variety store.
2. Make your own iron-on patch. Buy a piece of fabric and some iron-on bonding material. Cut the fabric and the bonding material to the same shape and size. Sew the two pieces together and iron on the patch.
3. Make a regular patch as shown in Figure 20-6. Cut a pattern from a piece of cardboard. Lay it on the fabric and cut around

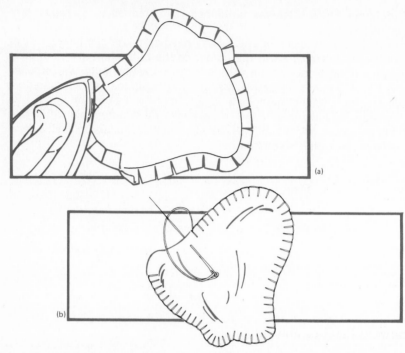

Fig. 20-6 Use your iron to fold ¼-in of material over the cardboard pattern (a). To sew on the appliqué, embroider or handstitch it to the clothing (b).

it, leaving an extra ¼ in [6 mm] all around for a hem. Fold this extra ¼ in of material (the *hem allowance*) over the cardboard with an iron so that you'll have a clear sewing line to follow. Snip small "V's" or make short slashes in the hem allowance so that the fabric fits around the edge and curves of the pattern as you iron. Remove the cardboard pattern and baste the patch, near the fold edge of the hem, before stitching it in place.

When attaching a patch or appliqué to a garment, pin it in position before sewing it. This way you can make sure that it stays in the position you want it. To sew on the patch, you can either embroider it or hand-stitch it. To embroider, use a blanket stitch or an outline stitch. An *outline stitch* is sewn like the back stitch, except that the needle goes all the way back to the previous stitch (instead of just ⅛ in [3 mm] back) on the surface of the fabric. Or, if you don't want the stitches to show too much, use the overcast stitch or slip stitch A.

Replacing Fasteners

There probably isn't anyone who hasn't lost a button, broken a zipper, or pulled off a snap at least once. Such accidents can be very annoying, but it's easy to replace clothes fasteners if you know how.

One way to prevent such accidents is to check the fasteners on any new garment you buy. If buttons, hooks and eyes, or snaps are not attached securely, take a few minutes to sew them tight. That way there's no chance they'll fall off while you're wearing the garment. Many manufacturers of more expensive clothing provide you with extra buttons to use in case of loss. This is especially helpful if the buttons are covered in fabric, since they may be hard to replace. If your clothes come with extra buttons, store them with the rest of your sewing equipment so you'll know where they are if you need them.

Hooks, eyes, and snaps should be sewn on with small overcast stitches, as shown in Figure 20-7. When you're finished, lock the thread twice by running the needle through the last two overcast stitches and then through the loop formed by the needle thread when it's pulled through.

Thread loops, instead of metal eyes, are often used at neckline closings. You can make a thread loop by running four strands of thread over and under the surface of the fabric, allowing for enough extra space in the threads to form a loop, as shown in Figure 20-8. Then work a buttonhole stitch over the strands. When you're finished, lock the thread into the fabric at the bottom of the loop.

Any button used as a fastener should have a *shank,* or metal stem. (Buttons that are used just for decoration don't need one since they won't be opened and closed.) Some jacket and coat buttons have built-in shanks, like the one shown in Figure 20-9.

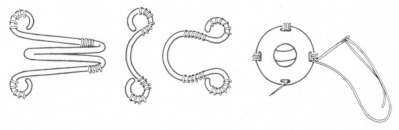

Fig. 20-7 Sew on hooks, eyes, and snaps with small overcasting stitches.

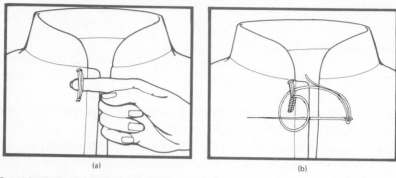

Fig. 20-8 When making a thread loop, allow enough slack so that your finger can fit comfortably under the threads (a). Work a buttonhole stitch over the threads to keep them together (b).

You attach such buttons by running at least six strands of heavy-duty thread through the shank and under the fabric at the bottom of the shank. Use a long needle because the eye has to be large enough for heavy-duty thread.

If a button has no built-in shank (two- and four-hole buttons don't), you can make one with thread as follows:

1.   Use heavy-duty single or double regular thread and a short needle. Knot the thread.

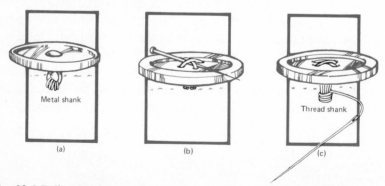

Fig. 20-9 Follow these steps in sewing on a button. (a) Use heavy-duty thread to sew on a button with a built-in shank. (b) Sew around a nail or a toothpick placed on top of the button to ensure that you leave an equal amount of space between the button and the fabric. (c) Remove the nail or toothpick and give the button a gentle pull so that the extra thread appears between the button and the fabric. Wrap the thread around the threads to make a strong shank.

2. Center the button over the spot where you want to sew it. With a pencil, make dots on the garment through each hole in the button.
3. Remove the button and insert the needle in one penciled dot, under the top layer of the fabric, and out through the dot diagonally across from it.
4. Place the button on the dots and bring the needle up through the same hole in the button.
5. To make sure you leave an even amount of space between the button and the fabric, place a thin nail (for heavy fabrics and large buttons) or a toothpick (for thinner fabrics and small buttons) on top of the button, as in Figure 20-9.
6. Holding the nail or toothpick in place with your thumb, bring the thread across it and insert the needle crosswise through the holes of the button into the spot where the thread knot is located.
7. To move the thread to the other hole of a four-hole button, push the needle into the spot where the knot is, run it underneath the surface, and bring it up through the adjacent hole. Repeat this step, ending with the needle and thread between the button and the garment.
8. To make the shank, remove the nail or toothpick and wrap the thread several times around the threads between the button and the fabric, as shown in Figure 20-9. Lock the thread a couple of times into the shank.

Buttons on heavy coats should be reinforced by using a small, flat button on the reverse side of the garment, directly under the outside button. Use the thread shank method in sewing on this type of button.

Replacing Zippers

Two of the most popular types of zippers are the lapped zipper and the centered zipper. The *lapped zipper* has a piece of material that overlaps the zipper. This type is usually used on slacks that have a fly front. The second type, the *centered zipper,* either has no material over it (as on the backs of many sweaters) or the material joins together as the zipper is pulled up (as on skirts with side zippers).

Both of these zippers are easy to replace. They should be sewn by hand, using the zipper, or pick, stitch.

When replacing a zipper:

- Measure the length of the teeth (not the length of the tape) of the broken zipper and buy one the same size, color, and type.
- Note how the original zipper is sewn in and try to follow the same sewing lines.
- Snip open any seams covering the top of the zipper tape and remove the old zipper (being careful not to stretch the seam) and any threads. This is where your small embroidery scissors or seam ripper will be especially handy.
- Trim the tape of the new zipper to the same size as the old one.
- Keep the zipper teeth closed while inserting it.

To replace a lapped zipper, pin the zipper tape under the extension side first. Figure 20-10 shows you which is the extension side.

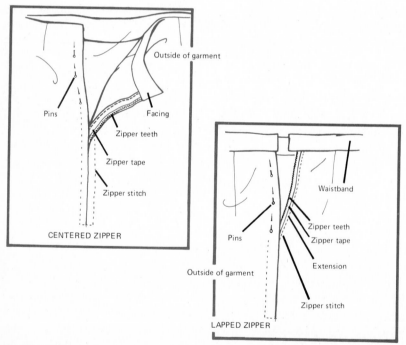

Fig. 20-10 These two illustrations show you how to position each type of zipper, how to pin it into place, and where to stitch the zipper tape.

The fold of the extension should touch the bottom of the teeth. Using the zipper stitch, stitch about ⅛ in [3 mm] from the fold line. Pin the top side of the garment to the left side of the tape. Starting at the bottom of the opening, zipper-stitch across, then up the left side. Resew the seams at the top into position over the zipper tape.

To replace a centered zipper, center the teeth on the seam opening. Pin both sides to the tape, using the ridge on the zipper tape as a guide. Working on the surface, zipper-stitch around the zipper, as shown in Figure 20-10.

Sewing Your Own

Although repairing and mending are necessary, they aren't very creative tasks. But now that you've learned the basic hand stitches, you're equipped to sew your own clothes, drapes, curtains, ties, scarves, and many more personal creations. Of course, the more advanced you get, the more you may need a sewing machine. But even if you just want to hand-sew, there are many things you can make. All you need is a needle and thread and a little imagination.

THINKING IT THROUGH

1. Making your own clothing repairs and alterations may not seem very exciting or even interesting. But it could mean a lot of money saved if the alternative is paying a dressmaker or tailor. Make a list of common repairs or alterations. What do dressmakers or tailors in your area charge for these services?
2. What are uses and applications of hand sewing besides clothing construction and repair? What crafts incorporate hand sewing?

PART FIVE

Time to Spare

Leisure:
A Timely Topic

"Life is going by too fast for me. I'm not accomplishing anything. . . . I'm not even learning anything. . . . Stop the clock!"[1]
—*Charlie Brown in* Peanuts

Do you sometimes feel, like Charlie, that time is your enemy rather than your most precious resource? Is this because time—unlike other resources—can't be saved for future use? Do you feel that you must make each day, each hour, each minute count—or it is lost forever? Do you feel you never have time to do the things you want to do?

Take a moment now and sit down and think about all the ways you spend your time. This is an important first step in taking control of your life. The way you use—or misuse—your time pretty well decides how satisfying your life is going to be.

Where Does the Time Go?

Ask yourself: What are the things you spend your lifetime doing? Try making a list of all your needs and responsibilities. Writing these things down will probably help you think them through. Your list may include some of the following:

1. Working or going to school. You may be doing either or both of these full- or part-time. These obligations most likely take the largest share of your time and energy.
2. Caring for your home. Whether you rent, buy, live on your own, live with your parents, or live with a roommate, your home still requires time and attention from you. Cleaning, painting, decorating, repairing—you are probably responsible for some of these chores.

[1]Text taken from *Peanuts* by Charles Schultz © 1976 United Feature Syndicate, Inc.

368

3. Caring for yourself. You must always make time to maintain your body. *Maintenance* includes such things as: buying and preparing food; choosing and washing your clothes; keeping healthy with exercise, vitamins, and medical care when necessary; bathing; and sleeping.
4. Going through the mechanics of living. You have certain responsibilities that are a small, fixed part of your daily or yearly routine. However small, they still take up your time. These include: arranging transportation, paying your income tax; buying insurance, paying your bills.
5. Developing relationships with others. Sometimes these relationships are an obligation and sometimes they are a joy. In any event, most people spend a large portion of their time with others, doing such things as coping with parents, getting along with co-workers, and seeing relatives and friends.
6. Enjoying leisure activities. Leisure is simply any free time you have that you spend on activities that interest you. The need for leisure is one that people neglect the most, for various reasons. One reason may be because some people know which leisure activities they *are not* interested in, but they haven't figured out which leisure-time activities they *are* interested in. So they do nothing. Other people fill their free time with things they enjoyed when they were children. Their use of leisure time has become a habit; they've never explored the many new possibilities now open to them as adults. In fact, if they are especially "good" at a particular activity, they may not wish to risk being "bad" at something new. Still other people haven't learned how to use their free time effectively—how to enjoy their leisure. They don't plan their time and so it is just wasted without being noticed. This doesn't mean you have to plan constant daily activities. But the point is that even a lazy afternoon's nap should be something that you want to do, not simply something you wind up doing.

In short, the problem of how to make time for leisure and what to do with it bothers many different people. Therefore, the focus of this part of the book will be on how to manage time for leisure activities and how to figure out which leisure activity is for you.

Time Traps

Each of us handles time in a different manner. This can mean using time effectively to satisfy and develop ourselves and or it can mean falling into some common but unsatisfying time traps. Let's look at the experiences other singles have had in coping with the time problem.

Procrastination   Lori, an office secretary, lived in Los Angeles. The cultural opportunities included the finest anywhere: museums, stage plays, ice shows, concerts, travel programs, sporting events, lectures, lessons, classes—almost everything. But she never went anywhere! "I thought I could always go," she said, "so I seldom

Fig. 21-1 Joining a theater group provides many opportunities for growth. You can make new friends, as well as try new skills such as acting. (Katherine Peticolas)

Fig. 21-2 In an activity like folk dancing, good coordination and expertise are less important than enthusiasm and interest. (Susan Berkowitz)

bothered. Going out was too much trouble—dressing, arranging transportation, maybe getting a friend to go with me. Later, I realized I had missed a lot of things that could have been fun."

When Lori moved to a small town where professional entertainment was sparse, she found that when something did come to town, *everyone* went and it was talked about for days. After she became a part of the community she started attending the local theater group plays, adult school classes, the local symphony concerts. "I'm really into the things the people do here," she said. "The community spirit more than makes up for the lack of professional talent and going to local events is always such a friendly thing."

Fear Does shyness or fear hold you back? Barbara had always been interested in dance, but was afraid to take any classes. She'd never been very "good" at doing gymnastics or at sports. She was convinced she was a klutz and didn't want to make a fool of herself trying. Then Barbara got to know Valerie, one of the people she worked with. Valerie belonged to a folk dancing club that met once a week to practice folk dances from around the world. When Barbara expressed interest in Valerie's dancing activities, Valerie invited her to join in. "Interest and enthusiasm," insisted Valerie, "are more important than being graceful or coordinated." Barbara held back for several weeks, but finally, one day, she went with Valerie to her class. Valerie was right. The dance club was made up of a motley group of people—men, women, young, old. Some were beginners and some very experienced dancers. They all just belonged for the fun of it. Barbara began to feel less and less self-conscious (although she never did get more graceful). She made a lot of new friends and never missed another weekly dance activity.

Busyness   Some people fall into the trap of "making work expand to fit the time available." Many people do this in order to feel important, as if busyness meant their lives were somehow worthwhile.

When Mary Ann got out of school, she took a part-time job so she would still have time to take classes or get further training. Also, she reasoned, a part-time job would leave her time to take up weaving, something she'd always wanted to try. Instead of taking classes or doing some weaving, Mary Ann found herself endlessly puttering about the house, keeping busy with small household tasks, but accomplishing little of real importance. Mary Ann, like a lot of people, felt guilty when she was quietly reading or weaving. This sometimes happens to people who were brought up in homes where only active, "productive" work was valued by the parents. Mary Ann felt more important and productive when she was constantly busy. She even liked to complain that she was too busy to get to her weaving.

Disorganization   David looked forward to being on his own as a chance to do what he wanted when he wanted. No more of his mother's nagging about yardwork, taking out the garbage, sweeping the garage—and no more being criticized for "wasting" all those hours in bed on weekends.

After three months on his own, though, his new life was disappointing to him. The place was a mess. Shopping, washing, cook-

Fig. 21-3 David always put off unpleasant chores like washing the dishes until every dish and pan in the place was dirty. Then, he had to spend twice as long getting them all clean again.

ing, cleaning—things he had never done at home—took up all his time. Sometimes he wished he was back in his old room with fewer responsibilities, better meals, and more real "free" time to do as he pleased. He had found endless responsibilities instead of new freedom.

Luckily, David acquired an "organized" roommate who had learned the basics of shopping, cooking, home maintenance, washing, and managing before he left home. Despite rationalization, most people do not find contentment or enjoy living in a "pigpen" environment. Dirty dishes, disorganization in meal planning and preparation, unkept clothes, and clutter everywhere lead to depression and feelings of poor self-worth and hopelessness.

David soon became more skillful in managing his time as well as learning how to do things on his own. He planned certain times to do things each day so that weekends and certain week-nights were free. He began to have a feeling of self-mastery. Time he had earned began to have more meaning and to be more fulfilling, just as did the money he earned himself. To work for something gives us a very special appreciation for it.

Inertia Watching television can take up a lot of a single's leisure time. It's very easy to simply sit and watch television out of inertia or boredom. Turning on the tube provides instant company, keeps us from hearing scary little noises when we are home alone, and helps us forget any unhappy experiences of the day.

It is estimated that the average American citizen watches television for an average of 18 hours a week. This is about equal to the time that is usually spent on a part-time job. This time could be spent otherwise, learning a new hobby or craft, continuing your education, or earning additional income. Properly used, this time could make a lot of dreams come true—dreams you may have gotten from watching TV!

Of course, there are some worthwhile things on television. If you are a sports fan, you can follow your favorite team. Some community colleges and universities offer courses during the early morning hours. Important national events can sometimes be witnessed in your home at a better vantage point than if you were there in person. There are all sorts of specials about animals, the sea, and outer space. Concerts and plays are sometimes broadcast.

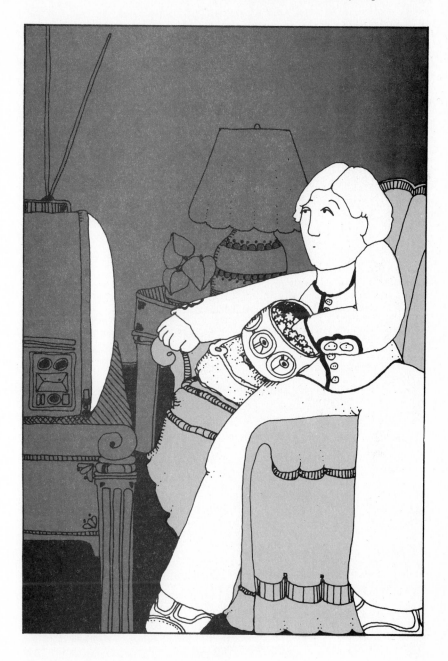

Fig. 21-4 Some people just sit and watch television all night because they are too bored or too tired to do anything else.

In general, though, people usually sit in one spot all evening and watch whatever happens to be broadcast. Hours of precious leisure time slip by as people watch television simply because they can't decide what else to do.

What purpose does television fill in your life? Are you bored?

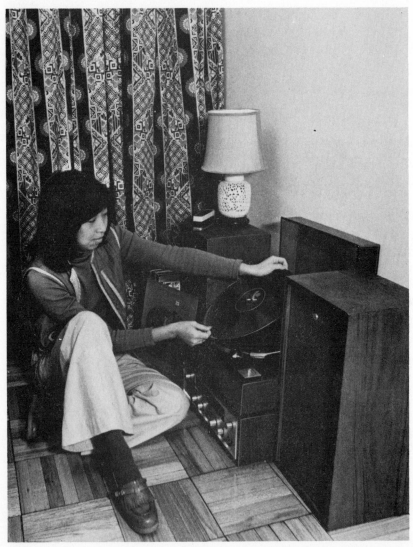

Fig. 21-5 Listening to your favorite records would probably be more fun than watching TV aimlessly. (Ginger Chih)

frustrated? tired? at a loss for anything else to do? lonely? When you find yourself watching TV for any of these reasons, ask yourself what else you could be doing. Here is a list of suggestions. What appeals to you?

- Telephone a friend.
- Catch up on studying.
- Make something.
- Read something.
- Write a letter (you might get a reply soon).
- Sleep (late shows can wipe you out).
- Listen to music.
- Invite a friend over for the evening.
- Take a walk.

Keeping Time

Next week, try recording where your hours are being spent. You might draw up a time log, like the one shown in Figure 21-6. Each day log in what you do and how long it takes you to do it. At the end of the week, evaluate how you've used your time. Have you been doing those things that are most important to you? Or do you find that you've been wasting precious hours? Can you make some time for leisure?

Learning Your ABCs

Alan Lakein, author of *How to Get Control of Your Time and Your Life*, has observed that many people never get anything done because they never get it started. We get distracted by all sorts of things. We get involved in some other, less important task; or there doesn't seem to be enough time to do what is really important to us. Lakein suggests that each person should set priorities for his or her daily tasks.

Highly important, must-do tasks are A's; tasks that are important but could be postponed are B's, and tasks that are repetitious, less important, and could be omitted are C's. Most people fill their time with B and C tasks. This is because C tasks are easier, and when

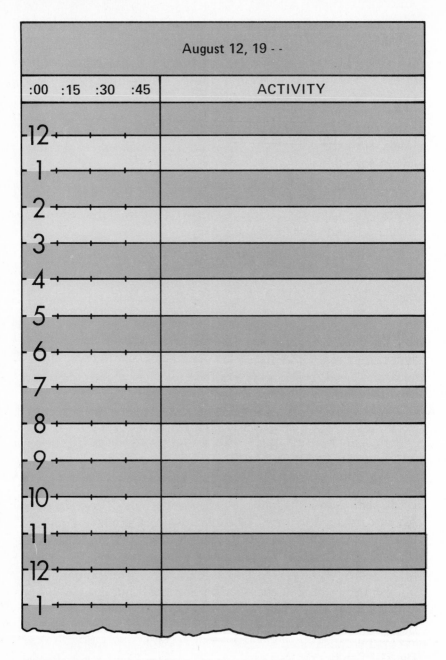

Fig. 21-6 Keep an hourly time log; write down what you do and how long it takes you to do it. Then, evaluate how you've spent your week.

Fig. 21-7 Bob has not learned to assign priorities to the things he wants to do. Instead of finishing his short story (an A task), he spent all day Saturday washing the windows (a C task).

you've accomplished them, you see immediate results. A tasks, however, are more difficult, are sometimes less enjoyable, and may not show immediate results.

For example, Bob spent all day Saturday washing windows rather than finishing the short story he'd begun ages ago and still hoped to publish someday. Lately, he's felt very frustrated with his writing. So he decided to wash the windows rather than work on his story. The strategy worked. When he finished the windows, Bob felt very proud of his accomplishment: The windows were certainly clean and sparkling.

Alan Lakein thinks that people should concentrate on accomplishing one A task and simply ignore all the C tasks. In the long run, he says, people feel more satisfied when they accomplish a challenging or difficult task. If Bob concentrated on improving his writing, he might someday publish that short story. But he may never get this done if he doesn't assign priorities and figure out what's most important to him.

Getting Started

Take a few minutes right now to decide how you really want to spend your time. Don't wait for the "perfect" time or let yourself get involved in some other activity. Try writing down a time schedule for yourself. Don't plan every moment, but allow time for what you want done. If you have to study math or chemistry, of if you want to write or sew or work on a new hobby, set aside an hour per day for that purpose only. Plan this time even if you have to get up earlier or stay up later to fit it in.

Each morning, set priorities for the day. Tackle one of your tasks, even if you can't possibly finish it right away. Take up that A task whenever you have a spare moment. Don't let yourself be distracted by any other job.

Get started fast. Most jobs are bigger to think about than to do. Plan to do the hardest things at a time when your energy level is highest. (For example, if you're a morning person, do them first thing in the morning.)

Don't hesitate to reward yourself when you've accomplished important tasks. Remember, you are your own best source of praise and encouragement!

THINKING IT THROUGH

1. A notable advertising poster of a few years back was entitled "The Face of the Enemy." The face was that of a clock. Do you feel that this is a fair way of depicting time or not? Why?
2. It's often said that "time goes by swiftly when you're having fun," or, on the other hand, that "the minutes seem like hours." Is there any truth in this? Do people really believe that some minutes or hours are actually shorter or longer than other minutes or hours?
3. Chapter 21 lists a number of categories into which a person's uses of time can be divided. Write down *one word* to describe your most important category of time use (not including eating, sleeping, and school attendance). Share your list with the other students in your class. Are there similarities and contrasts in the ways individuals think of their use of time?

Hobby Shopping

Now that you've learned how to make time for leisure activities, the next step is to decide what leisure activity you would like to start with. This decision can be a little difficult because there are so many activities available. The best way to start out is to decide what makes you happy.

Think back to the last happy experience you had. What exactly was it that made you feel happy? Was it because you were successful at something you tried?

In her book, *Success: You Can Make It Happen,* Dr. Lila Swell explains that there are eight major kinds of successful experiences. Each kind of successful experience satisfies a particular human need (and makes you happy). Look at Table 22-1. This table lists a wide variety of human needs. The needs have been grouped into categories. Read each category and list of needs carefully. Are any of these things important to you? Now think back to your successful experience. What *kind* of experience was it? Which category did it fall into? Aesthetic? (This means artistic or creative, as when you draw a picture.) Physical? Economic? Emotional? Social? More important, what needs did your happy experience satisfy? Were you praised by your peers? Did you make something on your own?

You may find that your experience fits into more than one category. Or that the experience satisfies many different kinds of needs. This is OK. It simply means that you should look for a leisure activity that also satisfies a variety of needs.

Know Your Needs

So now you know what your needs are. And you're probably wondering what *type* of hobby or leisure activity would satisfy all these needs. There are four basic types of hobbies—collecting, creating, educational, and performing. Each type of hobby offers satisfactions.

Table 22-1   HUMAN NEEDS[1]

Aesthetic	Need for beauty Need to create Need for nature
Physical	Need to have a beautiful body Need to master a sport

Economic	Need for material things, status, money,
	  nice clothes, luxurious home,
	  expensive car
	Need to sell things for a profit

Emotional	Need for approval from peers
	Need for recognition, awards,
	  promotions, raises, fame
	Need for pleasure
	Need for independence
	Need for emotional growth and
	  awareness
	Need to be special
	Need for security, for stable
	  relationships
	Need for new experiences

Social	Need to be with people Need to nurture and help others to grow Need for acceptance and popularity Need for intimacy and closeness Need to travel
Power	Need to compete and win Need to be in charge Need to influence Need to overcome difficult obstacles Need to do things on your own Need to organize
Religious	Need to be in harmony with God Need to work for church
Intellectual	Need to learn Need for academic degrees Need to communicate through writing and speaking Need to excel

[1]Copyright © 1976 by Lila Swell. Reprinted by permission of Simon and Schuster, a division of Gulf and Western Corporation.

Collecting   A natural habit for many people, collecting can become a very serious hobby. The two most popular (and well-
known) collection hobbies are stamps and antiques. However, the
possibilities for collection hobbies are almost unlimited. People collect coins, books, clocks, china, paintings, matchbooks, autographs,
stamps, seashells—the list is endless. Although the best part of the
collection hobby is the fun of looking for something special, the
hobby also satisfies many other needs. For example, collecting
coins, jewelry, paintings, stamps, etc., can satisfy a need for beauty
as well as the need for material possessions. Collecting gives you
an opportunity to trade or buy for profit; can bring approval and
admiration from your family and peers; can win you awards in
hobby shows; can satisfy your need to exercise your own judgment
and be independent.

Creating   Creating is an activity that a lot of people are afraid to
try. They get bogged down in worrying about whether what they
create is "good enough." They forget to relax and just enjoy the
process of making something.
   Creative hobbies can require a range of skills, from very simple
to rather complicated and precise. Of course, the enjoyment you
get out of a creative task depends on how much you like doing it,
not on how difficult it is. And, there are many, many creative hobbies for you to choose from. These include model making, cooking,
knitting, sewing, woodworking, sculpture, painting, leatherworking,
gardening, embroidery, weaving, macrame, photography, pottery,
decoupage, and so on.
   You'll find that a creative hobby can satisfy many of your needs.
Most obvious, of course, is the need for beauty. Another is the
need to produce something entirely by yourself. This can include
thinking of a pattern, shape, or design; gathering the materials you
need and want to use; and then making your project from beginning to end without anyone else's advice or help. Creative hobbies
also satisfy the need for peer-group recognition achieved through
hobby shows and sales; the need to learn new skills; and the need
to be special, to have a unique talent or interest.

Educational   As a high-school student, you might not think of
studying and going to classes as a "hobby"! However, for many

Fig. 22-1 A collecting hobby can be a lot of fun. Whether you collect stamps or seashells, it's always exciting to find and identify each new addition.

Fig. 22-2 In a creating hobby like pottery, the important thing is to let your imagination loose and make whatever pleases you. (Susan Berkowitz, Earthworks Pottery)

Fig. 22-3 You could use some of your leisure time to learn a skill just for fun—playing the piano, for example. (Joan Fisher)

people, learning new skills is a leisure-time activity that they really enjoy. They look upon learning as an adventure—exploring new territory and working hard to become competent or even skillful.

If you think you might like to try studying for fun, there are all kinds of educational hobbies you could choose from. They include studying plant life, animal life, or the stars; learning to dance, sing, or play a musical instrument; and learning to speak a foreign language. Remember, when you decide on an educational hobby, you only have to please yourself. You study and practice as much as you want to.

Although, of course, some people simply take classes in subjects they find interesting, many others go to night classes for further academic or vocational training. They may hope this additional education will improve their chances for promotions or raises. Or if they plan to switch careers altogether, they may be learning the skills necessary for the new field. Such further education may include computer programming, electronics, bookkeeping, and automotive repair. If you are interested in a different or specialized career, perhaps you can find out what "continuing ed" courses your local high school or community college offers.

An educational hobby suits many human needs. Your new knowledge and skills can earn approval from your peers and recognition from instructors and employers, make you independent and more self-confident, satisfy your need to learn and overcome obstacles. Attending classes provides an opportunity to meet new people and make friends.

Fig. 22-4 You could use some of your leisure time to learn a skill that will help advance your career—electronics or bookkeeping, for example. (Ginger Chih)

Performing Many people find pleasure in performing for others as well as in knowing they are improving their skills. Too often, however, a person will hang back from trying a performance hobby because of fear of failure. These people should realize that there are a great many performing hobbies, all requiring varying degrees of grace, expertise, and practice and many different kinds of skills.

If you think you would like to try a performing hobby, then see what your community offers. Are there municipal teams or leagues for baseball, basketball, tennis, bowling, volleyball, table tennis? Does your school sponsor swimming competitions or track meets? Is there a local orchestra, choir, theater group, ski club? Does your town have a roller- or ice-skating rink? Is there a bicycling club? Can you go to the local Y for exercise classes? Are there stables where you can rent horses to ride?

Performing hobbies can satisfy many human needs, especially the needs to master a sport and to compete and win. Related to these are the needs to win peer group approval, to gain recognition for achievement, to be with people, to gain independence, to overcome difficult obstacles, and to excel at something you consider important.

Factors to Consider

By now, you must have some ideas about which hobbies or leisure-time activities would satisfy your personal needs. Before you plunge in to try them, though, you should probably consider the following:

Location Where you live will affect your choice of recreational activities. What facilities are available in your community? Are there museums, theatres, swimming pools, tennis courts? What about the physical characteristics of the area? Are there lakes, deserts, or mountains nearby? What kind of climate does your area have—very cold, very hot, or moderate? Think about how these factors will influence your activity. For example, if you live in or near•the mountains, you could probably ski for most of the year.

Space The question of space is a very important one. Ample space can make the difference between whether you really enjoy your hobby or dread having to get involved in it. To avoid any

Fig. 22-5 One of the factors that may determine your choice of hobby is the facilities available. Check to see if there are tennis courts, swimming pools, skating rinks, and so on in your area. (Susan Berkowitz)

problems, first find out how much space you need for the activity you're thinking of. Then consider your living space. Do you live in a home with a basement or in a one-bedroom apartment? Does your dream of a darkroom compete with your need for a bedroom? Have you space for a greenhouse, or is a window box more your size? Can you leave your woodworking or sewing equipment out and close the door, or must you clean up when you finish for the day?

Money Some hobbies can be extremely expensive. It's a good idea to find out ahead of time just how much your hobby will cost you. Check out the cost of your materials or equipment, lessons, admission tickets or season passes, electricity, and transportation. Add all the costs up. Depending on how often you have to pay these costs, this tally should give you a pretty good idea of how much the hobby will cost you.

Finding out all the costs is only the first step, however. Now you should figure out how much money you have available for a hobby. Begin by writing down your monthly income after taxes. Subtract from this income all your "fixed expenses"—things you must pay for every single month. This would include your rent or mortgage payments, utility bills, retail installment loans, deposits in your savings accounts, etc. Next, subtract all your "variable expenses" — things that may change from month to month. Since these expenses are always changing, the best you can do is to figure out what is the *average amount* you spend on each variable item. These expenses include what you normally spend on food, clothing, home furnishings, transportation, toiletries, etc.

When you have subtracted all your fixed and variable expenses from your income, the amount remaining is what you have available to spend on hobbies or leisure activities. Now look back at the cost of the hobby you're thinking about. If the hobby requires more money than you have available, maybe you had better look for another hobby. Something else might cost less and give you just as much pleasure.

Time Sometimes it's hard to figure out how much time you would spend on a hobby. It all depends on how advanced you are, how much you enjoy it, how much time you have, how much time it

Monthly after-tax income	$500.00

Fixed expenses

Rent	150.00
Utilities (light and electricity)	100.00
Car loan	40.00
Savings deposit	10.00
Subtotal	$300.00

Variable expenses

Food	$100.00
Clothes	20.00
Transportation	40.00
Toiletries	10.00
Subtotal	$170.00
TOTAL left to spend on leisure activities	$30.00

Fig. 22-6 To figure out how much you can spend on recreation, first write down your monthly salary after taxes. Then subtract fixed expenses and variable expenses. The amount remaining is what you can comfortably spend on leisure activities.

Fig. 22-7 Shop around for equipment. The best buy is not always the most expensive and the best bargain is not always the cheapest. (Susan Berkowitz)

takes to get set up, etc. But you should really try to get some idea about the amount of time you would want to spend on a hobby you are interested in, and about how much time the hobby requires! Otherwise, you might invest in all the equipment and never find a chance to use it.

In Chapter 21, you made up a weekly time log. For the entire week, you recorded all your activities and how long you spend on them. Then you analyzed how you spend your time—whether or not it was on things that were important to you.

Now look back at your time log. How much time did you decide you could make for leisure? Is this enough time to enjoy your hobby thoroughly? Or will you always feel rushed to finish or cheated if you can't even get started?

Fig. 22-8 Choose a leisure-time activity that balances your work activities. If you are sitting indoors all day, you might like to balance this with a physically demanding sport like soccer. If you are physically active all day, you might prefer a quieter hobby like plant collecting. (Susan Berkowitz)

Balance   You will probably enjoy your leisure-time activity more if it balances your work-time activity. For example, people who do hard physical work, such as carpentry, might prefer a hobby that is less demanding physically, such as stamp collecting. However, on the other hand, people who are seated at desks all day long, as students are, might prefer a strenuous sport such as softball. Balancing your activities in this manner is good for your mind as well as for your body. You'll find it can be very refreshing to start a totally new task when you're thoroughly tired of doing something. A change of pace makes you feel interested and energetic all over again. So when choosing a hobby or an activity, first analyze what kind of antidote you need—a workout or a rest.

This chapter has focused mainly on sports and hobbies. There are, of course, many other activities that you can enjoy during your leisure time. Read on for some ideas about volunteer work, travel, camping, and more.

THINKING IT THROUGH

1. Do you have hobbies—activities to which you are committed outside of school and outside of organized youth activities? If so, what are they? If not, what are the factors that have kept you from becoming involved in a hobby? Do you think this will change later on in your life?

2. What if someone proposed to the School Board that every young person in school should be encouraged to get into a hobby—some kind of sport, collecting, creative, or performing activity that the young person could learn and stay with for a lifetime. According to the proposal, every student would be given time, equipment, information, and perhaps even small amounts of money for strictly private hobby activity. Do you think this would be a good idea or not? Why?

Time for Others

Volunteer work can be one of the most rewarding leisure time activities. There is no talent or skill that isn't in big demand every day of the year. If you are willing to help, you can always be sure that someone out there needs you.

What's In It for You?

Recent estimates of the number of unpaid volunteers in America have ranged between 38 and 45 million. This means that almost one in every three people 15 years of age or older participates in some form of volunteer service. That there are such large numbers of volunteers seems to indicate that these people find helping others very satisfying. There are several reasons for the great interest in volunteer work.

"Doing Good"   As we have said, many people everywhere try to help others through volunteer work. However, probably very few of these people have actually thought much about what really is involved in their helping relationship.

There is a simple truth about volunteer work that's easy to forget: Helping is a two-way process involving both the giver and receiver. This means that helping can provide benefits for both the helper and the helped, and yet it can also cause feelings that make each side uncomfortable and unhappy.

Helping others has always been called a deed we do "out of the goodness of our hearts." Often, though, as givers, we find it hard to be totally generous. We feel we deserve something in return—perhaps just simple thanks, or perhaps an improvement in the receiver's condition. Then, if the people we help are ungrateful—misusing or wasting the gift—or if they don't seem to "improve"

Fig. 23-1 Everyone has some training, talents, or experience that could be put to good use through volunteer work. If, for example, you play basketball well, you could volunteer to coach a team at the "Y." (National Council of YMCAs)

with our help, we are disappointed. Either we label them as undeserving, or we resolve that next time we will be more careful to tie strings to our giving—if indeed we do any more giving. It's hard to keep in mind that receivers may find it difficult to admit they need our help, or may find it embarrassing to have to rely on someone else. In addition, a person who accepts help must give up the known, however unpleasant, for something he or she has yet not experienced. This can be frightening. The best approach to volunteer work is not to worry about ultimate thanks or results, but

Fig. 23-2 Working at your local recycling center gives you a chance to help clean up the environment. Here, a volunteer tests soda cans to see if they are made of aluminum. (Susan Berkowitz)

to focus instead on the simple daily satisfactions that can be gained from helping others.

Spending time with older, handicapped, or underprivileged people allows you to learn about their lives and understand their feelings. Working as a candy-striper or teacher's aide is an opportunity to learn about the special needs people have when they are very sick or very young. Organizing or running the local recycling center gives you a chance to help clean up some small part of the environment.

Getting a Head Start on Your Career   Volunteer work can be an important boost to your career plans. Here are some of the many advantages to helping out in an organization or institution:

Experience   After you've graduated from school and are applying for a job, one question you will always be asked is, "What experience have you had?" This can be very frustrating if you have to answer "none." After a few such interviews, you begin to wonder how it is possible to gain experience if no one will hire you in the first place!

A good solution to the problem of how to get experience is to do some volunteer work. Experience in volunteer work can help you whether or not you know what kind of career you'll want after graduation. If you do already have career plans, then think about volunteer work in your particular field or in a related one. If you want to be a doctor or nurse, how about volunteering as a candy-striper in a hospital, or as a worker in a free or county clinic. If you want a secretarial career, check with your school's administrative office. Such offices are almost always understaffed and welcome any help with filing, typing, and answering phones. If you want to be a teacher, see if your school system utilizes teaching assistants and if you could use your free periods to volunteer as one. If this doesn't work out, try tutoring other students in subjects you are strong in.

Use your imagination in finding volunteer opportunities. Even if you haven't yet chosen a career, you will still find the experience

Fig. 23-3 If you are interested in a teaching career, one way to gain work experience is by assisting at a day-care center. (Dan Brinzac)

helpful later. Prospective employers will be pleased to see that you took the initiative, found a volunteer job, worked steadily at it, and were responsible and capable.

Information   Volunteering provides many other benefits besides work experience. As a volunteer, you will probably get to know a lot of professional people you might never meet otherwise. They are usually willing to share their knowledge with you, and this can be very valuable. For example, you might learn what's the best kind of training to get and where to get it. Or you might learn why and how certain tasks are done in the profession. Best of all, while doing volunteer work, you may hear about a job opening in your field. Just being there, knowing the people who run the program, and having some experience and knowledge could help qualify you for the job.

References   If, as a volunteer, you have done your best—been prompt, honest, and reliable—then you should be able to use your "boss" as a reference. (Someone who will tell a prospective employer about your work background is called a *reference*.) Usually you can ask your reference to write you a letter of recommendation or to allow you to use his or her name on an employment application. Volunteer work provides an unusual opportunity to gain "respectable" work references without actually having a full-time job.

Janice   Here's the story of one person whose volunteer work really paid off.

In Janice's hometown, a federally-funded consumer education program was administered by the local community college. Each semester the program accepted two or three student volunteers to assist the small staff. In return, the students received college credit for the experience they gained working in different phases of the program.

Over a period of several years, a number of students came and went, each dutifully completing the assigned tasks. The year Janice entered the community college, she was also "hired" by the consumer education program. Janice worked very hard and the staff really appreciated her. She was self-directed and did not need con-

Fig. 23-4 While she was a student, Janice was a volunteer worker in her school's consumer education program. She always worked very hard and impressed the staff with her interest and dedication.

stant supervising. She had innovative ideas to share and was prompt and uncomplaining about the work to be done. She was always neat and professional in her appearance and attitude. In general, the staff thought Janice fitted in perfectly.

Shortly after Janice graduated, the program unexpectantly expanded. There was more money in the budget to add another full-time staffer. Janice got the job. At a time of high unemployment, she was chosen over many older, more experienced applicants —some even with advanced degrees. The reason was that as far as the staff was concerned, Janice was familiar with the exact work that would be needed and had certainly proved herself capable.

Many such internships are available at high school and community college levels. As you look around at various volunteer programs and possibilities, don't overlook these internships for credit. They can be a great opportunity to get experience in the real world!

Getting to Know Your Neighbors   Although we sometimes find it hard to admit, at one time or another, we all need and want to be around other people. We like to hear their thoughts and experiences and tell them ours; go out and do things together; have someone to turn to for advice and help when necessary. If you live with your family and in the same neighborhood you grew up in, then you are probably surrounded by people you know, care about, and feel comfortable with. You probably know all your neighbors—next door, across the way, down the street. You may have a wide circle of friends—people you met in school, at camp, at municipal teams, at parties, or through mutual friends. Your relatives may live nearby or in the same town or state.

If this description fits you, then you should have no trouble satisfying your needs to be with people. However, if you or your family moved recently, you may not know anybody. This can be very lonely and can make going to school or to work just a little harder. You may spend all your time wishing someone would show an interest in you or would invite you over for a visit. If you keep waiting for other people to make the first move, though, you may wait forever. They may be busy with their own lives and simply not notice you. *You* have to take the first step to meet people.

Getting involved in volunteer work is a good way to reach out

Fig. 23-5 Getting involved in a local civics program like a park-cleanup is a good way to meet your neighbors as well as to accomplish something you believe in. (James H. Karales, Peter Arnold Photo Archives)

to people. Civic groups, for example, are an interesting way of making friends. When you join a conservation group or a tenants committee, you automatically meet a lot of people who share one of your special interests. As a group you will all work together for a common goal and experience the same advances and setbacks. Under these conditions, people usually draw closer together.

You might also consider volunteering for a school or church committee. Such a group is also usually based on a common, shared interest. In this case, it may be earning money for a new student lounge or gathering clothes for the needy. The people you meet are likely to be warm and friendly and will probably welcome your help.

Community volunteer work offers contact with a wide variety of people. If you reach out to them, you can satisfy all your "people" needs. They can become your neighbors—lending a hand and watching out for your safety. And, if you wish, they can be your friends—sharing your life and helping you to find happiness.

What Can You Do?

Maybe you are interested in doing some volunteer work, but don't know where to begin. How do you find out what kind of volunteer activities are available? Whom do you contact to join? What kinds of things do the volunteers get involved in?

The best way to find out what volunteer activities are available is simply to ask around. Talk to people you know at work, school, or church; ask them about any volunteer activities they do. Also keep your eyes open when you read the paper or watch TV. Very often there is news about various volunteer organizations and their functions. Look in the Yellow Pages under "volunteer" or "social services" to see what organizations are listed. Go to your local library and ask the librarian for information on volunteer groups.

When you've found an activity you think you might be interested in, call or write the director for information about what the group does and how to join. If it's a national organization and you're not sure where the regional chapter is in your area, write to the national headquarters. The people there will tell you about the chapter nearest you, or if there isn't a local chapter, they may tell you how to start one.

Listed below are some activities that beginning volunteers are often interested in. Read through the list. Does anything appeal to you?

- *Day care/head start.* If you like children, then you could work at your local day-care or head-start center. Your responsibilities might include assisting the teacher, playing with the kids, feeding them, and helping with arts and crafts activities and games.
- *Senior citizens.* Check to see if your high school or church has an "outreach" program for senior citizens. A typical program might utilize young people to assist senior citizens in a number of ways. For example, you might be asked to help out at group functions: putting on a handicrafts show, staging a play, or serving the Thanksgiving dinner. Or you might be asked to help senior citizens on a more individual basis. This could mean visiting elderly people in their homes, or spending time with them chatting, playing checkers, having lunch. Or it could be going with senior citizens to the grocery store, bank, etc., to help them

Fig. 23-6 Participating in a neighborhood senior-citizen program could mean simply spending some time with elderly people, chatting, playing bingo, or having lunch. (Ginger Chih)

with these tasks. Providing individual assistance is a perfect opportunity to get to know an older person closely.

- *Big Brother/Big Sister.* These well-known organizations have local branches over all the country. They try to provide adult role models and companionship to kids aged 8 to 16 who are from single-parent homes. A big brother's or big sister's main responsibility is to build a strong, caring friendship with a kid. Most often, this simply means listening and talking, going places together, and spending time together. You must be 18 or over to be a big brother or big sister. If you want to volunteer, call or write the local chapter for an application.
- *Boys Club.* Although the Boys Club is a program for boys 6 to 17 years old, it welcomes both male and female volunteers. The Boys Club offers kids a range of activities, and as a volunteer, you can participate in whatever interests you. You might, for

Fig. 23-7 The role of a Big Brother volunteer is to build a strong, caring friendship with a kid. (Big Brothers, Inc.)

example, assist with athletic competitions, or advise the science or photography club. Or you might tutor a kid in one of your stronger subjects. If you are 18 or older and are interested in offering your help, talk to the director of your local Boys Club.

- *Hospital volunteers.* Helping out in a hospital is probably the oldest and most traditional form of volunteer service. The volunteers' role in a hospital is a special one. They provide patients with many benefits and services that go beyond the usual medical care. These services can include: assisting patients in recreation areas, working on arts and crafts activities, escorting patients to other parts of the hospital, and going with patients on various outings. As a volunteer, you might also work in the clinics, helping people to cope with admission procedures: translating for non-English-speaking patients, filling out forms, reassuring anx-

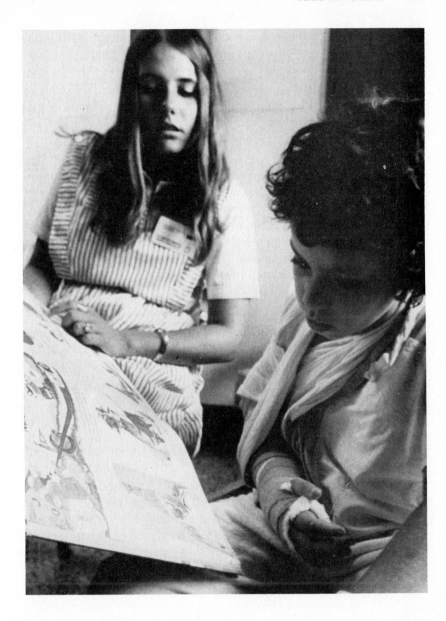

Fig. 23-8 The important qualifications for hospital work are concern, warmth, maturity, and reliability. As a volunteer, you may participate in a wide variety of activities—from working in the hospital library to making patients happy and comfortable. (St. Vincent's Hospital)

ious patients. You might work in the hospital library or administrative office, doing typing, filing, and other clerical tasks. You might be assigned to deliver toys on pediatric floors, or to help out in the gift shop. There is usually no age or experience requirement necessary for hospital volunteer work. The most important qualifications are concern, warmth, maturity, and reliability. Call your hospital to find out what kind of volunteer programs they have.

- *Recycling centers.* The easiest way to find out about working in your local recycling center is to take your trash for recycling! Once there, you will probably see volunteers tying up newspapers, sorting aluminum cans, crushing glass containers, and trucking tin and steel to steel companies. These volunteers usually began by bringing their own recyclables to the center and one day just started helping out. There is no age requirement.
- *Political parties/campaigns.* The people running political campaigns always need volunteer help. If you are enthusiastic about a particular candidate or platform, then you might consider volunteering your time and energy, as well as your vote. Of course, campaign work is not very glamorous—usually writing letters, stuffing envelopes, or handing out leaflets. But you may find it satisfying to play this role in the political system. To volunteer, simply call or visit the local campaign headquarters for the party or candidate you're interested in.
- *Legislators' offices.* Many legislators' offices—state senators and representatives, as well as city councilpersons—need volunteer office workers. These people do mostly clerical and administrative tasks. However, as a volunteer, you may also get the opportunity to participate in an investigation or do some research for proposed legislation. Working in a legislator's office gives you a closeup view of what a politician does after you help elect him or her. Again, call or write if you wish to volunteer your time.
- *Special-interest groups.* There are special-interest groups on every level in the political system—municipal, state, and national. These organizations promote a huge variety of causes.

If you feel strongly about some issue—a nuclear plant being built in your vicinity, or the pollution of a nearby river or lake— find out if there's a citizens group concerned with the problem. Call or write them to ask what you could do. Volunteers are almost never turned away by special-interest groups. Generally, the work here is much the same as in legislator's offices—a few hours a week of fairly routine clerical work. For people who wish to commit more time and energy, there may be some other opportunities.

So now you know a little more about how and why people volunteer their time. You may even have a fairly good idea about which volunteer activity you'd like to try. Well, then, pitch in!

THINKING IT THROUGH

1. Volunteer work has itself become a career for many young people. Professional fund-raisers are paid to direct volunteer workers soliciting money for churches, hospitals, schools, and other community institutions. Hospitals and charitable organizations have salaried staff members who organize the work of volunteers. Do you or do you not think this is a good idea? Why?

2. Most organizations that use volunteers will welcome anyone who wants to work; it is said that there are "never enough volunteers." What would you think of an organization that required an "employment application" from volunteers, limited the number of volunteers used, and "fired" any who were not doing satisfactory work? Would you approve or disapprove of this system? Why?

3. Investigate the opportunities for volunteer work in your community. After you have found three to five possibilities, select the one that you would choose if you were going to become a volunteer. What are your reasons for this choice?

Travel:
Wheels and Wings

America has always been a nation of travelers. Our heritage of wandering began with the earliest American settlers—the Indians. Many historians believe that the Indians migrated to the American continent from Asia via the Bering Strait. Once here, some of the tribes continued to wander in different directions—east, west, and south. Years later, the Indians' travel tradition was carried on by the early American colonists. These people, emigrants from Great Britain and Europe, sailed to the new land with curiosity and daring. Upon arrival, many of them settled down on the coast and began to build and farm. Many others, however, were restless and felt they had to move on—westward. Transportation in those days was on foot, on horseback, in ox carts, and in wagon trains.

Many years later, after the automobile was invented in 1896, travel became easier and quicker. People were able to travel longer distances and still return home in the same day. Eventually, as the car became more and more widely used, living in cities became less important. People were no longer limited to living close to schools, stores, work, and churches. They began to move out into the surrounding countryside, depending on their cars to get them wherever they had to go. "Suburbs," or residential areas, began to grow up outside the cities. A whole new way of life emerged—one in which people needed cars and drove everywhere.

Today, car-driving Americans still carry on the travel tradition. On holidays and weekends, an average of 60 million cars crowd the highways, all rushing somewhere. They are, it seems, always trying to squeeze the greatest distance out of the least amount of time.

You might guess, from such behavior, that all these people are only interested in *arriving* somewhere. In fact, however, *traveling* somewhere can also be a lot of fun. This chapter outlines a few preparations you should make before heading off on any trip.

Fig. 24-1 Americans are a car-conscious people; on every holiday and weekend, highways are clogged with thousands of motorists all rushing somewhere.

Fig. 24-2 Make sure your car is in top-notch condition before you leave home or your trip can be ruined. Check your tires for signs of weakness; pack a spare and a jack in your trunk; carry a pressure can that seals and inflates a flat tire.

By Car

As we have said, traveling by car is America's favorite means of transportation. Here are some helpful "rules of the road."

Car Checkout   Nothing ruins a vacation faster than unexpected car trouble along the way. Make sure your car is in top-notch condition before you leave home. Check the fan belt, battery, ignition and other electrical systems, tire tread, radiator and hoses, spark plugs, and brake fluid. By taking care of small problems at home, you reduce your chances of having larger ones on the road. It is wise to carry a pressure can that seals and inflates a flat tire, an extra fan belt, oil, and a jug of water.

Check your insurance coverage before leaving home. If you will be driving in Mexico, you may be required to purchase special automobile insurance at the border. Additional insurance is not needed when traveling in the United States or Canada.

If a mechanical problem develops while you are traveling, start looking for a reputable service place at once. If you are a member of a motor club, get their recommendation for a reliable mechanic. They will also tow you to the mechanic if the car has completely collapsed. If your auto insurance policy covers towing, obtain a receipt for charges so you can be reimbursed.

Before repairs begin, understand fully what is wrong and what the costs will be. Stay close by when the work is being done. Travelers are often ripped off in strange environments and so it pays to be skeptical even though most mechanics are honest.

Travel by car is seldom cheap for only one passenger, but if several people share expenses, it can be reasonable. To estimate mileage costs, figure out how many miles per gallon your car averages. Total up the miles estimated for travel both ways plus a generous allowance for sight-seeing or getting around at your destination. Add the cost of oil; this can be quite a bit on a long trip if your car is an "oil user" because of worn rings. Older automobiles that perform adequately for short-run hops around town are frequently not up to the rigors of steady driving at higher speeds. The big unknown in auto travel is unexpected car expense that might exceed budgeted funds. You should have extra money in the form of traveler's checks or a recognized credit card in order to avoid being stranded somewhere.

Fig. 24-3 Before you leave, estimate your travel expenses and take enough money along to cover them. For gas, figure out how many miles per gallon your car averages. Total up the number of miles you think you will cover on your trip. Work out how many gallons you will use and the cost per gallon. (Ginger Chih)

Where to Stay? You may be able to plot your route so that each night you will be staying with relatives or friends. If this is your plan, be sure and write or phone in advance so they will be expecting you. Be a considerate guest, pitching in to help with meal preparation or cleanup, making up beds, trying not to disrupt the routines of your hosts. Except in rare instances, some expense will still be involved—buying groceries, treating hosts to meals out, or taking an appreciative gift. Much depends on the closeness of the relationship and whether you will have a chance to reciprocate the hospitality. At any rate, try to figure out realistically how much staying over will cost you.

Taking along camping equipment is another possibility, but if you camp you have to stop earlier at night and will probably leave later in the morning, thereby reducing the miles that can be traveled comfortably. Are there good campgrounds along the route you are going? What are their fees? Are reservations necessary? Will you have room for camping gear in addition to luggage?

If you will be stopping in motels, hotels, or tourist rooms, you will find the cost of car travel going up. However, if you can plan ahead and get confirmed reservations, less expensive rooms can be obtained. Stopping at a budget chain is seldom possible without advance reservations. In popular areas, much confusion and frustration can result from not having reservations in advance; driving around surveying no-vacancy signs can make you wish you had stayed home. However, if this problem should arise, stop and explain your problem to a motel clerk. They are often willing to phone around for you, or they may know of a place off the main streets.

Eating Out Having a meal in a restaurant three times a day can be expensive. It is definitely worth the effort to carry a small ice chest. It is easy to stock milk, orange juice, cheese, butter, and fruit. A picnic lunch makes a welcome break from driving. You can always obtain breads, cold cuts, and other desired items from almost any store. Some people keep a picnic kit permanently packed with minimum dishes and eating utensils, a good knife, a can opener, salt and pepper, and aluminum foil. Instant coffee, tea bags, bouillon cubes, or instant soup packets can be worth their weight in gold when you are tired. Small portable hot plates are fantastic if an

Fig. 24-4 Eating daily in a restaurant while traveling can become very expensive. It's easy (and cheaper) to simply pack a picnic lunch and to store a can opener, dishes, and a knife in your car. (Susan Berkowitz)

electric outlet is available, or you can take along your corn popper or an inexpensive pot that heats water. If you "make do" for breakfast and lunch, you can splurge for a nice dinner out. If you are in a city where you especially want to eat at a famous place, and if the time of day is not important to you, remember that lunches are less expensive than dinners.

Going Somewhere?   Get maps and study them. Keep informed about changing road conditions due to weather. Decide about how far you should go every day. Automobile clubs will outline your entire trip for you and furnish guidebooks for each area as part of their service. If you plan to tour the entire United States, mapping out your route ahead of time is invaluable. And, for some trips, doing it yourself is part of the fun.

As you plan your route, try to decide which would be best—the freeways or secondary roads. Sometimes the latter are a wise choice. Secondary roads are almost always in excellent condition and usually aren't clogged with heavy traffic. And secondary roads often wind through small towns and the surrounding countryside. They can be more scenic than a superhighway. The back roads are

Fig. 24-5 Plan your route before you begin your trip. Decide how far you should go each day and which roads you will take. If possible, check on the condition of the roads you will be traveling. (Susan Berkowitz)

sometimes shorter as well as more interesting and relaxing. If a particular route looks appealing to you, you can always check it out in advance with the local highway patrol, highway department, or automobile association.

Take Your Time   If you are an experienced driver, you probably know that cars on superhighways sometimes travel in "packs." Have you ever been driving along quietly, when suddenly you were surrounded by a pack of 10 or 20 cars, all racing along at the speed limit (or faster)? Did you feel you had to join the pack? You shouldn't. Driving like this can make your trip tense and dangerous. A simple solution to this uncomfortable situation is to pull over in a safe "rest" area and let the pack go by. Sometimes you can have several miles of aloneness before another pack races by.

Look Around You   Have you ever been on a trip that you thought would never end? Do you know why that trip was so long, boring, and miserable? Could it be that you didn't take the time to look at the countryside you were driving through? Probably the greatest temptation when you're in a hurry to get somewhere is to ignore where you are. But, by doing this, you can cheat yourself out of some great experiences. Take a moment, stop the car, and look around you. Maybe you can go for a short walk. Are there mountains, meadows, deserts, beaches nearby? Is the area famous for its flora—cactus, pine trees, certain flowers, or ferns? Are there unusual birds or animals that you might catch a glimpse of?

After a break for such sight-seeing, you'll probably feel refreshed and ready to drive again. This could be the best trip you ever took!

By RV

Recreation vehicles can include tent campers, truck campers, travel trailers, and motor homes—all of which vary considerably in cost. RV's may be rented, purchased new or used, or even created from pickup trucks and used buses. In fact, RV's come in such a variety of styles and prices that you really have to shop around and learn about them in order to get full value for your money.

The greatest advantage of owning an RV is convenience; perhaps the least is saving money. Many people think that money saved on motels and restaurant meals will more than pay for an RV. The

Fig. 24-6 Make an effort to enjoy the traveling as well as the arriving. Stop your car for a moment and take a short walk. Look around at the countryside. (Susan Berkowitz)

more luxurious the vehicle, the less likely it is that this will be true. If you are planning to buy an RV, be sure to figure out the cost of decreased gas mileage, parking or storage of the vehicle, taxes and license fees, maintenance and repair, insurance, depreciation, and financing costs.

Most of the "rules of the road" for enjoying car travel also apply to RV's. However, there are some special considerations, listed below.

Fig. 24-7 The greatest asset of an RV is convenience; you can cook, sleep, and travel, all in the same vehicle. (Katherine Peticolas)

- Find out if there are any restrictions on RV's. Some highway departments prohibit RV's which carry containers of compressed gas from passing through tunnels. RV's are also prohibited from traveling on many bridges and parkways. A good map should list any such restrictions.
- Take the time to become familiar with the mechanical workings of your RV—both the engine and the appliances. Many things can go wrong if you do not follow proper operating instructions. The last thing you need on the road is a breakdown or other problem.
- Buy a copy of the *RVDA Directory*. This publication lists all RV dealers, which models they service, and what kinds of repairs they perform. It can be very helpful if problems do arise. To purchase a copy, write to this address: Recreation Vehicle Dealers

Association of North America, P.O. Box 2159, Boulder, Colorado 80302.

- Figure out how much you will need for gas. Most RV's get 8 to 12 miles per gallon. This isn't very good mileage and the costs of fuel on a cross-country trip can really pile up.
- If you are short on time and have the funds, consider flying to your destination, then renting an RV to see the countryside while there. Several national airlines can arrange such long-distance rentals.
- Before using an RV for a lengthy trip, think first about the compatibility of the people involved. Even the closest friends or family sometimes have trouble coping with constant togetherness in cramped quarters. The RV salesperson may say it "sleeps six or eight" but will that many people be happy and comfortable while awake? Think of a rainy day at camp and visualize where everyone would be. Is there adequate seating for meals? If you are considering a unit with "hookups," think about what it will be like without hookups, running on the battery.
- If you plan to stay in a trailer park or campground, you will need an up-to-date directory. One of the finest is *Woodall's Trailering Parks and Campgrounds*. This publication can be ordered from: 500 Hyacinth Place, Highland Park, Illinois 50035. The price is $6.95. (The directory is also available in bookstores in most areas.)

By Bus

If you don't like to drive, but you still want to travel, consider taking a bus. You'll find that bus routes connect most major cities and other areas of touring interest.

Here are some pointers that can help make bus travel more comfortable and fun.

- Arrive at the ticket counter early, for there are usually no reserved seats. Pay your fare in cash, and board the bus.
- You are allowed to check three bags weighing up to 150 pounds. Watch while the baggage is being loaded to make sure yours is included, for there is no guarantee that it will be put on the same bus.

- If you can, plan your travel in short stints. After 10 hours on the road (about 400 miles), it's easy to become very tired. Arriving late at night in a strange place can be confusing.
- Try to get on an express bus—one with limited stops. This will shorten your travel time.
- Figure out how much you will need for meals on the road. Eating in bus stations and local restaurants can be expensive, and so think about packing your own snacks. A feast of sandwiches, fruit, and cheese can be tucked into a carry-on bag and eaten at rest areas.

If you plan to travel cross-country, look into the travel passes offered by Trailways and Greyhound bus lines. These passes can be a real bargain. Trailways offers a 15-day, a 30-day, and a 60-day travel pass (Eaglepass). For a flat (and reasonable) rate, you can travel anywhere in the continental United States. There are no restrictions on how often you use the pass or what days you can travel. Greyhound offers 7-day, 15-day, and 30-day travel passes (called Ameripass). You are allowed unlimited travel in the United States and also Canada. If you have the time, you can really squeeze an inexpensive yet wide-ranging vacation out of one of these passes. Go to your local bus station to inquire about or buy yourself a travel pass.

By Train

Travel by train is not as popular as it once was. However, trains offer some advantages that buses and planes do not. For example, trains are not held up by traffic on the roads as buses are. And train travel is usually a good deal cheaper than plane fare. The disadvantages of train travel are the time it takes; the difficulty of finding a train that goes where you want to go; and the need to arrange transportation between the train station and your ultimate destination.

Nearly all passenger trains in the United States are owned and operated by Amtrak, except commuter lines. Amtrak operates a nationwide, computerized information and reservation system. You can obtain train travel information and reservations by contacting the nearest Amtrak station. If there isn't one near you, call an Am-

Fig. 24-8 If you plan to travel by train, be sure to look into Amtrak's U.S.A. Railpass, which offers unlimited travel for a flat rate during a certain period of time. (Ginger Chih)

trak-appointed travel agent or Amtrak's toll-free information number. To obtain the number for your area, dial (800) 555-1212. Reservations are necessary on almost all long-distance trips for coach, and must be made as much as a month in advance if sleeping arrangements are desired.

Amtrak offers a variety of money-saving arrangements, including family and group plans and package tours. The Amtrak travel pass, called U.S.A. Railpass, is another bargain. The pass, which may be bought for a 14-day, 21-day, or 30-day period offers unlimited travel in the continental United States. There are no restrictions on what days you travel or how often you use the pass.

If you like train travel, but only have the time and money for a short trip, call your local commuter train lines. Some lines offer a special, low same-day rate. You can board the train in the morning, travel to a nearby city or town, spend the day sight-seeing, and come home that evening. The fare for these day trips often comes to less than $15. It's a great opportunity to take a one-day vacation and an inexpensive way to visit a place you've never been.

By Plane

Flying is the best choice of transportation when your schedule is very tight, and you can't afford to spend much time getting to your destination. Shop around, though, to find the most convenient flight and the best buy for your travel dollars. There are several flight possibilities to look into. Choose the best one for you.

Commercial Airlines   Most airlines have a toll-free (800) number that you can call to ask prices and make reservations. When you do call, question the airline representative carefully. The fare you pay may vary considerably, depending on the time and day you travel; whether you ride first class or coach; how long you plan to stay; how far ahead of time you make your reservation (sometimes it is possible to get an excursion fare); and whether you go as part of a tour. Don't be afraid to ask whether the price quoted is the least expensive fare available. Also check on what meals or snacks are served. If there isn't a meal in flight, you may want to stash away some cheese and crackers to munch with the free soft drink or coffee that is usually served.

You are allowed to check two pieces of baggage on most domestic flights. An additional piece can be carried on board if it will fit under the seat. Label your bag clearly both inside and out, and report missing baggage immediately.

Allow plenty of time to get to the airport, check in, and walk to the gate. As a general rule of thumb, you should arrive at the airport about 1 hour before your flight takes off. If you are not a seasoned traveler you may think this is too much time. But in the larger airports, it takes quite a while to park your car, find the check-in

Fig. 24-9 If you don't allow enough time to get to the airport, check in, and walk to the departure gate, you may miss your flight.

Fig. 24-10 Travel as lightly as possible. Don't take along any more luggage than you can easily carry yourself.

area, and walk to the boarding gate. The airlines usually request that you check in a minimum of 30 minutes before departure.

Before entering the boarding gate, you and any carry-on cases will go through a brief security check. Because of the recent increase in plane hijackings, most airlines ask passengers to walk through metal detectors and other equipment. These machines are designed to sense the presence of guns, knives, and other dangerous weapons and to emit a signal to alert security personnel. Since belt buckles or keys sometimes set off the alarm, don't be nervous if you are asked to submit to a more thorough check. Remember that these procedures are for your protection.

Occasionally, as you get ready to board, you may find that you have been "bumped" from a flight because it's been overbooked. If you hold a confirmed reservation on a commercial carrier, you may be eligible for denied-boarding compensation. Ask for a written statement explaining the terms of this compensation to see whether you qualify. If you are bumped, don't leave the check-in area; airline personnel will do everything possible to get you to your destination.

Airplane travel can be very enjoyable if you make things easy on yourself. Here are some helpful tips:

- If you are disabled or have a very short time between plane connections, ask the airport personnel to arrange for an electric cart to transfer you directly on the field or move you swiftly through the corridors. There is no charge for this service, but it's a good policy to tip for the help or courtesy.
- Carrying luggage for a long distance can be extremely tiring. Make a point of traveling as lightly as possible. Don't pack any more luggage than you can easily carry yourself. If you must carry a lot of stuff, consider buying a suitcase with built-in wheels. Or try renting your own luggage dolly at the airport.
- If you get lost or have some other problem, go to the Traveler's Aid station, or talk to airport personnel.
- The larger airport complexes supply free buses to transfer travelers from one airline terminal to another. Be sure to take advantage of this service when you need it.
- When you come out of the airport, don't just jump into the nearest taxi and speed off to your hotel. Take your time and

check out the situation. The larger hotels often provide free transportation from the airport in small buses or limousines. Some airports run limousine and bus services to nearby cities. They usually charge a rather reasonable fee.

- If you must take a taxi, try to share one with some other travelers headed in the same direction. This way, you can split the cost.

Charter Flights   Traveling by charter can be much less expensive than flying on a commercial airline. For this reason, charters have become very popular and the number of packages offered has multiplied. Choose your charter flight carefully, however, because there have been some problems. Recently, the Civil Aeronautics Board canceled about 100 flights after some irregularities in charter arrangements were discovered. Passengers had complained that they had been delayed, inconvenienced, or cheated out of the membership and travel advances by unscrupulous promoters.

You may wonder how you can protect yourself from this kind of thing and still take advantage of charter flight benefits. The Office of Consumer Affairs offers the following guidelines for judging whether a charter flight is legitimate.

- Legal charter flights are not permitted to solicit passengers from the general public. Therefore, beware if the flight is advertised in a newspaper, on the radio, or on television.
- Legitimate charters must involve clubs or associations whose main purpose is not travel. Members must be in the club for at least six months before traveling. Beware if you are asked to join a club and accept a back-dated membership.
- If the promoters will not disclose the name of the airline that will perform the flight there may not be a contract. The charter flight may never take place.
- Find out how long the promoters have been in business. Are they using someone else's office and making extensive use of an answering service? Such cues can be a tip-off to possible unscrupulous dealings.

It's a good policy to think twice before purchasing a charter flight from an agent acting against CAB regulations. The passenger who knowingly buys a ticket on such a charter is breaking the law and running the risk of being stranded if the agent is unable or unwilling to complete flight arrangements. For more information about charters, send for the free booklet "Air Travelers' Fly-Rights." The address is: U.S. Civil Aeronautics Board, Washington, D.C. 20428.

By Bike

If you are interested in the travel, not the destination, then bicycling might be for you. On a bicycle you can start and stop when you want, watch the countryside as you ride, and explore side roads and interesting trails on your own. Whether you are taking a spin around the block or a two-week bike trip across the state, when you get on your bike, you're off on the road to adventure.

Fig. 24-11 Traveling by bike can be a lot of fun. You can stop and explore the countryside whenever you feel like it. (Susan Berkowitz)

The Basic Bike   Look for a bike that is well constructed and has a comfortable seat, good brakes, and safety lights. Choose a bike that is the correct size for your height and the proper model for the amount of traveling you plan to do. For example, 10-speed bikes are usually recommended for long-distance touring. Go to a reputable bike shop for help or read up on bikes in a cycling magazine.

While you're at it, get a good case-hardened bike lock and chain. Then, when securing your bike, be sure to chain the back wheel and body to something immovable—a tree, telephone pole, or bike rack. If possible, however, take your bike inside with you and keep it in sight. Be sure to have your driver's license number etched in the frame, and be sure to keep a record of the serial number of the bike.

Bikes are easily maintained. Try to learn how to do your own repairs. Look for a good repair book and follow it carefully whenever you start a repair. There are many such repair guides on the market; a good one is *The Complete Guide to Bike Repair*.

Biking Accessories   Although many accessories are available, only a few items are considered essential. These items—all safety features—include a mirror, a loud horn, clips to keep you pants from becoming entangled in the gears, and a "French armband" (a plastic light that shines white in front, and red in back). If you strap the armband below your left knee, the bobbing light will alert motorists to your presence. For added safety, wear iridescent clothing and put reflecting strips on the pedal edges, frame, and fenders.

Biking Travel Trips   When you ride, remember that you are considered a fast vehicle, not a slow pedestrian. Follow the same rules of the road as you do when driving a car. Here are a few tips to make the going easy:

- When traveling in a group, ride single file if there is traffic. Travel side roads whenever possible. Remember that bikes are prohibited on limited-access highways.
- Before leaving, plan your route and get yourself in shape physically. American Youth Hostels, Inc., suggests taking a month to work up to a 50-mile-a-day trip with a full backpack.
- Books such as the *AYH North American Bike Atlas* and *The*

Fig. 24-12 Lock your bike whenever you leave it; secure it to something im-movable—a tree, telephone pole, or bike rack. Have your driver's license number etched in the frame and the serial number of the bike recorded. (Joan Fisher)

Fig. 24-13 Before you leave, get yourself some good maps such as *AYH North American Bike Atlas*. Refer to them as you travel. (Erika Stone, Peter Arnold Photo Archives)

American Biking Atlas and Touring Guide indicate routes, sights to see, places to stay, the varying degrees of difficulty, and other information on numerous bike tours throughout the United States and Canada.

• If you ship your bike ahead on a public carrier, check to see what arrangements should be made. Most buses and airlines require that you carton the bike, which usually involves removing the handlebars, pedals, seat, and perhaps the front wheel. If you are traveling by car, try to buy or rent a bike rack for your car.

The Bikecentennial   In 1977 a Trans-America Bikecentennial was held to celebrate the 100th anniversary of the modern bicycle. About 4,000 people, ranging in age from an 8-year-old boy to an 86-year-old man, rode the route. Almost half the riders rode the entire trail, stretching 4,500 miles from coast to coast through winding back roads, rugged mountains, and rolling prairies. The rest of the riders rode only selected segments. The Bikecentennial was so popular that the organizers are planning to turn the program into an annual event. The bike route will be expanded by three "loop" trails starting near metropolitan areas in Virginia, Kentucky, and Oregon.

Does this kind of biking adventure appeal to you? Or do you feel hesitant? Maybe you fear a bike tour is too hard for you, or you don't know what to expect. Don't give up the idea of a bike tour until you've read about Ben's experience in the Bikecentennial.

Ben   Ben, a nonathletic high school student, joined the tour with some misgivings. He was worried about his ability to keep up with the group. Ben was not very experienced in bike riding. He didn't think he was in particularly good physical condition either. For two months before the trip, Ben tried to build up his body. He biked for 45 minutes daily. The weekend before the trip, he took a trial run with a full pack.

By the time the Bikecentennial arrived, Ben was ready. He had all the necessary equipment: a nylon trail tent, a 5-pound down sleeping bag, a rubberized ground pad, and a mess kit. He had put together all the equipment necessary for repairs: a spare tire and tube, three extra spokes, patching material, a freewheel assembly tool, and a few wrenches and screwdrivers. He had put aside some biking clothing: sneakers, three T-shirts, a heavy flannel shirt, two pairs of cotton riding shorts, jeans, three changes of underwear, three pairs of knee-length socks, toe clips, and a rubber-padded helmet. He had made up a first-aid kit: insect repellent, suntan lotion, sunburn ointment.

Ben packed his bike in a crate borrowed from a local bicycle shop. When he checked in at the airport, he was charged a small fee (about $10) by the airline to transport his bike. Ben flew from his home in Los Angeles to Missoula, Montana, to join the tour group. They set off at a speed of 10 to 12 miles an hour and covered about 55 miles a day. Altogether, they traveled bout 650 miles in 12 days.

Ben loved the Bikecentennial experience. He became friends with many of the other riders and enjoyed sharing campsites with them in the Grand Teton Mountains. He thought the beauty of the countryside alone made the trip worthwhile. He also enjoyed the feeling of being physically challenged in the morning and exhausted in the evening. "Altogether, it was just unforgettable," Ben said.

If you think you might also be interested in joining the Bikecentennial, write for more information. The address is: Bikecentennial, Box 8308, Missoula, Montana 59807.

THINKING IT THROUGH

1. Chapter 24 offers information in six important modes of recreational travel. Which mode of travel would you choose for a three-week trip? Why? Which would be the least favored? Why?

2. Based on your travel experiences or the experience of someone you know, share at least one "travel tip" with the rest of the class.

3. Make a list of five places (in the United States or abroad) that you would like to travel to. How much do you know about these places? What kinds of information would you need to get before making your travel plans? What is it about these places that most appeals to you?

Glossary

Accessories   The little extra personal touches in a room. Accessories fall into five categories: wall accessories, table and shelf accessories, room dividers, lighting, and houseplants. Accessories can be functional, decorative, or both.

Achievement motivation   A person's thoughts and feelings about doing things well, perhaps better than they've ever been done before.

Additive   Something added to food in processing. Additives may be natural or synthetic. They are used for many purposes, mainly preservation, flavoring, and color. Other purposes of additives are to increase nutritional value, to make food smoother or more crisp, or to make it easier to mix. The value and even the safety of many additives are questioned by critics.

Affiliation motive   A person's thoughts and feelings about having friends and helping other people.

Alkalies   Forms of salt. Three common alkalies used for cleaning are ammonia, baking soda, and borax.

Alloy   A combination of two or more metals.

Alternative futures   Thoughts about the different ways the future can happen. *Futurists* believe these thoughts can help us choose.

Ampere *(amp)*   A unit for measuring electricity. The amp number shown on fuses indicates the circuit's capacity.

Appearance quotient   An indication of how wise you are about how you dress.

Appliqué   A cutout decoration applied to a fabric.

Auger *(Also known as a plumber's snake.)*   A plumber's tool that is fed into a drain or toilet to unclog it.

Au gratin   Prepared for cooking with bread crumbs and cheese.

Back stitch   The strongest hand stitch; used for sewing areas that need extra reinforcement, such as side seams.

Basic color   Those colors that can be worn with many other colors, such as black, gray, white, beige, brown, and medium to dark blue.

Basting stitch   A temporary stitch used to hold fabric together.

Behaviorists   Psychologists who believe that people's personalities are formed only by outside forces.

Biodegradable A substance that can be broken down so as not to be harmful to the environment.

Blanket stitch An embroidery stitch used for sewing on patches and appliqués.

Bleed When colors run into each other during washing or dry cleaning.

Blend A combination of two or more fibers that are spun or twisted into yarn before being woven or knitted into a fabric.

Block To shape a knit garment to its original size when wet and dry it on a flat surface.

Bonnet The packing nut in a faucet.

Bouillon cube A tightly packed cube of dried meat juices, fat, and seasonings, to be mixed with water to make broth, soup stock, or a base for many other dishes.

Budget A plan in which you've figured out how much money you want to spend over a certain period of time.

Building manager The person who takes care of an apartment building. The building manager could be the landlord, or else someone employed by the landlord.

Building-on-basics (BOB) principle Building a wardrobe around basic colors and classic lines.

Buttonhole stitch Used to repair and make buttonholes.

Case goods Furniture without upholstery. Case goods include chests, tables, and desks.

Cash-and-carry A sales policy found in some stores. Cash-and-carry requires you to pay in cash (not credit) and to arrange delivery of the item home (the store doesn't provide this service).

Casserole A mixed dish, often designed as a one-dish meal, which is cooked in the oven for fairly long periods, usually without further attention.

Casters Removable wheels that can be attached to the legs of heavy furniture.

Catch stitch A A stretch stitch used especially for hemming sleeves and necklines on knit fabrics.

Catch stitch B Used for hemming knits and bulky fabrics although it doesn't stretch as much as catch stitch A.

Cellulosics Any fiber made from the cellulose (cotton and wood linters) of plants.

Celsius A scale of temperature on which 0° is the freezing point and 100° is the boiling point of water.

Centered zipper A zipper that either has no material over it or material that just joins together as the zipper is pulled up.

Chalk skirt marker A device used to mark hems with chalk while wearing the garment; when the bulblike handle is squeezed, chalk is transferred to the fabric at the desired hem level.

Circadian rhythms Differences in the "timing" of different people's minds and bodies. *Night people* and *morning people* are the best-known examples of how circadian rhythms may work.

Classic lines Fashions that have been steady favorites over a period of years.

Colander A large metal or plastic bowl with holes in it, used for washing food or draining water from cooked food.

Collapsible furniture Furniture that can be made more compact and stored when not in use. Folding chairs are one example.

Color Any combination of the three primary colors (yellow, blue, and red); also called hue or tone.

Combination stitch A strong stitch that combines the running and back stitches; used for seams and for mending.

Complete protein A food containing all eight amino acids not made by the human body but needed for making human body protein. Complete protein is usually provided by animal foods (meat, poultry, fish) or animal food products (eggs, milk, cheese).

Consensus Agreement by *all* people on an idea or answer.

Convenience food A food partially or completely prepared for use. Some need further preparation and cooking (instant cake mixes, for example), while others need only to be warmed and served (TV dinners, for example).

Conversation piece An object— or the way an object is displayed— that catches the eye and stirs up conversation about it.

Cool color Any color that has a lot of blue in it.

Credit rating A rating of a person's ability to borrow money and pay it back.

Cross-impact The way that two or more series of events may be expected to affect each other in the future.

Custom-made Clothes that are made especially for you, according to your exact measurements.

Decision A thoughtful choice made from among many possibilities. A *programmed decision* is a choice that is made automatically, with little or no thinking. A *novel decision* is one that may require much thought and worry.

Deep-pile fabrics Fabrics that are very thick, such as "fake fur."

Default When you do not live up to the terms of your lease; one example would be not paying the rent on time.

Defrosting Removing the built-up ice in a freezer by turning off the refrigerator and allowing the ice to melt away.

Dehydrated Processed to remove most or all water. Dehydrated foods are *reconstituted* by adding water to them.

Deposit A charge paid by the renter and held in trust (safe-keeping) by the landlord until the terms of the lease, or rental agreement, are met. All, or part, of a deposit may be returned to the renter.

Dolly A platform on wheels. Dollies are generally used to move heavy pieces of furniture around.

Double-duty furniture Furniture that can be put to more than one use. An example is a sofa that opens into a bed.

Dry cleaning A process by which clothes are washed in a chemical solution that cleans them and dries very quickly.

Eclectic A style of decorating in which many different styles of furnishings are put together. All that really matters is that the results are pleasing to the decorator.

Economist A person who studies the ways in which goods, work, and money are used and exchanged by people, industry, and government.

Efficiency expert An industrial engineer who studies how a task may be done best with least time and motion.

Ego Sigmund Freud's name for the personality, the part of every person that is seen and known to the outside world.

"Empty calories" Processed foods high in calories, but low or totally lacking in other nutritional elements such as protein, vitamins, and minerals. Snack foods and beverages made almost entirely of sugar or starch are the main examples.

Environment The whole framework of things, people, and forces, within which a person lives.

Esteem High value and respect given to a person or thing; self-esteem means putting high value on your own way of living.

Fabric Cloth that is made by weaving or knitting fibers.

Fad A short-lived fashion.

Fee A charge paid by the renter which is usually not returned.

Feedback Information from others about how well you are doing something *as you do it*. Feedback makes corrections possible as a task is being done.

Fiber Carbohydrate that is too tough to be digested by the body (such as membranes in an orange, "strings" in beans and celery). It serves, however, as "roughage," or bulk, in helping the body to eliminate wastes more effectively. The importance of fiber to bodily health is gaining increasing attention from doctors.

Fibers Long, thin threads that are spun or twisted into yarn and then woven or knitted into cloth.

Fixed spending The amount of time or money that is used in the same manner almost every week, month, or year.

Fixture Ceiling light.

Fluorescent light Light produced by passing electric current through a gas enclosed in a glass tube.

Focal point The part of a room that attracts attention. The focal point can be almost anything: a painting, a large wall hanging, a collection of favorite items, or a grouping of pictures.

Forecasting Trying to say clearly what will happen at some time in the future.

Frame The basic structure of furniture or the part of furniture that serves as the base.

Functional A term used to describe furniture that serves a definite purpose and is not just for decoration.

Furniture cutout *(Also called a template.)* An outline of a piece of furniture drawn to scale. You can use furniture cutouts with a room layout to decide how to arrange your furniture.

Futuristics *(also Futurism or Futurology)* The study of possible future events with the belief that choices can be made among them.

Grain line The yarn line in a fabric that runs either lengthwise or crosswise.

Guarantee The conditions under which an item may be replaced or fixed by the manufacturer. Most major appliances—radios, TVs, stereos, washing machines—come with a guarantee.

Hawthorne effect A change that occurs in the way people do things because they know what they are doing is being studied.

Health food A food claimed to have exceptional qualities of nutrition. As of the late 1970s, no government standards had been set to help people tell "health food" from other types, but such standards were being developed and debated.

Hem allowance The extra material left on fabric for the hem.

Hem, or blind, stitch Used for hemming because the stitches don't show on the surface of the fabric.

Hierarchy of needs A. H. Maslow's theory in which a series of five "steps" represent the important things that people want and need in life.

Hue *See Color.*

Id A term used by Sigmund Freud to mean the wild, animal-like part of a person's mind.

Identity A person's sense of being special and different from other people, for better or worse.

Incandescent light Light produced by passing electric current through a filament in a light bulb.

Incomplete protein A food with some, but not all, the amino acids needed by the body to make protein *(see Complete protein)*. Incomplete protein foods, such as beans, nuts, rice, and seeds, have to be eaten *at the same time* in certain combinations to provide complete protein.

Independent living Living *well* alone; having good control of and good feelings about your own life.

Ingredient A part of the whole; an element in a recipe.

Inseam The inside length of your leg.

Installment payments Payments that are to be made over a period of time in the future for something bought now. Finance charges, or interest, must usually be paid for such a plan.

Intensity The strength or weakness of a color.

Inventory agreement A listing of furniture and equipment included in the rental of a furnished apartment. By signing the agreement, the lessee becomes responsible for the furniture and equipment listed.

Joints The places where two or more parts of the frame meet in furniture.

Junk food Food of little nutritional value (see *Empty calories*).

Kapok A flossy fiber found in the pod of a kapok plant. Kapok is used in pillow stuffing.

Kinesthetic The way something feels to the touch.

Landlord The lessor or owner of a building that is rented to other persons. The landlord can be one or more individuals, or a corporation.

Lapped zipper A zipper that has material overlapping it.

Layout The way rooms are arranged. Also refers to the way pieces of furniture are arranged inside the room.

Lease A legal contract that spells out the rights and responsibilities of both landlord and tenant. The main purpose of a lease is to state the rent and the length of time for which a place is being rented.

Lessee *(Also called the tenant or renter.)* The person who signs the lease, agreeing to rent an apartment.

Lessor The landlord or owner of an apartment.

Liable A term meaning you are legally responsible. For example, a tenant is liable for repair of damages done to the rental while the lease is in effect.

Lifestyle The whole pattern of how a person lives. This includes not only food, dress, housing, and recreation, but also thoughts and feelings toward self and others.

Line The shape of a garment.

Manmade fibers There are two kinds: *cellulosics* (rayon and acetate), made from natural fibers and chemicals; and *synthetics* (nylon, acrylic, polyester, etc.), made from chemicals only.

Merchandising The skills of providing, pricing, and displaying goods for sale and increased sale.

Metabolism The total workings and pace of the body in handling and using nourishment. The metabolism of the individual may be as personal as a fingerprint.

Mixture A combination of two or more fibers used in knitting or weaving a fabric.

Motivation "Movement" from a set of thoughts and feelings (motive) to a goal.

Natural fibers Those made from nature's resources, such as silk, cotton, and wool.

Natural food A food made without preservatives, colorings, or flavorings. This term, like *Health food,* is often used carelessly. Government standards may be set for its exact meaning.

Neutral colors White, black, and gray.

Operant behavior Behavior in which a person initiates his or her own thoughts and actions.

Organic food Food grown without the use of synthetic fertilizers and insect-killers.

Outline stitch Similar to the back stitch; used for outlining patches and appliqués.

Overcasting Hand stitch used to sew on patches, appliqués, and fasteners, such as snaps, hooks, and eyes.

Passbook loan An amount of money borrowed from a savings bank where the borrower has a savings account. The person's savings remain in the bank to assure that the loan will be repaid.

Pasta Any food, like spaghetti or noodles, made from wheat mixed into a paste and then dried for storage.

Perishable foods Foods that will lose quality or spoil in a short time unless refrigerated.

Personality Everything about a person that can be seen and known to others.

Personal obstacles Anything—physical handicaps, environmental conditions, or other people—that may keep a person from getting to his or her goals.

Physiological needs Basic needs, like food and drink, that must be satisfied in order to keep a person alive. Physiological needs are the first step in Maslow's hierarchy of needs.

Pile The thickness of a fabric.

Pilling The formation of little, round fiber balls on a fabric.

Pin skirt marker A device used to mark hems by holding the garment in place while the pins are inserted by hand.

Plunger *(Also called the plumber's friend.)* A plumber's tool that is used to unclog a sink or toilet.

Policy holder The person who buys an insurance policy and pays the premium.

Polyunsaturated fats Fats with a chemical structure that keeps them in liquid form. These are usually vegetable fats. (See *Saturated fats.*)

Power motive A person's desire to lead other people or control what they do.

Primary colors Those colors (yellow, blue, and red) from which all other colors are made.

Probability A prediction of the possibility (or "odds") that something will happen one way or another.

Processed foods Foods changed

in some way by manufacturing methods.

Proportion   The way one part relates to another and to the whole. For example, the size and shape of a lamp shade should relate well to the height and shape of the base of the lamp. In addition, the lamp and shade should relate well both to the size and shape of the lamp table and to the room itself.

Psychiatrist   A medical doctor who specializes in treating the human mind and personality.

Psychologist   A person who studies and treats problems of the human mind and personality; not a medical doctor.

Pure colors   Bright, clear hues of full intensity.

Recycling   Making things—paper, aluminum, or other metals—usable again.

Rental agreement   A verbal or written month-to-month agreement that may be ended by either the tenant or the landlord by giving a month's notice.

Renter   *See Lessee.*

Respondent behavior   Behavior in which a person depends on others to tell him or her what to do and how to act; opposite of *operant behavior.*

Running stitch   The most basic hand stitch; used either for basting or as a permanent stitch for mending, seaming, and quilting.

Saturated fats   Fats with a chem-ical structure that gives them a solid form. These are usually animal fats (though coconut oil, a liquid, is also a saturated fat).

Scale   Size in relation to something else. A piece of furniture, for example, is in scale if its size fits in well with the other furniture in a room and with the room itself. Thus, large-sized furniture would be in scale in a large room and out of scale in a small room.

Scenario   A made-up story or play-like script about how things will happen to a person in the future; used by *futurists* to decide choices.

Scientific management   Movement started in the early 1900s to find faster and better ways of doing factory and office work.

Seam allowance   The extra material (about ¼ in [6 mm]) on either side of a seam.

Security deposit   An amount (usually one month's rent) paid by the renter and held by the landlord as a guarantee that the rental will be kept in good condition. The security deposit, except for the cost of repairing any damages, is returned when the renter moves out.

Self-actualization   The person's ability to be in complete tune with self and to use all feelings and talents to the fullest; also called self-realization.

Self-awareness   Knowledge of one's own mind and body.

Self-image   The person's picture

of self or personality; this may be different, and more or less realistic, than what others see.

Shade   Any color made darker by adding black.

Shank   The stem that's attached to a button.

Sharps   All-purpose sewing needles.

Skin color   Shade of skin; divided into fair, medium, dark, and black.

Skin tone   The amount of pink in your skin; divided into neutral, pink, or sallow.

Sleeve board   A tiny ironing board used for small areas.

Slip stitch A   Used for hemming and sewing on patches or for attaching any folded edge to a piece of fabric.

Slip stitch B   Used for joining two folded edges together.

Solitude   Being alone, but not lonely.

Soufflé   A type of dish made puffy and "airy" by the addition of stiffly beaten egg whites, with egg yolk and white sauce.

Staple   A basic food, such as flour or spices, used in a great many types of dishes and usually kept on hand in most kitchens.

Status   A person's standing with others.

Striving   Action given to reaching a goal.

Studs   The framework, or vertical strips of wood, within the wall.

Studs are usually placed 16 in (40 cm) apart and begin at the corner of a room. Large or heavy pictures, mirrors, and shelves should be hung over studs for extra support.

Superego   The part of the mind, described by Freud, which holds the rules for "right" behavior given by parents and the world.

Synthetic   A fabric made from chemicals, such as polyester or acrylic.

Template   See Furniture cutout.

Tenant   See Lessee.

Texture   The way something looks or feels.

Theory X, Theory Y   Opposed ideas about people's willingness to work. Douglas McGregor said that most bosses believed people dislike work (Theory X), but could improve output and feelings by understanding that people wanted to work (Theory Y).

Tint   Any color made lighter by adding white.

Tone   See Color.

Traffic patterns   The paths people take to get from one place to another. When you are decorating, figure out where the traffic patterns are, so you don't put furniture where people would want to walk.

Trunk   The portion of your body between the shoulders and legs.

Undernourishment   Lack of enough food for good health and survival, or lack of enough food of nutritional quality.

Underwriter's knot A knot tied with the wires when attaching a plug. An underwriter's knot will prevent the cord from pulling loose from the plug when subjected to normal strain.

Utilities Essential services such as water, gas, electricity, and telephone.

Value The amount of light (tint) and dark (shade) in a color.

Value conflict A clash of the values held by different people about the same subject; often a clash of different values (such as hard work and fun) held by the same person.

Variable spending Spending of time or money which may be increased or cut down from this week or this month to the next.

Variety meats The organ parts of meat animals, such as the liver, kidneys, and brains. These are extremely high in nutritional values.

Varnish A hard, protective coating on wood furniture. Polish this type of finish with a paste wax.

Velvet board A small, flexible piece of heavy-duty fabric or wood with tiny nails coming out of it; used for ironing pile fabrics such as velvet or corduroy.

Warm color A color that has a lot of red or yellow in it.

Warranty *See Guarantee*.

Whipped hem A stitch used to make a fine, narrow hem, such as is used on scarves and handkerchiefs.

Zipper, or pick, stitch A type of back stitch used to sew on zippers and for decorative stitching.

Index

452